THE ALLOCATION OF ROAD CAPITAL IN TWO-DIMENSIONAL SPACE

Studies in
Regional Science
and Urban Economics

Editors

ÅKE ANDERSSON
WALTER ISARD

Volume 5

NORTH-HOLLAND PUBLISHING COMPANY – AMSTERDAM · NEW YORK · OXFORD

The Allocation of Road Capital in Two-Dimensional Space

A Continuous Approach

TÖNU PUU
University of Umeå, Sweden

1979

NORTH-HOLLAND PUBLISHING COMPANY – AMSTERDAM · NEW YORK · OXFORD

Library of Congress Catalog Card Number 79-11740
ISBN North-Holland for this volume 0 444 85324 3

Publishers

NORTH-HOLLAND PUBLISHING COMPANY
AMSTERDAM · NEW YORK · OXFORD

Distributors for the U.S.A. and Canada

ELSEVIER NORTH-HOLLAND, INC.
52 VANDERBILT AVENUE
NEW YORK, N.Y. 10017

Library of Congress Cataloging in Publication Data

Puu, Tönu.
The allocation of road capital in two-dimensional space.

(Studies in regional science and urban economics ; v. 3)
Bibliography: p.
Includes indexes.
1. Roads--Finance--Mathematical models.
2. Roads--Economic aspects--Mathematical models.
I. Title. II. Series.
HE336.E3P87 388.1'1 79-11740
ISBN 0-444-85324-3

PRINTED IN THE NETHERLANDS

INTRODUCTION TO THE SERIES

Regional Science and Urban Economics are two interrelated fields of research which have developed very rapidly in the last three decades. The main theoretical foundation of these fields comes from economics but in recent years the interdisciplinary character has become more pronounced. The editors desire to have the interdisciplinary character of regional science as well as the development of spatial aspects of theoretical economics fully reflected in this book series. Material presented in this book series will fall in three different groups:

- interdisciplinary textbooks at the advanced level,
- monographs reflecting theoretical or applied work in spatial analysis,
- proceedings reflecting the advancement of the frontiers of regional science and urban economics.

In order to ensure homogeneity in this interdisciplinary field, books published in this series will:

- be theoretically oriented, i.e., analyse problems with a large degree of generality,
- employ formal methods from mathematics, econometrics, operations research and related fields, and
- focus on immediate or potential uses for regional and urban forecasting, planning and policy.

The Editors

To Gertrud and Margareta

ACKNOWLEDGEMENTS

My research on the subject dealt with in this book started about 1975, as a kind of hobby or therapy, to compensate for the monotonity of administering a university institute for general economics. Since I had previously not worked with regional problems there was a constant change of paradigm as I learned relevant mathematical methods and linked my own ideas to various existing bodies of knowledge in related fields.

The work was started at my own university in Umeå, Sweden, but most of it was carried out during a sabbatical leave of absence spent in the Federal Republic of Germany, 1977.

The project at its more advanced stages, and my stay in Germany, were financed by the Swedish Social Science Research Council, to which I wish to express my gratitude.

During my stay in Germany I was supplied with working facilities and access to libraries at several universities. Therefore I wish to thank Professor Rainer Thoss, of the University of Münster, and all the others at his institute, above all Mr Teo Kausel and Mr Kjell Wiik. By formally inviting me as a visiting professor to the University of Bonn, Professor Wilhelm Krelle helped me to profit from library resources and professional contacts there.

Several people have read preliminary versions of the work and have made valuable comments or suggestions for further development. For this I am indebted to Professor Åke E. Andersson (IIASA, Laxenburg, Austria), Professor Martin J. Beckmann (Technical University of München), Mr Alan Ingham (University of Southampton), Dr Karl C. Mosler (University of the German Defence, Hamburg), and Mr Urs Schweizer (University of Bonn).

During seminars arranged at the Universities of København, Oslo and Münster several useful comments were made.

Mathematical assistance has been provided by people at the Mathematics Department of Umeå University, especially by Dr Alf Jonsson and Dr Johan Karlsson, and by people at the Institute of Applied Mathematics at the Technical University of Göteborg, in particular Mr Kjell Holmåker. The deepest gratitude for mathematical help, however, is due to my friend Dr Anders Bàràny of the Department of Theoretical Physics, Uppsala University.

Finally, Dr Karl-Gustav Löfgren, at my own Department of Economics, Umeå University, has read parts of the manuscript, and has always listened patiently and made valuable comments whenever I have talked to him about the research documented in this book.

Umeå, November 1978 Tönu Puu

CONTENTS

Chapter 1

INTRODUCTION

The purpose of this book is to discuss the ways in which fixed transportation capital of a given total quantity should be allocated in two-dimensional space so that reasonable requirements for economic efficiency are met.

Transportation capital denotes either real capital in the sense of the length of a road network, or the monetary value of interest, amortization and maintenance cost per annum needed to keep up the network. We naturally specify a constraint on the total monetary capital. The proper question to pose is how given financial resources should be employed. In the main discussion, moreover, it is assumed that land acquisition costs for road building and the facility of construction are the same everywhere. This means that the constraint can be translated into one of given real capital. The aggregation problems are not too difficult in this case, in contrast to most aggregation problems where real capital is involved. We have a natural scalar measure for a total of road capital, namely the number of kilometers that the whole network contains. To use this, we have only to disregard different qualities of roads and their varying construction costs. It is true that due mainly to the costs of construction of exits and entrances a motorway is about five times as expensive as an ordinary road but, in view of the fact that we want some very general theorems on how the density of mesh should vary in space, abstraction from different qualities is defensible.

Economic efficiency means that the yearly sum of costs for fuel, wear of vehicles and travelling time for all transportation needed in a given geographical region is minimized. For simplicity this total cost is taken as proportionate to the total travel time. In the main text we go even further and regard it as proportionate to total transportation work in vehicle kilometers. This involves two abstractions. Taking travelling cost as proportionate to time means that we disregard differences between vehicles of different sizes. This is parallel to the abstraction from varying road quality. A more serious aspect is that in taking travel time as proportionate to travel distance we completely disregard the phenomenon of congestion.

Abstraction from congestion is, however, not so unreasonable as one may at first think. What I have in mind is not a small urban area, with which the "new urban economics" is concerned, but something like a vast country. In this case the deviations of most of the optimal communication paths or routes to avoid congestion nuclei are so small in comparison to their whole extensions that congestion costs becomc limited enough in relation to total communication cost to make the abstraction defensible. Congestion is a highly local phenomenon and can be avoided by moving the route a few kilometers.

The same defense may be used for the abstraction from varying land acquisition cost and varying construction facility. High land values too are very local phenomena, as are most impediments to construction. Again, siting a highway a few kilometers away from its best location contributes so little to capital and travel costs that we can defend the abstraction. From our macroscopic point of view these displacements are hardly visible.

The story is, of course, not quite as simple as that. In many industrialized countries congestion may extend over considerable regions, and the Alps are certainly impediments that cannot be avoided by putting the road a few kilometers to one side. If it were as simple to include congestion and other complications in the model as to leave them out then we would certainly prefer more realistic and more general assumptions. However, the inclusion of these phenomena in the general model makes certain variational problems insoluble from the very outset, so that we would not be able to carry out even the first steps of the analysis.

Therefore, we have excluded the complications from the main discussion, and concentrated on them in a final chapter, where other limitations on the scope of the analysis are introduced.

Let us now look a little more closely at the optimization problem: it is to minimize total travelling cost by choosing an appropriate spatial distribution of a given total of road capital. However, it is not a simple constrained minimization. We can first identify two different partial minimization problems.

If the spatial distribution of roads is a given datum, then we can ask which choice of routes for all the individual types of transport will minimize total transportation cost.[1]

Given the network of roads it is possible to decide which route is the least expensive for each individual transport. It is the shortest one if congestion is disregarded. In the absence of congestion we can also see that the solutions for all the individual paths are independent, since the best route for one transport is not then affected by whether only a few or a lot of other transports share parts of the same route. Hence, we can conjecture that total transportation cost is automatically minimized with the given network of roads when the transporters seek their individually optimal paths. If we take congestion into account, we cannot a priori exclude the possibility that total cost can be reduced by introducing tolls enforcing avoidance of the congested areas even more than would otherwise occur since individually optimal paths are no longer necessarily also socially optimal.

[1]The terms "transport", "trip" and "communication" are used synonymously for the transfer of a quantum of goods, messages or people from one location to another.

Provided that the need for transportation is specified in some way a distribution of traffic in the various parts of the region is associated with the solutions to the problems of finding optimal routes. This traffic distribution naturally leads us to the other partial minimization.

If we take the distribution of traffic in the region as a given datum, we may ask which allocation of road capital in space will minimize total transportation costs. By making the network most dense where traffic is heaviest we may expect to keep total transportation costs small. The reasons for this are obvious. If congestion is kept in the picture, then an increase of network density reduces the relative weight of traffic to capacity, thus reducing congestion and transfer times. If congestion is disregarded, then an increase of road capital still reduces the necessary detours, in excess of Euclidean distance, incurred when the actual network is followed. This is true because the smaller the mesh of the network, the closer a random path through it approximates to a straight line. But, having only a given total of network kilometers any increase of density at one point must be compensated for by a decrease of density at some other point. As a result of decreasing returns from successive increases of the density at one point, we may expect some optimal distribution of roads to correspond to each distribution of traffic. The assumption of decreasing returns seems reasonable, because the addition of a new shortcut to an existing network saves on average fewer detours the more ramified is the existing network, i.e. the more like straight lines the paths already are.

Thus, to an allocation of roads there is a corresponding minimum cost distribution of traffic, and to a distribution of traffic there is a corresponding minimum cost allocation of roads. Now, assume that both minimizations are attained simultaneously. Then, there is such an allocation of roads that the free choice of optimal paths by the individual travellers results in a distribution of traffic for which this allocation of roads is optimal. We have an equilibrium, obtained by the independent actions of individual travellers and some government agency responsible for the construction of roads.

We may now ask whether this equilibrium is also an optimum, so that the resulting total transportation cost is really the smallest that can be attained. The answer is obviously positive, provided that the constraints for the partial optimization problems are mutually independent. This qualification is, in fact, true. The relevant constraint when an optimal distribution of traffic with a given allocation of roads is sought is the prescribed need for transportation between all pairs of locations. This need for transportation is obviously independent of the constraint of a given total road capital that may be used in various parts of the region to increase network density and eliminate detours, which is relevant when an optimal allocation of roads with a given distribution of traffic is sought.

For readers who are economists, an analogy from duopoly theory may be helpful. The equilibrium corresponds to a Cournot solution where individual travellers choose optimal paths, taking the distribution of roads decided by the government agency as a given datum and where the government agency decides the allocation of roads, taking the distribution of traffic resulting from the decisions as to paths by the individuals as a given datum. The optimum, on the other hand, is a Stackelberg solution where the government agency is a "leader" and the individual transporters are "followers". Then the government agency takes into explicit consideration that any change of network influences the choice of routes and hence the distribution of traffic, whereas the individuals still take the distribution of road capital as something they are unable to influence by their choice of routes.

But, in contrast to ordinary duopoly, the government agency and the individual transporters presently do not have conflicting objectives. There is no competition for market shares but both categories of agents strive to minimize the same variable, namely total transportation cost. It is then not surprising that the solutions are identical in our case, whereas they are not usually so in duopoly theory. Striving for the same objective and independence for the constraints leads to a situation where the contribution of each agent to the total can be minimized, without interfering with the chances of others to do likewise and without destroying any benefits thus obtained by others.

Having outlined the problem something has to be said regarding the choice of a model. Several analogies from other sciences have been fruitfully employed for related problems. If population in the region is located only at a finite number of "nodes" or "vertices", then it is natural to regard roads as "arcs" or "edges" joining the locations at which people live, and to employ the theories of graphs and flows in graphs. Owing to the recent development of graph theory as a tool for the analysis of electrical networks as well as of computation algorithms, there are many general theorems available. The main weakness of this approach, however, is that graph theory is a branch of topology, so that the theorems tend to be of a topological character, making it difficult to say something about geometrical properties. The computational methods, where graphs are represented by matrices (whether incidence or adjacency matrices), do not easily lend themselves to representation of such geometrical properties as shapes and densities of networks.[2]

Even if population is dispersed in space by some continuous density function, one might still use the network representation of roads and a graph theoretical representation of problems and concepts, as Mosler (1976b) has recently done with considerable success. At the same time his treatment demonstrates that whereas graph theory is an efficient tool for the concise statement of problems, the conclusions are not obtained through theorems from this branch of mathematics.

[2]The methods are, however, suitable for the analysis of even large-scale planning models as the works by Holtgrefe (1975) and by Steenbrink (1974) demonstrate.

This leads to the natural question of whether it would not be possible to obtain conclusions of another type by using another analogy. Such a possibility is provided by geometrical optics and the kinematics of bodies moving under gravitational force. The methods used are from the calculus of variations. This paradigm was introduced into the field of transportation science by Beckmann (1952, 1953, 1960, 1976) and has been used more recently by Wardrop (1969), Angel and Hyman (1970, 1971, 1972a, 1972b, 1976), Zitron (1974) and Puu. As a matter of fact, Mosler too uses this analogy when transportation outside the network is considered. (As people live outside the vertices, they have to travel in the plane as well as on the network in Mosler's model.)

The region is then no longer regarded as a set of isolated points, but as a part of the plane delimited by a number of smooth arcs. In this model it is not feasible to regard the roads as arc segments. The natural concept suggested by the analogy is instead a scalar function, expressing the traversibility or the cost of transfer across a point in any direction. This traversibility must in some way depend on the density of the network (as a determinant of the necessity of detour taking) and on traffic (if congestion is considered). Provided the allocation of roads and the load of traffic are taken as given, so that the only problem is to find optimal paths, one does not need to bother with the exact nature of transfer cost. It is sufficiently convincing just to take traversibility as an analogy to the refraction index for light rays (the reciprocal of the velocity of light). This holds for most of the discussion where the paradigm is employed. In the present discussion, however, we have to make the dependence of transfer cost on road capital explicit. We will return to this matter later. We should just note that the cases which have been most popular are those where transfer cost is independent of direction, depending only on location coordinates; these cases are called isotropic. This naturally means the decisive abstraction from real networks as the facility of movement becomes equal in all directions.

There is another interesting feature in Beckmann's analysis, that no later authors in the field seem to have taken up, namely the hydrodynamic analogy of traffic flow. Traffic is understood in terms of vector fields, with field lines coincident with the paths taken, and with moduli representing traffic. As in hydrodynamics, the vector field can be related to the distribution of sinks by its divergence, which by definition represents the number of elements added to an incompressible flow. From this it follows that the measure of traffic provides for conservation or incompressibility. This does not hold for other measures, like the "cordon crossing" measures of traffic used by Angel and Hyman (1972a, 1972b, 1976).

It is surprising that Beckmann's idea has not been taken up, especially as hydrodynamic analogies have been very common in other branches of traffic research, especially in the investigations on perturbation waves in platoons of vehicles on crowded lanes, ever since the idea was introduced by Lighthill and Whitham (1955).

In our case there will be continuously distributed point sources and point sinks, specified by some transportation demand function, depending on pairs of locations in space. If we fix an origin or, equivalently, a destination, for all transports then the vector field representation can be employed. But, unlike the completely analyzed basic Beckmann case, where the movement of a single item of merchandise from excess supply sources to excess demand sinks is studied in terms of a single vector field, we presently deal with a continuum of vector fields when the whole need for transportation is considered. As the fields do not interfere with each other to merge into one resultant field, but have moduli that aggregate to total traffic, there are no analogies to physical phenomena. We are, however, still aided in some measure by hydrodynamics and its mathematical tools, namely vector analysis and complex calculus.

We have now outlined the problem, and the paradigm used. The data which determine the solution can be specified as the geometric shape and size of the region, and the size of population with its distribution in space.

In addition we require two substantial hypotheses about how trips or transports are distributed in the region (i.e. the transportation demand as a function of any pair of locations), and about how transfer cost is related to the quantity of road capital invested at any point.

As to the first mentioned, there is a class of empirically well established hypotheses in geography, namely the gravity and entropy models. The former was introduced by Stewart (1947) and specifies the demand for transportation, or "interaction", as proportionate to the population densities, and reciprocal to some positive power of the distance between the locations considered. The inspiration from Newtonian gravitation theory is obvious. This simple specification of the familiar properties of communication patterns is appealing to the intuition. It seems reasonable that the potential need for transportation should be obtained by the product of population densities at the locations concerned, as every pair of persons situated at equal distances are then assumed to need the same number of communications. That contacts are reduced by distance is also a familiar phenomenon and one not difficult to explain. Owing to the expense of long-distance communication it may be imagined that of every type of facility people will use the nearest available, and even abstain from such that are too distant, or prefer second-best solutions that are closer at hand. One can also accept that institutions needing very frequent contacts agglomerate in close proximity to each other.

Whatever the reasons the model was seen to fit empirical data well for such cases as aviation traffic and telephonic communications. Both the dependence on population density and on distance were observed in several instances. The exponent, i.e. the distance elasticity, of course, did vary from one application to another, but this was only to be expected, since the transportation of bulky merchandise would certainly be more sensitive to distance than telephone calls.

When regional economists started to use this model for single-purpose communications such as trips to work, substituting numbers of workers and working places for population densities, they rapidly ran into difficulties, as a doubling of workers and working places in the model would lead to a quadrupling of trips (instead of a doubling as would be reasonable). This absurdity was eliminated by the introduction of special balancing factors, but the ad hoc character of the amendment was felt to be very unsatisfactory. Before continuing we should emphasize that the proportionality for multipurpose trips to the product of population densities is not at all so absurd when we take into consideration that, in a growing society, the diversity of trip purposes increases together with population, and that the empirical support for the gravity model in some applications cannot be denied by absurdities occurring in other applications.

The natural challenge was, however, taken up by Wilson (1967, 1970), who developed his statistical entropy model. This was again done by analogy to physics – in particular statistical mechanics. Wilson wanted to describe a pattern of spatial interaction, or a distribution of transportation demand, as a macro state of a system. With a single-purpose communication, such as trips to work, and a finite number of locations, the matrix of numbers of trips from homes to working places is the macro state. The micro state is the complete attribution of each worker to a working place. Taking all micro states as equiprobable, Wilson wanted to show that one macro state is much more probable than any other macro state. By means of a constraint that prescribes a given total expenditure on communication, Wilson managed to prove the existence of a very sharp maximum probability, and demonstrated that it corresponds to a trip distribution where the proportionality to origin and destination densities is preserved, and also a distance dependence (slightly altered, being an exponential instead of a power function). The balancing factors, that provide the calibration to avoid the absurd quadrupling, are also derived within the theory.

This model has become so successful that it has almost completely superseded the gravity model in empirical applications. Economists have, however, been somewhat reluctant to accept a theory of this type, where the distribution of trips is derived independently of the locational decisions by the individuals that finally determine the communication pattern. Personally I agree with the skeptics and find it difficult to accept the constraint of fixed total transportation costs as something reflecting even idealized reality. But, more important than this is the fact that both models have the same basic features, and that all the people working within this field try to derive models of these same two varieties, whether by maximizing entropy in a macro system, or by maximizing utility for individual commuters (that choose locations for homes and for jobs), instead of trying to prove them false.

Hence, we can safely use such a model as a building block, without entering into detail as to its theoretical underpinnings. Since we are interested in multipurpose trips, we took the gravity model in its original form, without balancing factors. Except in a few places the distance dependence too has been disregarded altogether, so that the gravity and entropy models become indistinguishable. This is advantageous analytically. Moreover, there are some reasons for making things so simple in the present context. If the observed, contact-reducing effect of distance is due entirely to the expense of long-distance communication, so that people are content with second-best solutions closer to their location, we could argue that the whole need for transportation, even those trips that are rejected because they are too costly, should be taken into consideration in the planning of roads. We could even say that, provided people react to changes in the road network by refraining from transport that becomes too expensive, the goal of minimizing total costs becomes dubious, because it is possible that the cost could be reduced by making communication in general more difficult so that people refrain from a number of trips.

On the other hand, it would be reasonable to assume that at least a considerable part of the contact-reducing effect of distance is due to the spatial organization of the economy where those institutions needing many contacts, as already noted, are located close to each other. As it is not possible to disregard completely the distance dependence, some space is devoted to an examination of the difference it makes when this is brought into the picture. The effect is not so great. We have chosen the gravity variant, mainly because of its analytic advantages.

Things could be made even more complicated, as a change of infrastructure in the long run certainly affects location and hence the organization in space, which could in turn no longer be taken as a given datum; but then we would have to develop a complete theory for the space economy, which is not one of the purposes of this book.

Hence, knowing the transfer cost function we may, within the chosen model, determine optimal routes between any pair of locations in the region using the methods of variational calculus. If, in addition, we know how population is distributed in the region we may, through the hypothesis about how trips are distributed, derive a measure of traffic when we employ the hydrodynamic methods outlined.

But, this solves only the first of the partial optimization problems. In order to solve the second, i.e. to discover the optimal distribution of road capital when the distribution of traffic is a given datum, we have to relate transfer cost to the quantity of road capital invested by a specified mathematical relation.

As already mentioned, the general characteristics of such a relation are not difficult to find out. Obviously, a lot of road capital invested at one point means low transfer cost. The continuous model may be regarded as the limiting case of a network that is "microscopic" in mesh size. If the magnified picture of the microscopic network contained in a "point" is not completely filled with roads going in every imaginable direction everywhere, then in general it is not possible to take a straight line path between any two vertices of the network. The linear Euclidean distance has to be augmented by detours. Increasing road capital, by the addition to the network of new shortcuts, reduces these detours, but the reductions are subject to a law of diminishing returns, since a new shortcut saves fewer detours the more ramified is the existing network.

The simplest way of formalizing these ideas would be to let transfer cost be the sum of two terms: one linear or Euclidean cost that cannot be influenced and that provides an infimum when road capital goes to infinity, and one detour cost that is reciprocal to the quantity of road capital invested.

Apart from this general argument, the relation will be supported by a rigorous derivation. It is shown to hold for all networks that are conformal transformations of a regular network of roads intersecting six by six at every junction under angles of 60°. The basic network can hence be built up by equilateral triangle elements. It is also shown, following Mosler (1976b), that among all regular networks built by polygons this one is of the shape that requires the least detours when it is followed, i.e. the ratio between actual distance travelled and Euclidean distance is smaller than for any other regular network. The conformal transformations allow the density of the network to vary in any way over the region. Through the limiting process of mesh condensation the actual network disappears and paths that are sequences of arc segments joined with kinks almost turn into smooth curves. The actual length of a microscopic kinked path remains as information summed up by the transfer cost, specified at each point. When the cost or the length of a path is calculated, then a line integral of this transfer distance is taken along a path considered, and this is how paths following the network are transformed into paths taking any direction in the plane.

With this specification of the transfer cost function the optimal distribution of road capital, given the distribution of traffic, is solved so that road capital is proportionate to the square root of traffic.

I have included a section where data for Sweden 1973, concerning transportation work and road networks for a subdivision into local regions, are used to estimate a power curve for the relation between road capital and traffic (obtained from the primary data by division by areas). The fit is relatively good and the square root rule is within statistical confidence limits. The value of this should not be overrated, of course, but assuming that the Swedish road administration was reasonably successful in planning the network or roads (through its proper planning instruments) then the empirical data would provide some indirect confirmation of the continuous model in general and of the postulated relation between transfer cost and road capital in particular.

Apart from a discussion of the two partial optimization problems and an attempt to characterize the equilibrium distribution of traffic for a special case with a constant population on a unit disk, we discuss how transportation costs vary for different locations of origin. One might think that there would be a conflict of interest between people living centrally and peripherally, so that the former would desire centralized, the latter decentralized road capital. It turns out, however, that a solution that is optimal from the viewpoint of achieving minimum total travel costs is also optimal for almost any location. Depending on the exact location one would desire slightly more or less centralization of road capital, but everybody would profit from some degree of it. This, of course, is to a certain extent due to the fact that we disregard the dependence on distance, so that each location must communicate with all other locations with the same intensity, no matter how far off they are.

This is a quite unusual situation in the economics of public goods, among which roads should be counted. Conflicting interests, rather than consensus, are usually characteristic.

The final chapter takes up the problem of congestion and of differential land acquisition costs. However, the detour-reducing quality of roads is now disregarded and transfer costs are specified as only dependent on the ratio of traffic to road capital, which is used as a measure of congestion. Applicability is implicitly changed from a vast country to a limited urban area. There network density could well be taken as approximately constant, so that the main variation is in the ability of the roads to carry traffic. The introduction of differential land acquisition and construction costs is also natural, as at least land value certainly increases towards the center of the city.

In this simplified version the congestion case actually turns out to be less complicated than the subject matter of the main part of the book. First it is noted that, with any given distribution of traffic, the optimal ratio of road capital to traffic can be solved as a given function of the space coordinates, the form depending solely on the distribution of land acquisition costs. Then, we are able to demonstrate, by applying methods developed in the preceding chapters, that the total transportation cost, incurred when people seek minimum cost paths individually, is the smallest cost at which the need for transportation can be satisfied. Hence, in contrast to what economists usually argue, congestion tolls are not needed, because the congestion-delayed transfer velocity automatically acts as the signal or "price" needed to make individuals behave in accordance with the social optimum. The undeniable presence of "external effects" does not necessarily call for correcting tolls.

The qualification for this to hold true is that road capital be optimally allocated, which it seldom is in reality, due to the fact that changes of road distributions in response to changes in communication patterns are slow.

Only in the final chapter are the temporal aspects and the variations in traffic during the day taken into consideration. However, only one set of assumptions are specified, under which the conclusion still holds that correcting tolls are not needed. These are: (1) that all transportation needs are split into two parts, one that must be made at specified moments and one that can be made any time; (2) that these parts are proportional to their total; (3) that for the latter category of trips people prefer times when the trip is least time-consuming; and (4) that if several times are equivalent there may well be a preference for certain times, but that this preference is independent of the locations of origin and destination.

The conclusions are then not altered by introducing the temporal factor. All this warns us against the mechanical application of the economic theory of externalities. We have to recognize that tolls, or other corrective restrictions (which may prove more practicable), are second-best solutions instead of an optimal allocation of roads. It must be emphasized, however, that the objective only admits such external effects as delays on other communications but not such as damage to health and property through accidents and pollution of the environment.

Outline of the contents

This section outlines the organization of the book. In Chapter 2 the reader is familiarized with the problem of the optimal allocation of road capital, given a certain distribution of traffic, by means of a much simplified case, where the region is a one-dimensional interval. The population is assumed, as in a substantial part of the discussion, to be constant, so that one transport must join each pair of points in the region. This case is characterized by the fact that, as the region is an interval, any path or route must be a subinterval, determined by the two endpoints. Accordingly there is no latitude of choice as regards the path, and so the distribution of traffic is given independently of transfer costs. This means that the optimum allocation of road capital with the given distribution of traffic solves the whole optimum problem. In the derivation we develop a natural definition of traffic, geometrically interpreted as the product of the two interval lengths into which the whole interval is divided by the point at which traffic is calculated. This is accomplished by partial integration. The result is a simple parabolic traffic distribution. The optimum condition for the distribution of a given total quantity of road capital then prescribes that it is everywhere proportionate to the square root of traffic, so that the optimal traffic distribution is represented by an ellipse. The qualification for this is that the relation between road capital and transfer cost is a hyperbola, representing decreasing returns from successive increases of road capital at one point.

In Chapter 3 we introduce the general two-dimensional case. The chapter is devoted to developing a natural measure of traffic for the two-dimensional case with incompressibility or conservation properties. The task is accomplished by transforming an expression for total transportation costs, obtained by integrating the product of the cost of transportation and the number of transports between any two points, with respect to all possible origins and destinations. As each location is identified by two coordinates, the cost is originally obtained as a fourfold integral. This fourfold integral is transformed into a double integral, taken over all locations of the region, where the integrand is the product of transfer cost and the measure of traffic proposed, exactly as in the one-dimensional case. The difference is that now this traffic distribution can no longer be taken as a given entity as soon as the demand for transportation is specified. Rather, it is dependent upon the choice of paths and hence on the transfer cost function. The analytical tool is now Gauss's theorem, as integration by parts was in the one-dimensional case.

In Chapter 4 there is a discussion of the choice of optimal paths when the transfer cost function is a given datum. This variational problem is solved by minimizing the total transportation costs with the transfer cost function given. It is first noted that the minimization can be broken down into minimizing total transportation costs for each point of origin when, in the absence of congestion, there are no externalities. We then see that this is equivalent to minimizing the cost for each individual transport, which proves that tolls are superfluous. The result as such is trivial, but it can be applied in the last chapter to the congestion case and provides the same conclusion. The optimal paths are obtained by classical variational methods, and the sufficiency conditions are checked. The possibility is also discussed of employing plane conformal transformations to map curved optimal paths on straight lines, and conformal transformations onto curved surfaces such that the optimal paths become geodesics, i.e. straight in a generalized meaning.

In Chapter 5 the knowledge of optimal paths and of the proper definition of traffic is used to compute traffic distribution explicitly for two cases, namely when all paths are linear and when all paths are radial (going radially into the center and radially out again), respectively. For the sake of simplicity the region is taken as a unit disk and population is assumed to be constant in space. It is seen that the procedure requires the solution of a partial differential equation to obtain the measure of traffic passing across a point with one given starting point and going in one given direction. To obtain the measure of traffic passing across a point in all directions, from all possible points of origin in the region, we have to integrate twice subsequently with respect to the two coordinates that identify the origins. This procedure is so complicated that it was only possible to carry it out for the two simple cases of linear and radial paths. However, there are strong intuitive reasons for believing that the two distributions are important limiting cases, so that the trafffic distributions with any monotonically increasing and circularly symmetric transfer cost, implying convex paths, look like something between the distributions for the two cases solved.

Chapter 6 is devoted to a brief outline of the development of gravity and entropy models of interaction, and Chapter 7 to taking distance elasticity of transportation demand into the picture. The simple case treated is that of linear paths. Using the gravity model it is seen that the general conclusions are not much changed. The gravity model admits a solution where only one integration needs numerical quadrature, and this is done using Simpson's rule.

In Chapter 8 an attempt is made to develop a direct method to compute traffic distributions, so that the awkward method of solving one ordinary differential equation, one partial differential equation and subsequent double integration is not needed. It is seen that this procedure can be replaced by computing a fourfold integral directly. The method is illustrated by simulating random endpoints for transports, by numerical quadrature, and by a simple rough geometrical approximation. The method is similar to that of counting so-called cordon crossings, i.e. numbers of intersections of paths generated at random, with circles drawn concentrically with different radii. It can be seen, however, that the measures obtained in this way are correct, if the cordon crossings are not only counted, but weighted by the incidence angle secants.

In Chapter 9 the direct method is used to calculate traffic distributions with nonconstant populations.

In Chapter 10 the measure of transfer cost is formally related to road capital by a simplified model. It is first demonstrated that when the network of roads is built by elements that are equilateral triangles then the average distance, including detours, along the network equals the Euclidean distance plus a term that is reciprocal to the density of roads, measured as the length of the network per unit area. This relation is seen to be independent of mesh, so that it still holds true when at the limit the mesh vanishes in size. As the crucial elements, i.e. intersection angles of roads and linear magnification factors, are unchanged or independent of direction, respectively, we discover that the relation still holds true if the network is obtained from the one built by equilateral triangles after conformal mappings. We also supply some reasons for the choice of the basic network. It is seen that, as compared to other networks built by tesellations of regular polygons, the one used minimizes the necessity to make detours, whereas criteria designed to determine the accessibility to the network to inhabitants living inside an elementary polygon, delineated by the roads, cannot discriminate between the regular networks. In this way the network type, for which the intuitively appealing hyperbola relation holds true, is the most efficient amongst the regular ones. In this chapter we see how the kinked paths along the real network in the limit become smooth curves, that can take on any shape, whereas the length of the kinked actual paths in relation to the smooth approximations are summarized in the concept of transfer cost (time or distance) for each point.

In Chapter 11 we use this specification of the transfer cost function to derive the optimal allocation of road capital (given in total quantity) when the distribution of traffic is a given datum. Again the square root rule appears, i.e. road capital is prescribed to be proportionate to the square root of traffic. The partial optimality rule is hence simple to derive, and is the same as in the one-dimensional case. The equilibrium-optimum, however, cannot be specified. To do it as well as possible, we take a simple class of power function and try to discover which member of this family of functions is the one (amongst those where a given total of road capital is distributed) which minimizes total transportation costs. It is seen that in this class of functions the best one represents some concentration of road capital to the central parts of the region.

Chapter 12 supplies some empirical evidence for the method used (the continuous model and the hyperbola relation between transfer cost and road capital). There are data available for a subdivision of Sweden into 275 local communities, about local road networks and local transportation work. Through division by areas, measures of traffic and of road capital are obtained, and a power curve is fitted by least squares. The power function explains 65 percent of the variation in road capital. After renewed estimation by generalized least squares, to correct for heteroscedasticity, an exponent of 0.46 is obtained. This is pretty close to the optimal 0.50 prescribed by the square root rule and, in fact, within 99 percent confidence limits. Hence, the empirical data would seem to support the theory developed, provided we assume that the planning authorities have been efficient in planning, by their proper means, of course.

In Chapter 13 we look at how communication costs would be distributed for different locations, to see if there are strongly conflicting interests as regards the location of roads for people living in different parts of the region. We see that, provided at least that the need for transportation in the first approximation is not distance-dependent and that we confine the discussion to the same class of power functions as in the discussion of optima-equilibria, surprisingly a globally optimal road capital concentration is almost optimal for everybody living in the region.

Finally, in Chapter 14 congestion and differential land acquisition costs are taken into consideration. The focal interest is changed from a vast country to a limited urban area. Network density is assumed to be almost constant, and only transfer time, i.e. the reciprocal of velocity, is taken into consideration. This transfer time is assumed to be determined by a measure of congestion that is simply the ratio of traffic to road capital (as representing the capacity to carry traffic). We see that, if land acquisition costs are constant in space, then road capital should be proportionate to traffic (not to its square root). We also see that total transportation is then minimized when total traffic is also, i.e. when the paths are straight lines. But, as congestion is constant, road capital being proportionate to traffic, the individual transporters automatically choose straight lines, so that no tolls are needed. The result is trivial in view of the fact that congestion is constant. Therefore it is interesting to bring differential land acquisition costs into the picture, so that congestion is no longer constant. With cheaper roads in the periphery it is preferable to increase road capital there more than in proportion to traffic, so that congestion increases as one moves to the center. As we discover, however, the paths chosen by individuals are still socially optimal, so that the increasing transfer time in congested areas automatically acts as the "price" or "signal" needed, again making tolls superfluous.

It is unavoidable that the discussion should become somewhat technical. To aid the reader without any knowledge in the fields of vector analysis, complex variables, the calculus of variations and differential geometry, five appendices devoted to these subjects have been added. The appendices are written from my subjective point of view. Being an economist, with a general knowledge in calculus and ordinary optimization, I have myself felt a strong need to supplement my existing knowledge with the fundamentals of the fields enumerated above. As they are usually methodological tools employed in physics they do not occur in the ordinary reading of a general economist. This may not be a suitable choice of items to be explained for readers with different backgrounds, but it has been impossible to adapt the choice of material in the appendices to suit all potential classes of readers.

Appendix A deals with vector analysis which is needed for Chapters 3, 4, 5, 8 and 14. Appendix B, concerning the calculus of variations, is a requisite for Chapters 4 and 14. Appendix C, which concerns complex analysis, is needed for the reading of Chapters 4 and 10. Appendix D, concerning differential geometry, is only used in Chapter 4. Appendix E, on tensors, supplements the material of Appendix D.

Apart from these techniques, summarized in the appendices, the reader is assumed to have some knowledge of calculus, above all of handling multiple integrals and ordinary differential equations. (The partial differential equations that occur are so simple that they do not require any additional knowledge.) Some knowledge of elementary statistical techniques, least squares and generalized least squares regression, and simple testing of regression coefficients, as well as simple simulation techniques and programming in BASIC are also necessary. In addition, some knowledge of graph theory and of physics, especially optics, particle kinematics and statistical mechanics, would be helpful.

The methods enumerated are, however, only necessary if one wants to understand all the material, and to continue a line of research from any of the loose ends left. For a more informative reading, I hope that the book is sufficiently self-contained, and that the main ideas communicate themselves even if the reader does not bother with the formal derivations at all.

Chapter 2

THE ONE-DIMENSIONAL CASE

We now discuss the one-dimensional case in some detail in order to familiarize the reader with the problems discussed and the assumptions made. The one-dimensional case is so much simpler than the two-dimensional that it is almost trivial.

Hence, assume as region the interval $(-1, 1)$, where population is uniformly distributed so that, assuming every pair of individuals to need one transport each unit time period, there is one transport between each pair of points.

Locations are identified by the variable x. The point of origin for a transport is denoted x_0 and the point of destination x_1.

Assume now that the cost of moving across a point is denoted f, and is equal to $a+b/l$, where l is road capital invested in the point. As was said in Chapter 1, this reflects an assumption that there is always the necessity to move across a linear distance. Increased road capital eliminates undesirable detours, hence reducing transfer cost f, subject to the law of diminishing returns from successive increases. In the one-dimensional case the geometric model makes no sense (it will be formally derived for the two-dimensional case), so let us say that the specification is the simplest way of expressing the facts that there is an infimum cost for moving across a point, that the actual cost can be reduced by increasing road capital but that, due to diminishing returns, the infimum cost can only be reached with an infinite amount of road capital.

2.1. Cost and traffic

These assumptions make it possible to calculate the cost for one transport. If the transfer cost function is given as $f(x)$, we get

$$I=\int_{x_0}^{x_1} f(x)\mathrm{d}x \tag{1}$$

as the cost of transportation from x_0 to x_1, provided that the point of destination is to the right of the point of origin. Otherwise, we would have to put a minus sign before the integral.

We are now able to compute total transportation costs for the whole region as

$$2\int_{-1}^{1}\int_{x_0}^{1} I\,\mathrm{d}x_1\mathrm{d}x_0 = 2\int_{-1}^{1}\int_{x_0}^{1}\int_{x_0}^{x_1} f(x)\,\mathrm{d}x\,\mathrm{d}x_1\mathrm{d}x_0. \tag{2}$$

The factor 2 is necessary because the integral only accounts for trips going to the right. Trips leftwards could be calculated by another integral, but we can see directly that they are equal in number and have the same cost as the corresponding trips rightwards.

We can now transform the triple integral into a single integral by integrating partially twice. The right-hand member of the preceding equation first transforms to

$$2\int_{-1}^{1}\left(x_1\int_{x_0}^{x_1} f(x)\,\mathrm{d}x\Big|_{x_1=x_0}^{x_1=1} - \int_{x_0}^{1} x_1 f(x_1)\,\mathrm{d}x_1\right)\mathrm{d}x_0 = 2\int_{-1}^{1}\int_{x_0}^{1}(1-x)f(x)\,\mathrm{d}x\,\mathrm{d}x_0. \tag{3}$$

We have simply used the partial integration formula for x_1 and, in the last transformation, substituted the symbol x for x_1, which is always allowed when the integration limits are the same.

Next, we do the same with respect to x_0, i.e. use integration by parts. Hence, eq. (3) transforms to

$$2\left(x_0\int_{x_0}^{1}(1-x)f(x)\,\mathrm{d}x\Big|_{x_0=-1}^{x_0=1} + \int_{-1}^{1} x_0(1-x_0)f(x_0)\,\mathrm{d}x_0\right) = 2\int_{-1}^{1}(1-x^2)f(x)\,\mathrm{d}x, \tag{4}$$

where again in the last transformation we have substituted x for x_0.

The complicated triple integral has thus been transformed into a single integral. The factor $2(1-x^2)$ has the following simple interpretation. A point x in the interval $(-1,1)$ divides the interval into the two subintervals $(-1,x)$ and $(x,1)$, the lengths of which are $(1+x)$ and $(1-x)$, respectively. As one transport starts at each point and ends at each point, the total number of transports through x, going from the interval on the left of x to the interval on the right of x, is $(1+x)(1-x)=(1-x^2)$. The same number of transports go from the right to the left. We can thus intuitively interpret $2(1-x^2)$ as the measure of *traffic going through the point* x. Traffic is maximal when we are at the origin, i.e. the midpoint of the interval, and decreases symmetrically to both sides so that it is zero at both endpoints of the interval considered.

This produces a nice interpretation of the last integral. Total communication costs, originally obtained as the double integral $2\int\int I\,\mathrm{d}x_1\mathrm{d}x_0$, equal the single integral of traffic multiplied by transfer cost $2\int(1-x^2)f(x)\mathrm{d}x$.

2.2. Complications in the two-dimensional case

We can stop here to consider what the two-dimensional case would look like. First, the definition of I above is nonproblematic. There is only one route that the transporters can use, namely the part of the line segment between the endpoints. In two-dimensional space, on the other hand, the individual transporters have to choose an appropriate path so that the cost is minimized, given the transfer cost function. To determine these paths we must solve a problem in variational calculus, and we have had to devote a whole chapter to it.

Secondly, the passage from the triple integral to the single in the present case would be equivalent to a passage from a fourfold integral to a double. The derivation is much more complicated than that using integration by parts. It is done by applying Gauss's theorem in the plane, which in fact provides a type of formula for integration "by parts".

Thirdly, the distribution of traffic, which has been seen to be given and *independent of* $f(x)$ is, in the two-dimensional case, an outcome of the choice of transportation routes and hence depends on the form of the f-function. It is quite complicated to compute a traffic distribution corresponding to a given transfer cost function. Actually it involves the following steps: (i) solving the variational problem, which requires the solution of a (usually nonlinear) differential equation of the second order; moreover (ii) solving a partial differential equation the form of which depends on the solution of the first one; and finally (iii) taking a double integral. Alternatively, it is shown that in some cases the three steps can be replaced by an evaluation of a fourfold integral. As the reader can understand, we are only able to obtain explicit solutions for very special cases.

2.3. Optimal distribution of road capital

Returning to our one-dimensional introductory case, we would want to minimize

$$2\int_{-1}^{1}(1-x^2)f(x)\mathrm{d}x, \tag{5}$$

which is total communication costs, subject to the postulated constraint

$$f(x)=a+b/l(x), \tag{6}$$

and the additional constraint

$$\int_{-1}^{1} l(x)\mathrm{d}x=\text{constant}, \tag{7}$$

expressing the fact that a given total amount of road capital is to be distributed. The minimization is made by choosing l as an appropriate function of x.

This is an (infinite-dimensional) constrained minimization problem that can easily be handled by a Lagrangian method. The solution is obviously obtained from the first-order condition $-2(1-x^2)b/l^2+\mu=0$, which may be written

$$l=\gamma\sqrt{(1-x^2)},$$

where $\gamma^2=2b/\mu$ and μ is the original Lagrange multiplier (see fig. 2.1). The value of the proportionality constant γ can easily be calculated to equal the ratio of the constant total road capital to the integral of the square root of traffic (that equals $\pi/2$). Hence, the optimum distribution of road capital is solved. It is also

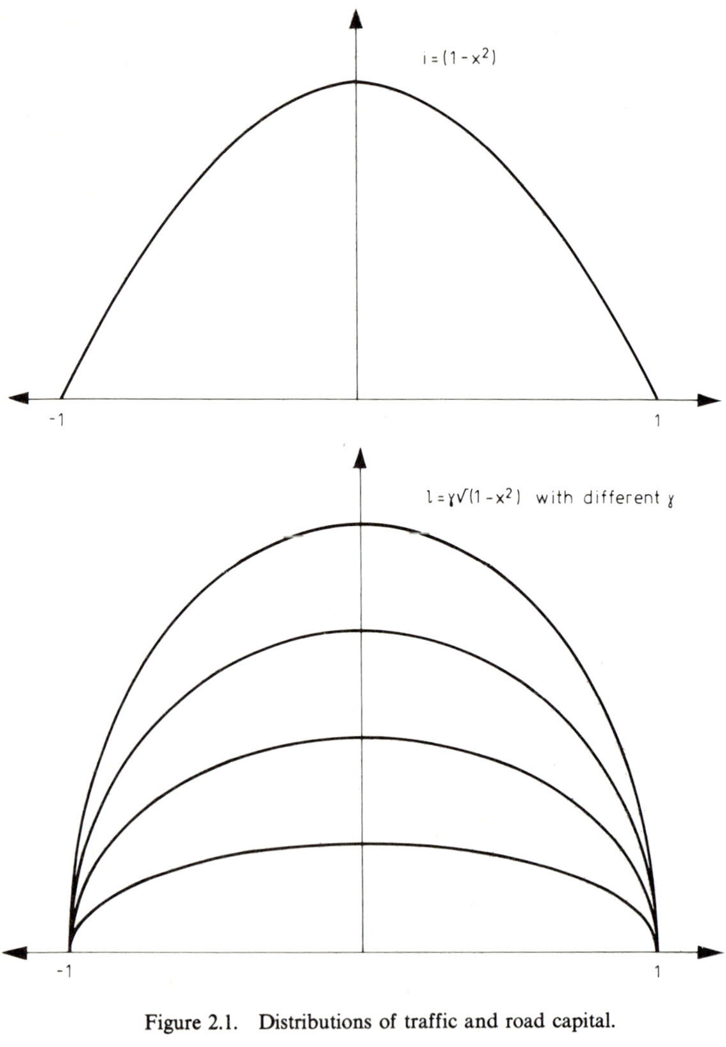

Figure 2.1. Distributions of traffic and road capital.

obvious that it is an equilibrium that will be attained independently of congestion tolls. As a matter of fact the question of whether congestion tolls are needed is not meaningful in the one-dimensional case, because it is not possible to redistribute traffic by tolls (at least insofar as the time aspects with varying loads over the day are not introduced). Trips joining points at different sides of the center simply must cross this congested center. In the two-dimensional case this becomes far from trivial, since it is possible to force the transporters to make spatial deviations around congestion centers.

As was said in Chapter 1, however, we will first disregard congestion and only take it up in the final chapter. The same holds true for the case of differential land acquisition costs for road-building in various parts of the region.

Other generalizations, treated casually and again left, are cases of nonequal distributions of population and dependence on distance for transportation demand.

However, although we leave aside all these complications and assume the region to have an extraordinarily simple shape, by taking a unit disk, we will not actually be able to derive an equilibrium or optimum distribution of road capital in the two-dimensional case. What we can do is to identify the best member within a special class of functions, and to provide some general considerations.

To be more exact, the square root relation between road capital and traffic still holds true and is almost as simple to derive as in the one-dimensional case. It is also supported by some empirical evidence. But, owing to the difficulties of computing traffic distributions, the circle cannot be closed.

2.4. The one-dimensional region in the "new urban economics"

The idea of a one-dimensional region was used by Solow and Vickrey (1971) in an attempt to discover the optimal allocation of urban space between roads and residences and the variation of rent from the center to the outskirts appropriate for striking the optimum. The "long narrow city" was an excessive simplification needed to make the task tractable. Later, Solow (1972) generalized the model to two dimensions, but the generalization is spurious, because there are only radial communications with a CBD ("central business district") in the model. The two-dimensional model is then simply the image of the one-dimensional model rotated around the center. By this, of course, magnitudes are altered because line segments turn into rings with areal dimension, but otherwise things remain the same. Angel and Hyman (1976) criticize the "new urban economics" for ignoring the real two-dimensional character of space, because the radial communication with a CBD leaves the most interesting and difficult matters out of the picture, and of course they are right in this. However, one must make simplifications in order to obtain manageable models and Solow is well aware of this. This is also why we are not going to complicate the discussion with the fact that land used for road construction is taken from residential or other uses, or with the attempt to derive a land rent gradient. Since I am not going to enter into this most interesting field of land-use theory, which has given rise to much literature following the works of Wingo (1961) and Alonso (1965), I have contented myself with the mention of one single contribution.

Since we disregard the discussion of land-use alternatives – for housing and for road construction – we will also disregard the most interesting modern literature in the vein of von Thünen (1921). Instead of confining all production in a CBD, this branch of regional economics studies the spatial arrangement of rings for the production of various goods and the allocation of land to these productive activities in competition with the demand for road construction. Together with the spatial arrangement for the production of different commodities a land rent structure emerges from the model. Here I will only refer to one of many contributions on this subject, namely a most interesting work by Schweizer and Varaiya (1976), where they manage to derive interesting theorems on the direction of movement of half-finished goods. But, in this discussion too, there is a single CBD to which all transportation goes radially. Even if production is no longer concentrated there, it is the market place for finished consumer goods and because of the radial transport the most interesting features of two-dimensional space are lost.

In order to concentrate on them, I have to disregard the allocation of various productive activities in space as well as residential land use and the variation of rent. Even though an integration of these problems would be most desirable, at present I have to exclude them from the picture and take the whole locational pattern of production as well as housing as a given datum.

Chapter 3

TRANSPORTATION COSTS AND THE INTENSITY OF TRAFFIC

S denotes the region and G its boundary. The boundary is assumed to be positively oriented, so that moving along it in the positive direction means that the interior of the region will be on the left-hand side. G is, of course, a closed curve, which is sectionally smooth and delimits a convex region. On S is defined a continuous population density function $p(x,y)$; P denotes total population, i.e. the surface integral of this function over the region.

According to assumptions the number of transports from a point ξ,η to a point x,y is $p(\xi,\eta)p(x,y)$. When only those transports which started at a fixed point are considered this product is written $\bar{p}p$, where $\bar{p}$ is population at the fixed point of origin ξ,η.

Assume that transportation facilities are given. According to the assumptions they are represented by a positive and continuously differentiable transfer cost function, denoted by $f(x,y)$, and likewise defined on S. A certain transportation path or route is given parametrically by $x(\tau)$ and $y(\tau)$, where τ is the length of arc along the path, measured from the point of origin ξ,η. The cost for a certain transport is then given by the definite integral

$$I(t)=\int_0^t f\,\mathrm{d}\tau. \tag{8}$$

If we only consider transports radiating outwards from one single fixed point ξ,η, then it is obvious that the optimal route to any intermediate point on an optimal route must coincide with part of the latter.[1] It follows from definition (8), according to which transportation costs are "additive", i.e. obtainable by integration, that such a policy must be followed if the paths be candidates for optimality. The result then is that there is only *one* path going through each point of S, except the singular point ξ,η to which all the paths converge. Hence they constitute a set of field lines.

[1]This fact implies that we abstract from costs associated with changes of means of transportation. Such costs may make it profitable to use a certain path only if it is followed over a sufficiently long distance.

3.1. A measure of traffic with "conservation" properties

Let us further associate with each point of the region (except the singular ξ,η) a scalar quantity denoting the local intensity of traffic, or rather the *partial* local intensity of traffic, flowing in a certain direction and having the given point ξ,η as origin. Later we will define the *total* local intensity of traffic, flowing across the point in all directions and starting at all the points of the region.

But for a given point of origin we have only one set of field lines and we may therefore associate with each point – still excepting ξ,η – a vector field whose direction is the direction of the path and whose modulus is the partial intensity of traffic. We denote the vector field $\boldsymbol{v}$. The partial intensity of traffic is hence $|\boldsymbol{v}|$, and the direction taken by it is given by the unit vector $\boldsymbol{v}/|\boldsymbol{v}|=(\cos\theta,\sin\theta)$. Accordingly, $\boldsymbol{v}$ is a field defined everywhere on S, except at ξ,η where there is a singularity.

With a certain field $\boldsymbol{v}$ we may also associate a scalar function $I(x,y)$ defined on S and expressing the cost of transportation from ξ,η to the point x,y according to (8) when the field lines of $\boldsymbol{v}$ are used as transportation paths.

So far we have not said anything about how the modulus of $\boldsymbol{v}$ is determined only about its direction, which is the direction of a system of arbitrary transportation paths. The modulus must be determined by two things, namely how many transports end at each point in the region and how many transports flow across its boundary.

We know from vector analysis that the divergence of a vector field tells us how additional elements are added to a flow at each point. In the present case there is a "sink" or a negative "source" $-\bar{p}p$ at each point as $\bar{p}p$ transports are delivered there. Accordingly, the divergence of $\boldsymbol{v}$ equals $-\bar{p}p$, i.e.

$$\nabla\cdot\boldsymbol{v}=-\bar{p}p. \tag{9}$$

This imposes one constraint on $\boldsymbol{v}$. The other constraint is that no transports go across the boundary G to the exterior of the region, i.e. $\boldsymbol{v}\cdot\boldsymbol{n}=0$ on G where $\boldsymbol{n}$ is the unit outward normal to the boundary curve. These conditions together with the field lines determine the field $\boldsymbol{v}$ everywhere, except at the singular point of origin.

Let us next compute the cost for all transports originating at ξ,η, denoted by $C(\xi,\eta)$. Since I, according to (8), is the cost of transportation from the point of origin to an arbitrary point x,y, and as $\bar{p}p$ is the number of transports ending there, the whole cost incurred is

$$C(\xi,\eta)=\int\int_S I\bar{p}p\,\mathrm{d}x\,\mathrm{d}y. \tag{10}$$

We shall now transform this expression into another one, expressed in terms of the transfer cost f and the partial intensity of traffic $|\boldsymbol{v}|$. First, we note from (9) that we may write

$$C(\xi,\eta) = -\int\int_S I\nabla \cdot \boldsymbol{v}\,\mathrm{d}x\,\mathrm{d}y. \tag{11}$$

Next we see that according to a standard formula in vector analysis

$$\nabla \cdot (I\boldsymbol{v}) = \nabla I \cdot \boldsymbol{v} + I\nabla \cdot \boldsymbol{v}. \tag{12}$$

According to Gauss's divergence theorem for two-dimensional space the surface integral of the divergence of a vector field over a region equals the line integral of the outward normal component of the vector taken along the boundary. For this to be applicable the region must be delimited by a closed boundary curve (as assumed) and the vector field must be regular everywhere.

There is a problem, namely the singularity at the point ξ, η which prevents the latter condition from being fulfilled for the region S itself. We may, however, easily overcome this difficulty by surrounding the singular point by a second boundary curve and excluding the portion of S lying inside this curve. The new region is denoted by S' and the curve that delimits the excluded part is denoted Γ. It is assumed that Γ, like G, is positively oriented. For Γ we take a niveau curve for $I=$constant. Hence, we may decrease the excluded portion indefinitely by taking smaller values for I. In the limit, as I goes to zero, S' goes to S. For all S', no matter how small I is, Gauss's theorem is applicable. Hence,

$$\int\int_{S'} \nabla \cdot (I\boldsymbol{v})\,\mathrm{d}x\,\mathrm{d}y = \int_\Gamma I\boldsymbol{v} \cdot \boldsymbol{n}\,\mathrm{d}s, \tag{13}$$

since we do not need to write down the line integral along G when the normal component of $\boldsymbol{v}$ vanishes (because, according to assumptions, no transports go across the boundary G). As before, in eq. (13) the vector $\boldsymbol{n}$ is the unit outward normal to the boundary Γ. However, as I is constant along Γ, we may move I outside the integration sign in the right-hand member of (13).

Next, we apply Gauss's theorem to $\nabla \cdot \boldsymbol{v} = -\bar{p}p$ for the same region S'. This yields

$$\int_\Gamma \boldsymbol{v} \cdot \boldsymbol{n}\,\mathrm{d}s = -\bar{p}\int\int_{S'} p\,\mathrm{d}x\,\mathrm{d}y \tag{14}$$

since again the line integral along G vanishes for the same reason as in (13). (The factor $\bar{p}$ has been moved outside the integration signs since it denotes population at the fixed point of origin and hence is independent of the space coordinates x,y of the variable endpoint.)

In the limit, as I goes to zero, the right-hand member of (14) approaches $-\bar{p}P$, where, as before, P is total population of the region. Notice that the limiting value $\bar{p}P$ denotes the number of transports emanating from the singular point ξ, η. It is intuitively obvious that this number of transports is obtained as the product of total population in the region and the population of the singular point of origin.

What has been said is that the right-hand member of (13) in the limit is the product of two factors, namely I which goes to zero and the integral (14) which goes to the finite number $-\bar{p}P$. Hence, the right-hand member of (13) goes to zero, whereas the region of integration in the left-hand member of (13) goes to the whole region S. This means that the improper integral

$$\int\int_S \nabla\cdot(I\boldsymbol{v})\,\mathrm{d}x\,\mathrm{d}y=0. \tag{15}$$

Application of this to (12) and the use of expression (11) yields

$$C(\xi,\eta)=\int\int_S \nabla I\cdot\boldsymbol{v}\,\mathrm{d}x\,\mathrm{d}y. \tag{16}$$

But, as $\boldsymbol{v}/|\boldsymbol{v}|$ is a unit vector in the direction of the transportation path we see that $\mathrm{d}I/\mathrm{d}t=\nabla I\cdot\boldsymbol{v}/|\boldsymbol{v}|$ and this, according to (8) equals f. Hence $\nabla I\cdot\boldsymbol{v}=f|\boldsymbol{v}|$ and

$$C(\xi,\eta)=\int\int_S f|\boldsymbol{v}|\mathrm{d}x\,\mathrm{d}y. \tag{17}$$

This is the final transformation of (10). The total cost for all transports originating at ξ,η, initially expressed in terms of the transportation cost I to each point and the number $\bar{p}p$ of transports ending there, is now obtained in terms of the transfer cost f across a point and the partial intensity $|\boldsymbol{v}|$ of traffic there. Expressions (10) and (17) tell us how much all transportation costs are for individuals situated at ξ,η. The expressions may be used to discover how profitable various points are for individuals from the point of view of centrality of location.

But, in order to discuss equilibrium and optimality for the whole region, we need the cost of transportation for all individuals living at all the points of the region. This latter cost is

$$\int\int_S C(\xi,\eta)\,\mathrm{d}\xi\,\mathrm{d}\eta \tag{18}$$

or, if we define the *total* intensity of traffic

$$i(x,y)=\int\int_S|\boldsymbol{v}|\mathrm{d}\xi,\mathrm{d}\eta, \tag{19}$$

we get total cost according to (18) and (17) as

$$\int\int_S f(x,y)i(x,y)\,\mathrm{d}x\,\mathrm{d}y. \tag{20}$$

This is the expression that the road-building authorities will attempt to minimize.

We finish this chapter by pointing out two important facts that will be useful later. The first is that the derivations in this chapter are by no means dependent on the simplicity of eq. (9). We could have introduced a distance dependence as well, replacing $\bar{p}p$ by $\bar{p}p/\tau^{\varepsilon}$, where τ denotes distance along the path chosen, and where ε is a distance elasticity. Instead of this gravity model we could have used the entropy model where the distance dependence is specified as $e^{-\beta\tau}$ instead of $\tau^{-\varepsilon}$. Instead of the potential defined by the product of population densities we could have used asymmetric densities of origins $O(\xi,\eta)$ and destinations $D(x,y)$. We could also have multiplied origin and destination densities by special balancing factors $A(\xi,\eta), B(x,y)$. Whatever we had been using in the right-hand member of (9) all the substitutions made could still be made in the same manner and the derivation would hold. In short, the right-hand member of (9) could be replaced by any transportation demand function of the pairs of locational coordinates ξ,η and x,y, and everything would hold true.

3.2. Total traffic and total transportation work

The second fact is that if we replace f in eq. (8) by a unit constant, then we at once note that $I=t$. Next, we see from (10) and (17) that

$$\int\int_S t\bar{p}p \, \mathrm{d}x \, \mathrm{d}y = \int\int_S |v| \mathrm{d}x \, \mathrm{d}y. \tag{21}$$

Integrating once more with respect to ξ,η on S we get

$$\int\int_S\int\int_S t\bar{p}p \, \mathrm{d}x \, \mathrm{d}y \, \mathrm{d}\xi \, \mathrm{d}\eta = \int\int_S i \, \mathrm{d}x \, \mathrm{d}y. \tag{22}$$

But, the left-hand member is an integral with respect to all origins and all destinations of the number of transports multiplied by the length of each transport. It is therefore a measure of what is usually called *transportation work*. In the right-hand member we, on the other hand, have the integral of the traffic distribution function on the region. This may be called *total traffic*. We conclude that *total traffic is always equal to total transportation work*. This fact again holds if the right-hand member in (9) is replaced by a more general transportation demand function.

If the local intensity of traffic i happens to be a constant in the right-hand member, then the latter equals this constant traffic intensity, multiplied by the area of the region. As we have seen it must equal total transportation work. This means that if we can assume that traffic intensity is constant in some region and we have empirical data on transportation work in total vehicle translocation distance, then we can obtain a measure of the traffic intensity from the data by division by area.

Chapter 4

OPTIMAL PATHS

We are now ready to discuss the first of the partial optimization problems outlined in Chapter 1, namely to find the distribution of traffic, i, and the vector fields $\boldsymbol{v}$ (one for each ξ,η), that minimize eq. (20) when the transfer cost function $f(x,y)$ is taken as a given datum. In passing, it may be noted that in the one-dimensional case this was no problem at all since traffic distribution was given and not subject to choice.

4.1. Social and individual cost minima

We could proceed in two different ways. We could determine the optimal path for each individual transport separately, or we could solve the minimization of total cost. It was conjectured in Chapter 1 that, in the absence of congestion, the deliberate free choice of best routes by individuals automatically minimizes the aggregate. Intuitively one can see that this is obvious, since in the absence of externalities each individual can seek his minimum contribution to the total cost without affecting the cost for anybody else. We can, however, formally prove that this is the case, by first solving the problem of minimizing total transportation cost, and then transforming the expression thus obtained to the one that can be obtained directly as the optimal solution for the individual.

We can write (20) in the following manner:

$$\int\int_S\int\int_S f(x,y)\,|\boldsymbol{v}(x,y,\xi,\eta)|\,\mathrm{d}x\,\mathrm{d}y\,\mathrm{d}\xi\,\mathrm{d}\eta. \tag{23}$$

This must be minimized subject to $\nabla\cdot\boldsymbol{v}(x,y,\xi,\eta) = -\bar{p}p$. Observe that the divergence of $\boldsymbol{v} = (v_1(x,y,\xi,\eta),\ v_2(x,y,\xi,\eta))$ is taken with respect to the variables x,y, i.e. it equals $\partial v_1/\partial x + \partial v_2/\partial y$, and that it must hold separately for all ξ,η. The constraints simply specify that the need for transportation be satisfied. In addition we assume that the region is insulated, i.e. that $\boldsymbol{v}\cdot\boldsymbol{n} = 0$ on G. This constraint too must hold separately for each ξ,η, i.e. for each vector field.

Both constraints – the prescribed distribution of sinks and the boundary condition – therefore hold for each vector field separately. Thus, if we minimize (17) for each ξ,η subject to its proper constraints, this does not interfere with the other minimizations, and we can obviously break the minimization of (20) down to the minimization of (17), subject to (9) and the boundary constraint that $\boldsymbol{v}\cdot\boldsymbol{n}$ be zero on G.

For given ξ,η this problem is nearly identical to the one solved by Beckmann (1952) for the flow of a merchandise from excess supply sources to excess demand sinks. The only difference is that, whereas in his model there is no net outflow from singular points, in the present case all the transports delivered by a single vector field flow out from the singular point ξ,η. The different sources come into the picture only when we regard the whole continuum of vector fields, and this makes the present case much more complicated.

The constrained minimization problem is identical to the unconstrained minimization of

$$\int\int_S (f|\boldsymbol{v}|+\lambda(\bar{p}p+\nabla\cdot\boldsymbol{v}))\,\mathrm{d}x\,\mathrm{d}y, \tag{24}$$

where λ is some Lagrange function of the space coordinates x,y.

The Euler equation for minimization of (24) is

$$f\boldsymbol{v}/|\boldsymbol{v}|=\nabla\lambda, \tag{25}$$

which means that the vector field $f\boldsymbol{v}/|\boldsymbol{v}|$ is the gradient of a potential function λ. The field lines of $\boldsymbol{v}$ coincide with the field lines of $\nabla\lambda$, even though the two fields are by no means identical, the difference being a scalar factor $f/|\boldsymbol{v}|$.

It can easily be seen that the line integral of (25), taken along an *optimal* transportation path, is

$$\int_0^t f\,\mathrm{d}\tau=\int_0^t \nabla\lambda\cdot\boldsymbol{v}/|\boldsymbol{v}|\,\mathrm{d}\tau \tag{26}$$

because $(\boldsymbol{v}/|\boldsymbol{v}|)^2=1$. But, $\nabla\lambda\cdot\boldsymbol{v}/|\boldsymbol{v}|\,\mathrm{d}\tau=\mathrm{d}\lambda$ is an exact differential, hence the line integral (26) is independent of the integration path. Provided that we arbitrarily put the potential λ equal to zero in ξ,η, the right-hand member of (26) equals λ. The left-hand side, according to (8), equals I. Thus, we may write

$$\lambda=I. \tag{27}$$

The field (25) proves to be the gradient of I, and this in turn means that the field lines of $\boldsymbol{v}$ cut the isopotential curves for I orthogonally.

We now see how (25) determines the field lines for $\boldsymbol{v}$. As the curl of a gradient is always zero, we know that $\nabla\times\nabla\lambda=0$. From (25)

$$\nabla\times(f\boldsymbol{v}/|\boldsymbol{v}|)=0. \tag{28}$$

But, according to the formula for the curl, analogous to formula (12) for the divergence, it is true that

$$\nabla f\times\boldsymbol{v}/|\boldsymbol{v}|+f\nabla\times(\boldsymbol{v}/|\boldsymbol{v}|)=0. \tag{29}$$

Since $\boldsymbol{v}/|\boldsymbol{v}|$ is now a unit vector, the first term, according to the definition of a "cross" product, equals the *sine* of the angle between the gradient of f and the vector $\boldsymbol{v}$, multiplied by the modulus of the gradient. Let ω denote the angle of the gradient, and θ denote the angle of the vector $\boldsymbol{v}$.

The angle in question is then $|\theta-\omega|$. From the definition of the "dot" product we know that the first term with the cross replaced by a dot equals the *cosine* of $\theta-\omega$, multiplied by the modulus of the gradient. Hence

$$(\nabla f\times \boldsymbol{v}/|\boldsymbol{v}|)/(\nabla f\cdot \boldsymbol{v}/|\boldsymbol{v}|)=\sin(|\theta-\omega|)/\cos(\theta-\omega).$$

But, $\nabla f\cdot \boldsymbol{v}/|\boldsymbol{v}|=\mathrm{d}f/\mathrm{d}\tau$. Using these results in (29) and multiplying by $\cos(\theta-\omega)$ we obtain

$$\mathrm{d}f/\mathrm{d}\tau\sin(|\theta-\omega|)+f\nabla\times(\boldsymbol{v}/|\boldsymbol{v}|)\cos(\theta-\omega)=0. \tag{30}$$

The derivation does not cover two special cases, namely when $f=$constant, so that $\nabla f=0$ everywhere, and when $\nabla f\cdot \boldsymbol{v}/|\boldsymbol{v}|=0$ because the two vectors are orthogonal. For this we need two special arguments. When $\nabla f=0$, we cannot define ω, but owing to (29) then, the first term being zero, we have $f\nabla\times(\boldsymbol{v}/|\boldsymbol{v}|)=0$. On the other hand $\mathrm{d}f/\mathrm{d}\tau=0$ along any path and hence (30) holds. In the second case, when $\nabla f\cdot \boldsymbol{v}/|\boldsymbol{v}|=0$, eq. (30) simply stipulates that $\cos(\theta-\omega)$ being zero, then $\mathrm{d}f/\mathrm{d}\tau$ be zero. When the vectors are orthogonal, the path does not intersect the isocurve for f, but has a point of tangency. From an infinitesimal perspective then the path follows the isocurve, and the result that f be constant, which is all that (30) prescribes, is obvious.

Since $\boldsymbol{v}/|\boldsymbol{v}|$ according to the definition of θ now equals the vector $(\cos\theta, \sin\theta)$, we see, according to the definition of a curl, that $\nabla\times(\boldsymbol{v}/|\boldsymbol{v}|)=\cos\theta\,\partial\theta/\partial x+\sin\theta\,\partial\theta/\partial y$. The reader may notice that we have been using curls as well as cross products as operating on two-dimensional vectors and the result has been scalars. Strictly, they operate on three-dimensional vectors and result in three-dimensional vectors, so that formulae like (30) are nonsensical. But we can interpret the two-dimensional vectors with which we deal as three-dimensional vectors in space with a zero third component. Then all cross products and curls are three-dimensional vectors pointing right out from the plane where everything interesting happens. We are completely disinterested in this direction, the only thing of interest being the scalar value of the sole nonzero element of the resultant vector. Identifying the resultant vector with this scalar value of its nonzero component, which is abusive, cannot lead to confusion, while it makes it possible to profit from the notational economy of vector operators. Since the vector $(\cos\theta,\sin\theta)$ is now of unit length and points in the direction of the transportation path, we find that $\cos\theta=\mathrm{d}x/\mathrm{d}\tau$ and that $\sin\theta=\mathrm{d}y/\mathrm{d}\tau$. Collecting these results we obtain

$$\nabla\times(\boldsymbol{v}/|\boldsymbol{v}|)=\mathrm{d}\theta/\mathrm{d}\tau. \tag{31}$$

If we now substitute this into (30) we see that we may write

$$\mathrm{d}/\mathrm{d}\tau(f\sin(|\theta-\omega|))+f\cos(\theta-\omega)\,\mathrm{d}\omega/\mathrm{d}\tau=0. \tag{32}$$

In the case where ω is constant, i.e. the gradient of f always points in the same direction, we obtain

$$d/d\tau\,(f\sin(|\theta-\omega|))=0 \tag{33}$$

or

$$f\sin(|\theta-\omega|)=c, \tag{34}$$

where c is a constant. Eq. (34) tells us that the angle which the transportation path makes with the direction of the steepest increase of transfer cost decreases along the path if the transfer cost increases along it. Hence, the path is attracted towards the direction of the steepest increase of f, if the path goes in the direction of increasing f.

The result is analogous to that for the problem of finding the paths of light rays in an isotropic medium. Where the medium consists of two layers of different homogeneous media, eq. (34) gives Snell's law for the refraction of light in a separation point between the two layers. It is interesting to note that this law for the analogous case of transportation over two media, such as by land and by sea, was given by Palander (1935).

4.2. Optimal paths and circular symmetry

Suppose now that we specify the transfer cost function so that it depends only upon the distance r of the point from the origin of the coordinate system, i.e. $f(x,y)=f(r)$, where $r=\sqrt{(x^2+y^2)}$. The reason for this is that we shall later specify the region S as a unit disk with a circularly symmetric distribution of population. We may without further analysis state that the transfer cost function for such a region must have circular symmetry in order to be a candidate for an equilibrium or an optimum. If we put the origin in the center of the disk, we obtain the formula $f(r)$. For such a transfer cost function eq. (32) may be expressed in a simpler way. It should be noticed that (34) is not valid for the present case since the angle of the gradient of f changes when one moves from one point to another.

As ω is the angle of the gradient, we obtain by differentiation $\nabla f= f'(x/r,y/r)=f'(\cos\omega,\sin\omega)$. This immediately gives $x=r\cos\omega$ and $y=\sin\omega$. Hence, r and ω (fortunately) turn out to be polar coordinates for x,y.

Differentiating the expressions for x,y in polar coordinates with respect to arc length τ, measured along the transportation path, we obtain

$$\dot{x}=\dot{r}\cos\omega-r\dot{\omega}\sin\omega; \qquad \dot{y}=\dot{r}\sin\omega+r\dot{\omega}\cos\omega,$$

where the dot above the variables indicates differentiation with respect to arc length. However, as θ is the angle of the transportation path we have

$$\dot{x}=\cos\theta; \qquad \dot{y}=\sin\theta.$$

We substitute these in the former equations and solve for $\dot{r}$ and $r\dot{\omega}$. Then, employing the formulae for the cosine and the sine of a difference, we obtain

$$\cos(\theta-\omega)=\dot{r}; \qquad \sin(\theta-\omega)=r\dot{\omega}.$$

Eq. (32) may therefore be written

$$\mathrm{d}/\mathrm{d}\tau\,(fr\dot{\omega})+f\dot{r}\dot{\omega}=0 \tag{35}$$

or

$$\mathrm{d}/\mathrm{d}\tau\,(fr^2\dot{\omega})=0. \tag{36}$$

This, however, implies that

$$fr^2\dot{\omega}=c, \tag{37}$$

where c is a constant.[1] Now the infinitesimal arc $\mathrm{d}\tau$ expressed in polar coordinates is $\sqrt{(r^2+r'^2)}\,\mathrm{d}\omega$, where $r'=\mathrm{d}r/\mathrm{d}\omega$. Thus, we obtain $\dot{\omega}=1/\sqrt{(r^2+r'^2)}$ which, substituted into (37), yields

$$fr^2=c\sqrt{(r^2+r'^2)}. \tag{38}$$

This is a differential equation for the optimal path in terms of polar coordinates r and ω. It may be observed that this equation may also be derived directly as the Euler equation for minimizing

$$\int f(r)\,\mathrm{d}\tau=\int f(r)\sqrt{(r^2+r'^2)}\,\mathrm{d}\omega=\int f(r)\sqrt{(1+r^2\omega'^2)}\,\mathrm{d}r,$$

that is relevant for the individual transporter. Hence, we have proved that the individual transporters actually minimize total cost.

4.3. Curvature of paths

We can learn something about the general character of the solution curves to (38) if we differentiate the equation with respect to ω. After elimination of c by substitution from (38) this yields

$$f'r(r^2+r'^2)=f(rr''-2r'^2-r^2). \tag{39}$$

Hence, the expression $(rr''-2r'^2-r^2)$ has the same sign as f', because all the other factors are positive. This is interesting, since the curvature of the solution curve depends on this expression.

Let us derive the curvature vector $\boldsymbol{k}$. To do this we imagine the solution curve to be given by two equations, $x=r(\omega)\cos\omega$ and $y=r(\omega)\sin\omega$, parameterized by ω. The tangent vector obtained by differentiation with respect to ω is $(r'\cos\omega-r\sin\omega, r'\sin\omega+r\cos\omega)$. From this the unit tangent vector $\boldsymbol{t}$, or the tangent vector

[1]There is a striking similarity between the present case and the theory of particles moving under a central force in classical mechanics.

obtained by differentiating with respect to the "natural" arc length parameter, is obtained by division with the length of the tangent vector in terms of ω, i.e. by $\sqrt{(r^2+r'^2)}$. Hence,

$$t=(r'\cos\omega - r\sin\omega, r'\sin\omega + r\cos\omega)/\sqrt{(r^2+r'^2)}. \tag{40}$$

We next differentiate the tangent vector to obtain the curvature vector but, since we are only able to perform the differentiation with respect to the actual parameter ω, whereas the curvature is obtained by differentiation with respect to the natural parameter, we must again divide the result by the factor $\sqrt{(r^2+r'^2)}$. Hence, we first get

$$(r^2+r'^2)^{3/2}\,\mathrm{d}t/\mathrm{d}\omega = (rr''-2r'^2-r^2)(r\cos\omega + r'\sin\omega, r\sin\omega - r'\cos\omega),$$

and thereafter

$$k=\frac{(rr''-2r'^2-r^2)}{(r^2+r'^2)^2}(r\cos\omega + r'\sin\omega, r\sin\omega - r'\cos\omega). \tag{41}$$

Observe that k can be zero only in one single instance, namely when it happens that the expression $(rr''-2r'^2-r^2)$ is zero. But we have seen that the sign of the latter expression is uniquely determined by f'. If the function is always monotonic, with a positive or negative derivative, then there cannot be any points of inflection on the solution curves. This is so because the curvature vector is zero at any inflection point. When the derivative has a constant sign everywhere we conclude that the curves are always curved to the same side, and are thus all convex or concave, depending on the constant sign of f'.

We can easily see which sign is related to convexity to the origin and which sign is related to concavity. Note that we can speak of convexity and concavity to the origin because, with a circularly symmetric transfer cost function, all solution curves can be obtained from some other solution curve by rotation around the origin. The direction of the curvature can be obtained by checking the sign of the projection of the curvature vector k on the outward radial $(\cos\omega, \sin\omega)$. We obtain

$$k\cdot(\cos\omega, \sin\omega) = r(rr''-2r'^2-r^2)/(r^2+r'^2)^2. \tag{42}$$

However, we have seen that $(rr''-2r'^2-r^2)$ has the same sign as f'. Hence, the projection of the curvature vector on the radial is away from the origin if f' is positive, and towards the origin if f' is negative. This means that the curves, all of them and everywhere, are convex to the origin if and only if transfer cost increases with radius vector, and are concave if and only if transfer cost decreases.

Intuitively one finds this appealing since in the neutral case of constant transfer cost the best paths are the shortest, i.e. segments of straight lines, and also because in the cases of monotonic transfer cost functions the paths should deviate from straight lines into those parts, close to or off from the origin, where transfer is particularly cheap.

The formal analysis has made it possible to relate exclusively convex paths with monotonically increasing transfer cost and exclusively concave paths with monotonically decreasing transfer cost.

It should be emphasized that the relation is one of necessity as well as of sufficiency. Another result of a general qualitative character is the rotational symmetry of the solution curves. This is intuitively obvious, but could also be derived formally. Interchanging dependent and independent variables in (38) yields $\omega' = c/\sqrt{(f(r)^2 r^4 - c^2)}$ after solving for the derivative. Integration obviously yields a second constant that is additive to ω, and this proves the rotational symmetry.

4.4. Sufficiency conditions

Up to now we have only discussed the solution curves to the Euler equations as if they actually were the extremals sought. As is known the case is not as simple as that. In order to be certain that a solution to a Euler equation provides an extremal we must check the Jacobi condition that there are no conjugate points (or kinetic foci) on the solution curves between the relevant endpoints, so that the solution curves from a given starting point really are embedded into a central field, and we must check the Weierstrass condition that the E-function does not change sign. The Weierstrass condition can be replaced by the simpler Legendre condition.

The latter can easily be checked. Recalling that extremals, minimizing $\int f\sqrt{(r^2 + r'^2)}\,\mathrm{d}\omega$, are sought, and putting $F = f\sqrt{(r^2 + r'^2)}$, we see that the Legendre conditions require

$$F_{r'r'} = fr^2/(r^2 + r'^2)^{3/2} \tag{43}$$

to be non-negative for a minimum and nonpositive for a maximum. As the expression is indeed non-negative, we have a minimum, provided that the check for conjugate points holds. Because the non-negativity holds for any value substituted for r', we know that any minimum would be a strong one, so that the extremal is optimal within a family of similar curves that need not be close to the extremal in slope when they are close in terms of deviation distance.

The checking of the Jacobi conditions is a little more complicated, and may be done in several different ways. One, which we shall employ in the examples below (with a transfer cost of the power variety), is to eliminate one of the arbitrary constants in the solution by fixing one endpoint, and to determine an envelope to the central field of radiating solution curves. Because the conjugate points belong to the envelope, the check is straightforward. But for this we must know the explicit solution, which is not available with an unspecified transfer cost function.

Another way is to look at Jacobi's differential equation. Before doing this we must, however, change dependent and independent variables. Otherwise the calculations will become very complicated. Thus, taking the radius instead of the angle as independent variable, we minimize $\int f\sqrt{(1+r^2\omega'^2)}\,\mathrm{d}r$. This is simply due to another way of expressing arc length. We can check that the Euler equation is $fr^2\omega' = c\sqrt{(1+r^2\omega'^2)}$ which, as it should, transforms into (38) by the identity $r'\omega' \equiv 1$.

Putting now $G = f\sqrt{(1+r^2\omega'^2)}$, we can write the Jacobi equation as $(G_{\omega\omega} - \mathrm{d}G_{\omega\omega'}/\mathrm{d}r)u - \mathrm{d}(G_{\omega'\omega'}u')/\mathrm{d}r = 0$. Here u is the derivative of ω with respect to the one remaining parameter in the solution, when the other one is eliminated by fixing a starting point. For an envelope this partial derivative must be zero, and thus we must ascertain whether u takes on a zero value, except at the fixed starting point. If so, we have a conjugate point.

But ω does not appear explicitly in G, and hence all the partial derivatives with respect to ω vanish identically. The only nonzero derivative in the Jacobi equation is $G_{\omega'\omega'} = fr^2/(1+r^2\omega'^2)^{3/2}$ and hence a first integral of the Jacobi equation is

$$fr^2u'/(1+r^2\omega'^2)^{3/2} = \text{constant}. \tag{44}$$

If the constant is nonzero, we see that u' has a constant sign, all the other factors being non-negative. In those cases, u cannot have more than one zero, and hence no conjugate points exist. If the constant is zero, then u' is identically zero along the path, and hence u could be zero along the whole path. This shows that the envelope, if it exists, coincides with the whole extension of a solution curve. Within an area delimited by such a bounding curve, there are no conjugate points. Hence, the solution curves constitute a central field and, the Legendre conditions being fulfilled, in fact represent minimum cost extremals. However, from symmetry it follows that such bounding curves can only be radials. This will be further illustrated in the sequel, but we can see that many of the qualitative results obtained in the example hold for any circularly symmetric transfer cost function.

4.5. Power functions: the paths

Let us now, as an illustration, specify the transfer cost function as $f(r) = r^n$. If n is positive it is cheaper to travel in the central parts of the region; if n is negative it is cheaper to travel in the peripheral parts. We see that the costs saved by travelling in the cheap part of the region are greater, the greater is the absolute value of n. It is to be expected that with n different from zero the paths deviate from straight line segments so that they are convex to the origin if n is positive, and concave to the origin if n is negative. If $n=0$ the transfer cost is the same everywhere and it is to be expected that the optimal paths are straight line segments.

All this is verified by the formal solutions. If $f=r^n$, eq. (38) becomes

$$r^{n+2}=c\sqrt{(r^2+r'^2)} \tag{45}$$

or

$$rr''=(n+2)r'^2+(n+1)r^2. \tag{46}$$

This second-order differential equation has a solution in terms of elementary functions. The general solution may be written

$$R\cos(\Omega+b)=a \tag{47}$$

where, for convenience, we have defined two intermediate variables:

$$R=r^{(n+1)} \quad \text{and} \quad \Omega=(n+1)\omega.$$

Before continuing with the general case, we notice that the solution does not work when $n=-1$. Then we have instead $\ln r=a+b\omega$, or

$$r=A\,\mathrm{e}^{b\omega}, \tag{48}$$

with $a=\ln A$. This is the equation of a logarithmic spiral.

Let us check the sufficiency conditions. Take first the Jacobi condition. Fix a starting point r_0, ω_0, then $r_0=A\,\mathrm{e}^{b\omega_0}$ and we can try to construct a central field by eliminating A. This yields

$$r=r_0\,\mathrm{e}^{b(\omega-\omega_0)}. \tag{49}$$

We can try to find the equation of an envelope by differentiating with respect to the remaining parameter and putting the derivative equal to zero. Hence,

$$r_0(\omega-\omega_0)\,\mathrm{e}^{b(\omega-\omega_0)}=0$$

would be required to hold. But this is obviously only possible, unless the starting point is at the origin, when $\omega=\omega_0$. Hence, there can be no envelope except the radial through the starting point.

In this case we can also use Jacobi's differential equation and solve it by quadrature. As $f=1/r$, we have $F=\sqrt{(1+r^2\omega'^2)}/r$. But from the solution, $r'=br$ and, accordingly, $\omega'=1/(br)$. Because F does not contain ω, Jacobi's equation takes the form $F_{\omega'\omega'}u'=\text{constant}$. Substituting, we obtain

$$u'=K/r, \tag{50}$$

where K is a constant incorporating the original constant as well as the factor $(1+1/b^2)^{3/2}$. Integrating, and using the knowledge that $u=0$ at the starting point, we get

$$u=K(\ln r-\ln r_0), \tag{51}$$

which can only become zero at the starting point. Hence, Jacobi's test holds.

As to the Legendre condition, we have already employed

$$F_{\omega'\omega'} = r/(1+1/b^2)^{3/2}, \tag{52}$$

which can never become nonpositive. Hence, we have strong minima by virtue of the sufficiency conditions.

We can also easily obtain the isotransportation costs. As $r' = br$, we have $\sqrt{(r^2+r'^2)} = r\sqrt{(1+b^2)}$. Because $f = 1/r$, we get $I = \int\sqrt{(1+b^2)}\,d\omega = \sqrt{(1+b^2)}(\omega_1-\omega_0)$. But we also have $b = (\ln r_1 - \ln r_0)/(\omega_1-\omega_0)$ from the solution. Thus,

$$I = \sqrt{\left((\ln r_1 - \ln r_0)^2 + (\omega_1-\omega_0)^2\right)} \tag{53}$$

is an expression for the transportation cost between two points given in polar coordinates, computed along the optimal paths.

In fig. 4.1 are drawn the optimal paths from a given starting point and the corresponding isocosts. The paths are dashed, while the isocosts are drawn as continuous lines, a practice we shall adhere to. Note that the plane is divided into two parts that are "mirror images" of each other. This is due to the fact that the continuations of the logarithmic spirals after 180°, although locally optimal in a strong sense, are globally suboptimal.

After this exercise with a special case, which we shall encounter again in another example later on, we are prepared to return to the general case of power functions.

Solution (47) has two parameters, a and b, that are determined by the endpoints. If we fix one of the endpoints r_0, ω_0 or r_1, ω_1, say the starting point r_0, ω_0, one parameter can be eliminated. We obtain $R\cos(\Omega+b) = R_0\cos(\Omega_0+b)$, which yields a central field with b as the sole remaining parameter. Let us now find the envelope to the family of curves in this central field. An envelope is

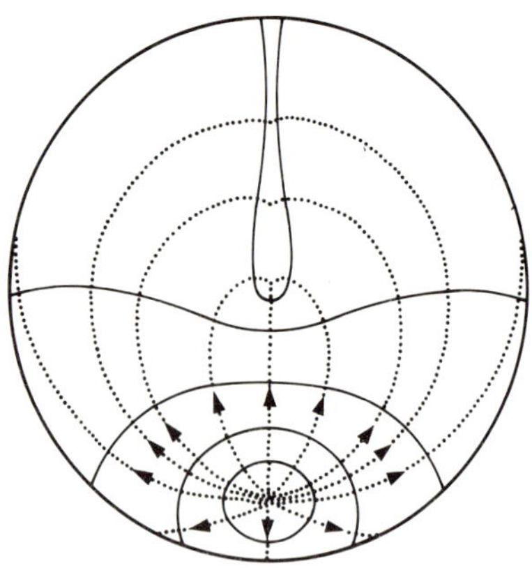

Figure 4.1

obtained if we differentiate the equations of the curves with respect to the parameter and use the new equation thus obtained together with the old one. The differentiation yields $R\sin(\Omega+b)=R_0\sin(\Omega_0+b)$. If we now divide the two equations, member by member, we get $\tan(\Omega+b)=\tan(\Omega_0+b)$, where R and R_0 have disappeared. As $\tan(\Omega_0\pm\pi+b)=\tan(\Omega_0+b)$, we see that the envelope consists of a pair of radials with angles $\Omega_0\pm\pi$ or, in the original coordinates, $\omega_0\pm\pi/(n+1)$.

Now, the points conjugate to the starting point all lie on the envelope. These conjugate points play a central role in the Jacobi conditions for the sufficiency of a solution to a Euler equation to be an extremal. We see that if the acute angle between the endpoints does not exceed $\pi/(n+1)$, then the paths do not contain any conjugate points and therefore the Jacobi conditions are satisfied. In this case (47) can provide a solution. The Legendre–Weierstrass condition, on the other hand, is a check on the sign of $r^{(n+2)}/(r^2+r'^2)^{3/2}$, which is non-negative. The fulfillment of the combined Jacobi and Legendre–Weierstrass conditions ascertains that the solution (47) indeed provides a strong minimum.

It should be observed that expression (47) is the equation of a straight line expressed in polar coordinates when $n=0$, i.e. $r\cos(\omega+b)=a$.

If the critical angle, $\pi/(n+1)$ is exceeded, then the solution must be obtained by another method, because this case is not covered by (47). Let us therefore interchange dependent and independent variables in eq. (45) and write $r^{n+2}\omega'=c\surd(1+r^2\omega'^2)$, by virtue of $\omega'r'\equiv 1$. We then immediately see that, for $c=0$, $\omega=$constant is a solution. (For $c\neq 0$, the solutions are those already obtained.) Hence, radials are possible solutions, and this is the case with any n. The only difference is the sector in which these solutions are relevant.

Now, if $\omega_0\neq\omega_1$, which in general is the case, then a radial solution cannot be a curve with a continuously turning tangent. For a pair of radials joining the endpoints the discontinuity point for the tangent can only be the origin if, as it should be, the curve is made in one piece. We must therefore check the relevant transversality conditions for this discontinuity. These imply that, with $F=r^n\surd(1+r^2\omega'^2)$, the expressions $(F-\omega'F_{\omega'})=r^n/\surd(1+r^2\omega'^2)$ and $F_{\omega'}=r^{n+2}\omega'/\surd(1+r^2\omega'^2)$ be equal for the two intersecting radials. Now, for both radials $\omega'=0$, and in the origin $r=0$. Thus, both test expressions are zero for both intersecting radials, and the transversality conditions are satisfied.

We finally have to check the sufficiency conditions for these radial paths. For a family of radiating straight lines there is obviously no envelope and therefore no conjugate points that can lie on the paths. This means that the Jacobi conditions are fulfilled for radial paths going straight into the center and out again. The Legendre–Weierstrass test is now a check on the sign of the expression $r^{n+2}/(1+r^2\omega'^2)^{3/2}$. As this is non-negative, we again have a strong minimum. These curves are local extrema even when the critical angle is not exceeded, but in comparison with the solutions (47) they are, in this case, globally suboptimal. They are relevant solutions when the critical angle is exceeded and (47) cannot provide a solution.

The solution curves are illustrated below (with n equal to 1 and 2, respectively) for a fixed point of origin. Fixing the point removes one degree of freedom so that a one-parameter family of curves results. Hence, fig. 4.2a, b shows sets of field lines of the type discussed in Chapter 3. (Strictly speaking only the wedges where the paths are curved are regular enough for the discussion above to be applicable. The scattering at the center introduces a new singularity. Fortunately, however, the radial paths are very easy to handle by special direct means.)

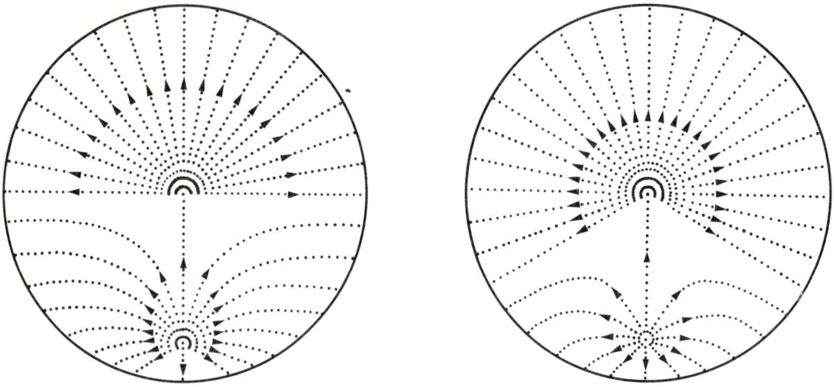

(a) $n=1$; (b) $n=2$.

Figure 4.2.

4.6. Power functions: isopotentials

We may also easily obtain the isopotential curves for I (or λ).[2] Where solution (47) is relevant we have $r'=\mathrm{d}r/\mathrm{d}\omega=r\tan(\Omega+b)$. Hence, the infinitesimal arc

$$\mathrm{d}\tau=\sqrt{(r^2+r'^2)}\,\mathrm{d}\omega=r\sqrt{(1+\tan^2(\Omega+b))}\,\mathrm{d}\omega=r/\cos(\Omega+b)\,\mathrm{d}\omega.$$

Inserting this, together with $f=r^n$, into (8), we obtain $I=\int R/\cos(\Omega+b)\,\mathrm{d}\omega$, recalling that $r^{n+1}=R$. Substitution from (47) next yields $I=a\int\cos^{-2}(\Omega+b)\,\mathrm{d}\omega$. This integral equals $a\tan(\Omega+b)/(n+1)$ and thus we obtain

$$(n+1)I=a(\tan(\Omega_1+b)-\tan(\Omega_0+b))=R_1\sin(\Omega_1+b)-R_0\sin(\Omega_0+b).$$

The last equation holds because (47) must be true for both endpoints, i.e.

[2]Isodapans in Weber's terminology, as used by Palander (1935).

because $a=R_0\cos(\Omega_0+b)=R_1\cos(\Omega_1+b)$. Taking squares of the last expression for $(n+1)I$, i.e. of $R_1\sin(\Omega_1+b)-R_0\sin(\Omega_0+b)$, and of $R_1\cos(\Omega_1+b)-R_0\cos(\Omega_0+b)=0$, and adding, we obtain $(n+1)^2I^2=R_0^2+R_1^2-2R_0R_1\cos(\Omega_1-\Omega_0)$ when the formula for the cosine of a difference is used. Hence,

$$(n+1)I=\sqrt{\left(R_0^2+R_1^2-2R_0R_1\cos(\Omega_1-\Omega_0)\right)}, \tag{54}$$

where the indices 0 and 1 denote the endpoints. This expression is again relevant if the angle of the radii vectors to the endpoints, i.e. $|\omega_1-\omega_0|$, does not exceed $\pi/(n+1)$. Of course, the acute angle is the relevant criterion.

For larger angles the paths are radial, as we have seen, and thus the infinitesimal arc $d\tau=\pm dr$ as $d\omega=0$ on the paths. The sign is chosen according to whether the path is directed away from or towards the origin. The positive sign is, accordingly, chosen for paths from the center to point 1, and the negative sign for paths from point 0 to the center. Hence, the indefinite integral $\int\pm r^n dr$ being equal to $\pm r^{n+1}/(n+1)=\pm R/(n+1)$, we see that $(n+1)I=R_1-(-R_0)$ or

$$(n+1)I=R_0+R_1. \tag{55}$$

Observe that, for the special case of n equal to zero, formula (54) gives the linear distance between the endpoints and (55) gives the radial distance between them, obtained as the sum of the radii vectors. (The isopotential curves for $I=$constant according to (54) thus become concentric circles, centered around the starting point, when $n=0$. In this case the critical angle is π and hence no paths are radial.)

Fig. 4.3a, b shows the sets of isopotential curves, together with the corresponding optimal paths, for the cases already illustrated. It can be seen that the paths cut the isocurves for constant I orthogonally, as is stated above.

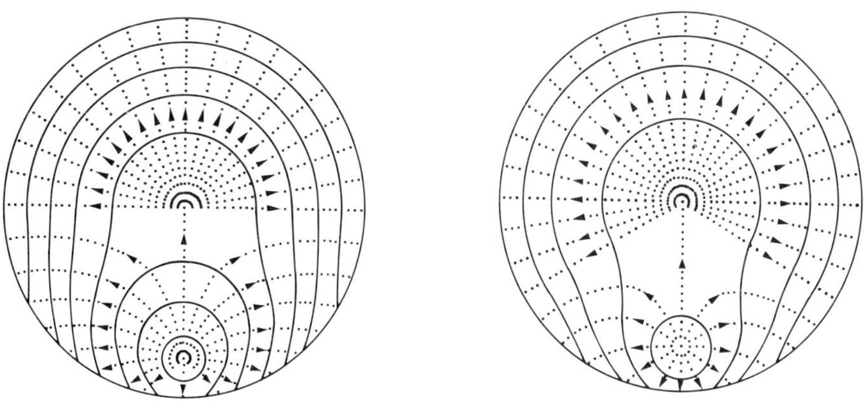

(a) $n=1$; (b) $n=2$.

Figure 4.3.

4.7. Power functions: conformal mapping and Riemann surfaces

There is, however, another way of representing these solutions. If we regard R and Ω as polar coordinates for *new* rectangular coordinates X and Y, so that $X = R\cos\Omega$ and $Y = R\sin\Omega$, we obtain a quite interesting mapping from x and y to X and Y.

In order to characterize this mapping we may see how single points, curves, and the whole region are affected by it. As regards the individual points we see that they are moved by both rotation and radial projection because the angle ω is changed to the angle $\Omega = (n+1)\omega$ and the radius vector r is changed to the radius vector $R = r^{n+1}$.

Assuming n to be non-negative (i.e. assuming that the concentration of road capital – if there is any – is to the central part of the region), we see that the angles rotate counterclockwise and that the points of the unit disk are projected towards the center.

If we imagine that each point represents one "person" in the population, so that population is uniformly distributed on the original disk, then the uniformity is obviously distorted by the mapping. The exact extent of this distortion is given by the Jacobian of the mapping, which equals

$$\partial(X,Y)/\partial(x,y) = ((n+1)r^n)^2. \tag{56}$$

Hence, if $\mathrm{d}x\,\mathrm{d}y$ people live in the infinitesimal rectangle of area $\mathrm{d}x\,\mathrm{d}y$ of the original disk, it follows that $\mathrm{d}X\,\mathrm{d}Y/((n+1)r^n)^2$ people live in the rectangle of area $\mathrm{d}X\,\mathrm{d}Y$ of the transformed region. Since n is non-negative this means a concentration of population to the central parts, or possibly that its distribution is left unchanged in the limiting case.

The next question is: what happens to curves? The curves of special interest are the solution curves for transportation paths. We have seen that they are of two different kinds: in the sector where the solution (47) is relevant the paths are curved, whereas they are radial outside the sector. The remarkable thing now is that the curved paths are mapped into straight line segments, whereas the radial paths are left radial. This fact will be very useful.

Thus, a situation with a uniform distribution of population and curved transportation paths is translatable to an imaginary situation where population is clustered but transportation paths are linear. If n is positive, so that transfer is cheapest in the central parts and the optimal paths deviate from the straight line by being convex to the origin, the clustering of population is to the central parts. Both agglomeration of people and cheapness of transfer cause traffic to be most intense in the central parts of the region.

The third characterization of the mapping concerns the transformation of the shape of the region, i.e. the unit disk. From one point of view it is not changed at all. Every point of the original unit disk is mapped into a new unit disk, and there is some point of the original disk that corresponds to every point of the new one – even though, as we have seen, the density of points is altered.

However, the correspondence is not one-to-one. By the rotation the new disk is covered $(n+1)$-fold number of times. The wedge of the original disk, where the paths were curved, is magnified to a whole disk itself, and the rest of the original disk, where the paths were radial, makes n additional disks.

We may therefore think of the new region as made up of $(n+1)$ identical disk-shaped sheets, slit up along the positive real axes and joined to one continuous surface with the free edges joined across the other sheets. This is a so-called Riemann surface, well known from the study of mappings. See fig. 4.4 for the case $n=1$, which is equivalent to fig. 4.2a. The surface has been bent by force to make its character easy to visualize. Once this force is removed the surface falls flat. Thus, instead of looking at the solutions as in figs. 4.2 and 4.3, we may reason in terms of $(n+1)$ unit disks, one on top of the other, with linear paths on the bottom floor and radial paths on the top floors (one and two respectively for the two cases illustrated). This picture may be used for all starting points, and the different floors may be thought to be completely "independent" in the sense that all transports are generated by the gravity hypothesis on each of them. We only have to keep in mind that $1/(n+1)$ of the population "lives" on each floor, and that it is concentrated towards the center by the inverse Jacobian of the mapping.

Calculation shows that

$$\begin{aligned} \partial X/\partial x &= (n+1)r^n \cos n\omega = \partial Y/\partial y, \\ -\partial X/\partial y &= (n+1)r^n \sin n\omega = \partial Y/\partial x. \end{aligned} \tag{57}$$

Hence, the Cauchy–Riemann differential equations are fulfilled and the mapping is *conformal*. This implies that it may be represented by an *analytical* complex function of a complex variable. Let us define the complex variables $z=x+\mathrm{i}y$ and $Z=X+\mathrm{i}Y$. (Observe that $\mathrm{i}=\sqrt{-1}$ and does not have the meaning than it has in the rest of the text.)

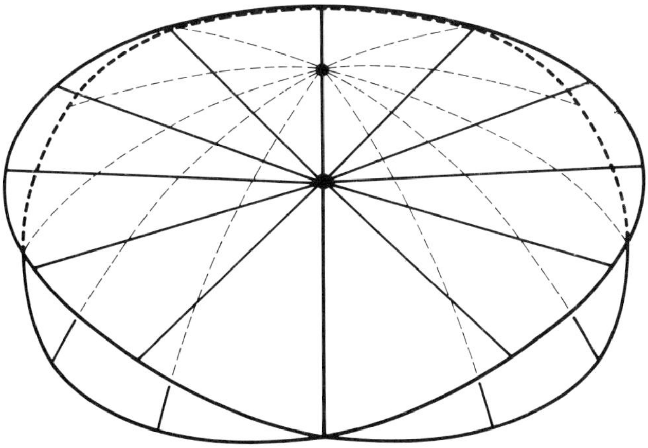

Figure 4.4

According to definition, the derivative of the analytic function sought is $\partial X/\partial x + \mathrm{i}\partial Y/\partial x$. Inserting from (57) we obtain $(n+1)r^n(\cos n\omega + \mathrm{i}\sin n\omega)$. But, according to de Moivre's theorem, the parenthesis equals $(\cos\omega + \mathrm{i}\sin\omega)^n$. Using this and inserting the rectangular coordinates $x = r\cos\omega$ and $y = r\sin\omega$, we obtain the derivative of the analytic function as $(n+1)\,(x+\mathrm{i}y)^n = (n+1)z^n$.

As the function is analytic we may use normal rules for integration. Thus,

$$Z = z^{n+1} \tag{58}$$

is the simple analytic function required to transform the quite complicated solution curves for the case $f = r^n$ to segments of straight lines.

In a most elegant exposition, Wardrop (1969) has demonstrated the possibility of using complex calculus for solving problems concerning the choice of best paths. Our objective was to minimize the integral $\int f \mathrm{d}\tau = \int r^n \mathrm{d}\tau$. But we have seen that $\mathrm{d}Z/\mathrm{d}z = (n+1)z^n$. Hence, $|\mathrm{d}Z/\mathrm{d}z| = (n+1)r^n$, because $|z|^2 = z\bar{z} = (x+\mathrm{i}y)\,(x-\mathrm{i}y) = (x^2+y^2) = r^2$, by virtue of elementary complex algebra. Moreover, we have, analogously,

$$|\mathrm{d}z|^2 = \mathrm{d}z\,\overline{\mathrm{d}z} = (\mathrm{d}x + \mathrm{i}\mathrm{d}y)\,(\mathrm{d}x - \mathrm{i}\mathrm{d}y) = \left((\mathrm{d}x)^2 + (\mathrm{d}y)^2\right) = (\mathrm{d}\tau)^2,$$

or, in short, $\mathrm{d}\tau = |\mathrm{d}z|$. Substituting into the minimand, we see that we can look for an extremal of the functional

$$\int |\mathrm{d}Z/\mathrm{d}z|\,|\mathrm{d}z| = \int |\mathrm{d}Z| \tag{59}$$

which only deviates by the factor $(n+1)$ – a constant – from the original minimand. But, $|\mathrm{d}Z|$ is the arc length in the Z-plane, and hence the extremals are trivially straight-line segments.

The problem with Wardrop's approach is to find a transformation $z \Rightarrow Z$ so that the modulus of its derivative, i.e. $|\mathrm{d}Z/\mathrm{d}z|$, is proportional to the transfer cost function f. When we have circular symmetry so that f only depends on r, the class of power functions, r^n, is the only possibility for f. This is observed by Wardrop.

On this account Angel and Hyman (1976) criticize Wardrop. To me, however, their criticism seems exaggerated, since Wardrop has nowhere suggested that this type of approach is applicable in any case. He has only pointed at possible solutions in special cases, where his type of analysis becomes strikingly simple and elegant. I must admit, however, that I have not been able to find any manageable way of handling or applying the complex polynomial cases that he suggests as another possibility.

4.8. Paths as geodesics on a curved surface

Angel and Hyman (1976) prefer another paradigm, which in contrast to conformal transformations of plane regions onto plane regions is applicable under very general circumstances, namely when plane regions are mapped onto patches of curved surfaces. The idea seems to owe its origin to Warntz (1967). Its content is that the actual region in the plane is mapped onto a curved surface, so constructed that the images of actual optimal paths in the plane are "straight" on the surface in the sense of being geodesics, and so that communication cost between any two locations is equal to the length of the geodesic passing through the image points of these locations. This construction seems to be possible with very general classes of transfer cost functions. Angel and Hyman have exemplified several such constructions.

Assume that we have a transformation from the x,y-plane to the ξ,η,ζ-space. Given certain regularity conditions, this represents a surface in three-dimensional space, parameterized by the rectangular coordinates of the plane where the original region is. The three component functions in this transformation make it possible to find image points on the surface.

Next, define the three first fundamental coefficients of the surface in terms of the parameterization:

$$\begin{aligned} E &= (\xi_x,\eta_x,\zeta_x)\cdot(\xi_x,\eta_x,\zeta_x), \\ F &= (\xi_x,\eta_x,\zeta_x)\cdot(\xi_y,\eta_y,\zeta_y), \\ G &= (\xi_y,\eta_y,\zeta_y)\cdot(\xi_y,\eta_y,\zeta_y). \end{aligned} \tag{60}$$

It should be noticed that these coefficients, probably the most important concepts in Gaussian theory, are properties of the surface and not of the parameterization. Even if the coefficients change with the parameterization, important expressions obtained in terms of them, like arc lengths, areas, angles between intersecting curves and Gaussian curvature of the surface, are invariants with respect to the parameterization.

The length of a curve on the surface is now

$$\int \left(E(\mathrm{d}x/\mathrm{d}\tau)^2+2F(\mathrm{d}x/\mathrm{d}\tau)(\mathrm{d}y/\mathrm{d}\tau)+G(\mathrm{d}y/\mathrm{d}\tau)^2\right)^{1/2}\mathrm{d}\tau. \tag{61}$$

If this be a measure of transportation cost it must be equal to the expression

$$\int f(x,y)\left((\mathrm{d}x/\mathrm{d}\tau)^2+(\mathrm{d}y/\mathrm{d}\tau)^2\right)^{1/2}\mathrm{d}\tau. \tag{62}$$

Because the equality must hold for any path, then obviously the integrands must be equal at all corresponding points in the plane and on the surface.

If we restrict ourselves to conformal transformations, then the images of the coordinate lines for x and y constant on the surface intersect under right angles, and hence F due to definition (60) vanishes identically on the surface. This is so because a conformal mapping does not alter angles between intersecting curves. In addition, we know that the linear magnification factor is the same in all directions for a conformal mapping, in particular in the two coordinate line directions. Hence, $E=G$ in addition to $F=0$. This implies that we must find a transformation $x,y \Rightarrow \xi, \eta, \zeta$, such that

$$\sqrt{E} = \sqrt{G} = f(x,y) \qquad F = 0 \tag{63}$$

hold.

4.9. Conformality to the plane

There is a good reason why we should concentrate our interest on conformal transformations. We have required equality to hold for the integrands in (61) and (62) for all corresponding points. Now, we can without loss of generality suppose that the curve in the parameter plane has been parameterized by arc length. Hence $(\mathrm{d}x/\mathrm{d}\tau)^2 + (\mathrm{d}y/\mathrm{d}\tau)^2 = 1$, and we can put $\mathrm{d}x/\mathrm{d}\tau = \cos\theta$, $\mathrm{d}y/\mathrm{d}\tau = \sin\theta$. Substituting into (61) and (62) and equating the squares of the integrands we obtain

$$E\cos^2\theta + 2F\cos\theta\sin\theta + G\sin^2\theta = f(x,y)^2,$$

which must hold for *all directions* θ when we deal with isotropic transportation. Now, putting in turn $\theta = 0$ and $\theta = \pi/2$, we get $E = G = f^2$. But, as we substitute this into the preceding equation, we get

$$F\cos\theta\sin\theta = 0,$$

which again must hold for all θ. And this is only possible when $F = 0$. This means that (63) must be fulfilled. Hence, in fact only conformal mappings work with an isotropic transportation problem. Since the transfer cost function determines the first fundamental coefficients we know that the whole metric structure for the "cost surface" is given. The surface may be transformed only by isometries, i.e. by bending without tearing or elastic stretching, and these leave the metric structure unchanged. Among the metric properties are linear and areal magnification which transform, for example, population densities in a specific manner. As Angel and Hyman (1976) notice, it is impossible to employ yet another transformation to make such densities constant.

4.10. Existence

From the fact that with (63) the first fundamental form (the integrand of (61) squared) is positive definite we conclude that, owing to the fundamental theorem of surfaces, a cost surface exists for any isotropic transportation problem. This does not mean that the surface needs to be simple or easy to parameterize.

Finding a parameterization amounts to solving the system of differential equations

$$\begin{aligned}
&\xi_x\xi_x+\eta_x\eta_x+\zeta_x\zeta_x=f(x,y)^2,\\
&\xi_x\xi_y+\eta_x\eta_y+\zeta_x\zeta_y=0,\\
&\xi_y\xi_y+\eta_y\eta_y+\zeta_y\zeta_y=f(x,y)^2,
\end{aligned}\tag{64}$$

which is not always so simple.

4.11. Conic surfaces

We exemplify the solution by a case treated by Angel and Hyman (1976), namely when $f=1/r$. If we use the transformation $\xi=x/\surd(x^2+y^2), \eta=y/\surd(x^2+y^2)$, $\zeta=\ln\surd(x^2+y^2)$, then the plane is mapped on to a cylinder with unit radius and extending to infinity in the directions of both ζ-axes, as suggested by Angel and Hyman. As $\xi_x=y^2/(x^2+y^2)^{3/2}$, $\xi_y=\eta_x=-xy/(x^2+y^2)^{3/2}$ and $\eta_y=x^2/(x^2+y^2)^{3/2}$, whereas $\zeta_x=x/(x^2+y^2)$ and $\zeta_y=y/(x^2+y^2)$, we obtain the left-hand members of the first and last equation in (64) equal to $1/(x^2+y^2)=1/r^2$ which, indeed, equals f^2. The left-hand member of the middle equation can easily be checked to add to zero.

On the cylinder, optimal paths are helices or straight lines, which are actually special helices of infinite torsion. Helices are geodesics as the geodesic curvature is zero on them.

As the cylinder can be cut along any of its generators and unfolded into an infinite plane strip of width 2π, we suspect that a mapping onto a plane region is possible. In fact, the transformation $\xi=\ln\surd(x^2+y^2), \eta=\arctan y/x$, chosen in an appropriate interval, and $\zeta=$constant will do as well. The geodesics, helices on the cylinder, turn into straight lines.

This demonstrates that in the case we have chosen for illustration Wardrop's method could be used. In fact, $Z=\ln z$, with $|\mathrm{d}Z/\mathrm{d}z|=1/r=f$, transforms the optimal paths to straight lines. The case is illustrated in fig. 4.5. In general, as Angel and Hyman (1976) underline, the plane representation is not possible.

Angel and Hyman mention another exception, namely when, more generally, $f=r^n$, with $-1<n<0$. Then it is possible to map the plane conformally onto a cone. The optimal paths again are geodesics. If we now cut the cone along a straight line from its apex, we can roll it up, like the cylinder, to a plane sector in this case, where the geodesics are again straight lines. As the reader understands, this possibility is only open when the three-dimensional surface, on which the optimal paths are geodesics, is "isometric" to the plane. Strictly speaking, the word "isometry" is incorrect as, for example, a cylinder and a plane strip are not

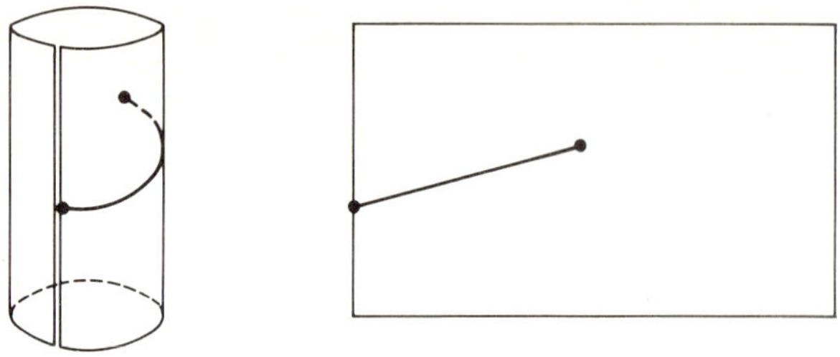

Figure 4.5

even isomorphic. This is demonstrated by the fact that a closed curve on a plane strip can always be shrunk together to a point, whereas a circle on the cylinder cannot. However, the difference being due to the topological property of simple connectedness, the abuse is not confusing. As both Wardrop (1969) and Angel and Hyman (1976) stress, the circularly symmetric, two-dimensional construction is limited to the cases already mentioned. In these cases the three-dimensional representation is not at all necessary, as Wardrop's procedure is equivalent to Angel's and Hyman's. The conic case is shown in fig. 4.6.

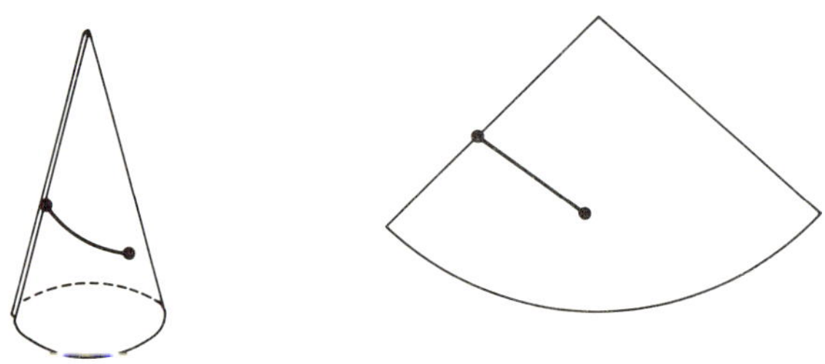

Figure 4.6

4.12. Spherical surfaces

However, even though we are not able to unfold curved surfaces to plane areas by a simple cut, so that the geodesics turn into straight lines, we can sometimes map the curved surface on the plane so that the images of the geodesics become other simple types of curves. We illustrate this with another transfer cost function, discussed by Angel and Hyman, namely the case $f=4/(4+r^2)$. Then it is possible to show that the optimal paths, as Angel and Hyman demonstrate, can be regarded as geodesics on a sphere. Actually, Angel and Hyman discuss a slightly more general case, where $(4+r^2)$ is replaced by $(b+ar^2)$ with ab equal to four times the radius of the relevant sphere. In our case the radius is unity. The numerator is necessary in order to make distances on the sphere equal to, and not only proportionate to, the transportation cost.

Now, it is well known that geodesics on a sphere are great circles. Moreover, as a *stereographic projection*, i.e. a projection of the sphere that rests on a plane onto this plane, by rays from the north pole, is a conformal mapping that maps all circles on circles, including straight lines (that are circles with infinite radius), we can represent the optimal paths on the plane as circular arcs. The sphere used in stereographic projections is well known from its use in representing complex numbers on the so called Riemann sphere, and hence the properties of this mapping are well investigated.

We are, however, running ahead of the argument. Let us first prove that the optimal paths can actually be represented on the unit sphere as geodesics, the lengths of which equal the transportation cost, by constructing the appropriate mapping $x,y \Rightarrow \xi,\eta,\zeta$. For this reason put $\xi = 4x/(4+x^2+y^2)$, $\eta = 4y/(4+x^2+y^2)$, and $\zeta = 2(x^2+y^2)/(4+x^2+y^2)$. The tangents to the parameter curves can now be obtained as

$$(\xi_x,\eta_x,\zeta_x) = (16-4x^2+4y^2, -8xy, 16x)/(4+x^2+y^2)^2,$$

$$(\xi_y,\eta_y,\zeta_y) = (-8xy, 16+4x^2-4y^2, 16y)/(4+x^2+y^2)^2.$$

From these tangent vectors the first fundamental coefficients are readily obtained as dot products. We have $F=0$, and $E=G=16/(4+x^2+y^2)^2$. The square root of the latter actually equals $4/(4+x^2+y^2)=f$, as $x^2+y^2=r^2$. Hence, the mapping is conformal, because the coordinate lines cut each other perpendicularly, whereas the magnification factor is the same in both coordinate directions. As the linear magnification factor equals transfer cost, it follows that arcs on the sphere represent transportation cost. Minimum cost is thus incurred when a geodesic is followed, and geodesics are great circles, as we know.

This latter fact can also be formally proved in the following way. First, we can compute the unit normal to the sphere,

$$\begin{aligned} N &= \partial/\partial x(\xi,\eta,\zeta)\times\partial/\partial y(\xi,\eta,\zeta)/|\partial/\partial x(\xi,\eta,\zeta)\times\partial/\partial y(\xi,\eta,\zeta)| \\ &= -(4x,4y,x^2+y^2-4)/(4+x^2+y^2). \end{aligned}$$

The reader may observe that this normal vector actually has the components $(\xi,\eta,\zeta-1)$. Owing to the parameterization formulae, its length is unity and it points inwards to the center of the sphere. We have not yet proved that the parameterization yields a sphere, but the reader may check that $(\xi^2+\eta^2+(\zeta-1)^2)\equiv 1$. The asymmetry for the third coordinate is due to the fact that the sphere is put on the plane where the zero of the vertical axis is at the point of tangency. The center of the sphere is thus at $\zeta=1$.

Next, the curvature vector can also be computed, whatever the parameterization, as $\boldsymbol{k} = -(4x,4y,x^2+y^2-4)/(4+x^2+y^2)$, if the curve is a great circle. The osculating circle of such a curve is obviously the great circle itself and its center is at the center of the sphere. Now, the geodesic curvature is $\kappa_g = \boldsymbol{k}\cdot(\boldsymbol{N}\times\boldsymbol{t})$, which can be computed as the determinant of the matrix made up by the components of the three vectors. However, since $\boldsymbol{k}$ and $\boldsymbol{N}$ are proportionate, the determinant is zero, and so is the geodesic curvature. Hence, great circles are geodesics.

We have now proved that optimal paths are great circles on the unit sphere. As stated previously we know that by stereographic projection circles on the sphere are projected onto circles in the plane. Let us now check whether the solution curves to the original variational problem can be circles.

The Euler equation to be satisfied is $fr^2 = c\sqrt{(r^2+r'^2)}$, with $f=4/(4+r^2)$. Substituting f, differentiating once with respect to ω, and eliminating c by the Euler equation, we arrive at

$$(r^2+4)rr'' - 8r'^2 + r^4 - 4r^2 = 0, \tag{65}$$

which is a second order differential equation and is not so easy to solve. But, as we know that the solutions are circular arcs, we can try the paths

$$x = r\cos\omega = a + \rho\cos t, \tag{66}$$
$$y = r\sin\omega = b + \rho\sin t,$$

where we have parametrically given circles with the centers in a, b and with ρ as radii. We can solve for $\rho\cos t$ and for $\rho\sin t$, take squares and add. This yields

$$r^2 - 2r(a\cos\omega + b\sin\omega) - K = 0, \tag{67}$$

where we define $K = \rho^2 - a^2 - b^2$. This K must be a constant for each circle since it only depends on the center and the radius.

Observe that we have been able to drop the parameter t, so that we have the equation of the circle in polar coordinates. The easiest way of handling this expression is to differentiate it twice subsequently with respect to ω. Then we arrive at two new equations, involving derivatives of r (with respect to ω) up to second order. From the three equations arrived at, including the original one, we can eliminate the trigonometric expressions involving ω and obtain

$$(r^2+K)rr'' - 2Kr'^2 + r^4 - Kr^2 = 0. \tag{68}$$

We conclude that this second order differential equation is in perfect agreement with the preceding one, obtained from the Euler equation, provided that we put $K=4$.

Thus, a circle whose center is at distance $\sqrt{(a^2+b^2)}$ from the origin, at the same time as its radius is $\rho = \sqrt{(4+a^2+b^2)}$, is the solution for an optimal path when the transfer cost function is $f=4/(4+r^2)$. For the solution the spherical representation was of great help, as the differential equation is relatively complicated. The case is illustrated in fig. 4.7.

Fig. 4.8 shows a set of optimal paths, radiating out from a fixed point of origin. The paths are dashed as before, whereas the isotransportation costs are

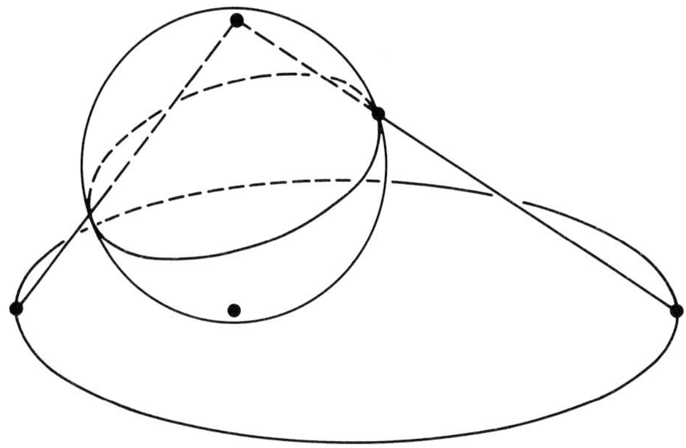

Figure 4.7

drawn continuous. As is seen, all the paths again intersect in another focus, symmetric to the point of origin. This focus actually is a degenerate "envelope" containing conjugate points, so that an extremal can only be the shortest part of the whole circular arc, contained completely in the right- or left-half plane, whichever is relevant.

The fact that the circular paths all assemble in another focus, symmetric to the origin, can be seen in the following way. Putting the paths in parametric

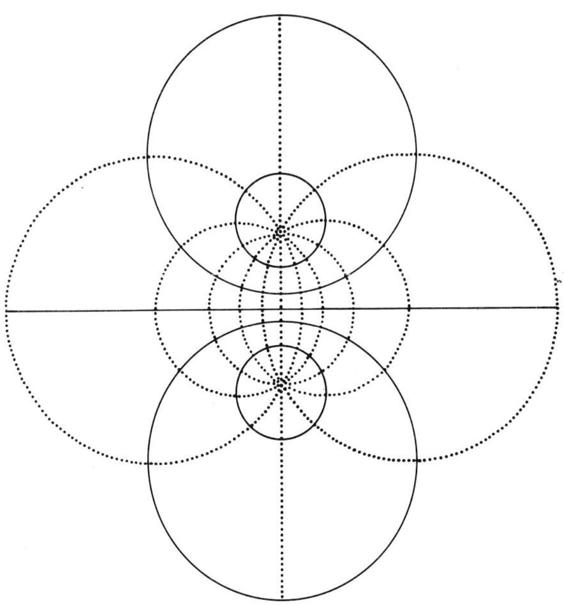

Figure 4.8

form and using the fact that $\rho^2=(a^2+b^2+4)$, we have that

$$x_0=a+\sqrt{(a^2+b^2+4)}\cos(t+\phi),$$
$$y_0=b+\sqrt{(a^2+b^2+4)}\sin(t+\phi), \tag{69}$$

for all the paths that pass through x_0,y_0. We remember that a,b are the coordinates of the center of the circular arc in question. The phase lag or lead ϕ is introduced to make the representation more general and to make it possible to let x_0,y_0 correspond to $t=0$ for all the paths originating at that point. Observe, however, that t is by no means any arc length parameter; it is in a constant proportion to arc length for each path, but the proportion changes from path to path.

But, independently of this, we can, by moving the constants to the left, taking squares, adding, and cancelling equal terms in the members, obtain

$$x_0a+y_0b=(x_0^2+y_0^2-4)/2. \tag{70}$$

When x_0,y_0 are given, i.e. when we only regard curves passing through the fixed point of origin, this is the equation of a straight line in the variables a,b. In passing we notice that we have at the same time dropped the parameter and the variable phase lag.

Since a,b are now the coordinates of the centers of the circular arcs, we conclude that *all the centers of the circles that pass through* x_0,y_0 *lie on a straight line*. This implies the existence of a symmetric focus to the starting point. Dropping a normal to the equation for a,b from x_0,y_0 we obtain the coordinates of the point of intersection as

$$a=x_0(x_0^2+y_0^2-4)/(2x_0^2+2y_0^2),$$
$$b=y_0(x_0^2+y_0^2-4)/(2x_0^2+2y_0^2).$$

Obviously, the two foci where the circles intersect must lie symmetrically with respect to this point. For the starting point we have already introduced the notation x_0,y_0. Let us for the other focus put x_1,y_1 as coordinates. Then, according to symmetry, $a=(x_0+x_1)/2$ and $b=(y_0+y_1)/2$. Substituting for a,b we can solve

$$x_1=-4x_0/(x_0^2+y_0^2); \qquad y_1=-4y_0/(x_0^2+y_0^2) \tag{71}$$

as the coordinates for the other focus.

In the case illustrated we have put $x_0=0$ and $y_0=2$. By the formulae, $x_1=0$ and $y_1=-2$. For this case it may be noticed that the curves are the coordinate curves for a familiar coordinate transformation, i.e. the *bipolar* one. By tilting the diagram, moving the origin to a symmetric position and changing scale by a single factor, we can transform any case to this one. Such changes, involving magnification, rotation and translation combined, are linear conformal maps of a type usually called *loxodromic*.

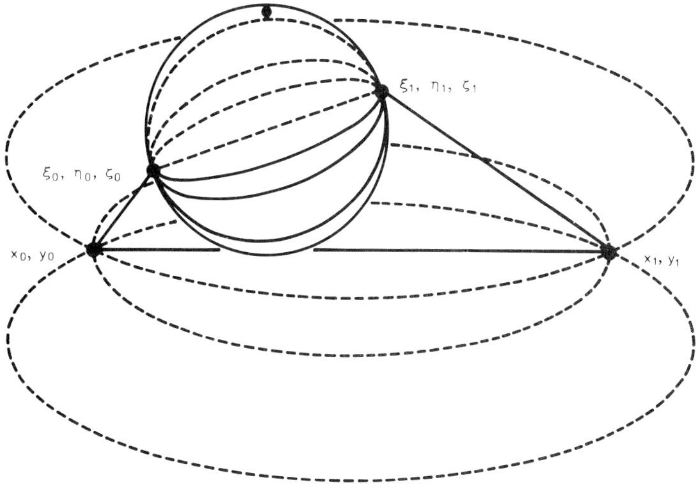

Figure 4.9

More generally, the two foci can be located anywhere in the plane, provided that they are in a certain relationship to each other, namely being image points of two opposite poles of the sphere used in the stereographic projection. As on the sphere optimal paths are great circles, the set of optimal paths that pass through a point has a common intersection point on the opposite side of the sphere. Thus, all the projections of the great circles passing through the two poles of the sphere are mapped on circles in the plane that pass through two given points collinear with the origin (see fig. 4.9).

We can see this by computing the image points on the sphere of the two foci x_0,y_0 and x_1,y_1. According to the formulae for the projection we have $\xi_0 = 4x_0/(4+x_0^2+y_0^2)$, $\eta_0 = 4y_0/(4+x_0^2+y_0^2)$ and $\zeta_0 = 2(x_0^2+y_0^2)/(4+x_0^2+y_0^2)$. But, we can calculate by formulae (71) for x_1,y_1 in terms of x_0,y_0 that $\xi_1 = -4x_0/(4+x_0^2+y_0^2)$, $\eta_1 = -4y_0/(4+x_0^2+y_0^2)$ and $\zeta_1 = 8/(4+x_0^2+y_0^2)$. Hence, we have

$$\xi_0+\xi_1=0; \qquad \eta_0+\eta_1=0; \qquad \zeta_0+\zeta_1=2, \tag{72}$$

which proves that the points (ξ_0,η_0,ζ_0) and (ξ_1,η_1,ζ_1) are opposite poles on the sphere.

Chapter 5

THE PARTIAL AND THE TOTAL INTENSITY OF TRAFFIC

5.1. Linear paths

We now discuss the distribution of traffic on the unit disk starting with the simplest case, namely with $f=1$. As can be seen immediately from eq. (47), all paths become linear (in x,y space) and hence we may write the parametrical equations for a solution curve in terms of arc length τ as

$$x=\xi+\tau\cos\theta; \qquad y=\eta+\tau\sin\theta, \tag{73}$$

where θ is a constant for each path.

We see that τ equals $\sqrt{((x-\xi)^2+(y-\eta)^2)}$ and that hence $\nabla\tau=(\cos\theta,\sin\theta)=\boldsymbol{v}/|\boldsymbol{v}|$. This means that

$$\boldsymbol{v}=|\boldsymbol{v}|\nabla\tau. \tag{74}$$

In order to determine $\boldsymbol{v}$ we must also take into consideration eq. (9), stating that $\nabla\cdot\boldsymbol{v}=-\bar{p}p$, and the boundary condition, stating that $\boldsymbol{v}\cdot\boldsymbol{n}=0$ on G. Assume for simplicity that the population is equally distributed throughout the region, i.e. that $p(x,y)=1$ everywhere. Hence, we have $\nabla\cdot\boldsymbol{v}=-1$, and this applied to (74) yields (according to the same relation as was used in (12) above) $\nabla|\boldsymbol{v}|\cdot\nabla\tau+|\boldsymbol{v}|\nabla^2\tau=-1$. Computing the Laplacian $\nabla^2\tau$ to equal $1/\tau$ we get the partial differential equation

$$\nabla|\boldsymbol{v}|\cdot\nabla\tau+|\boldsymbol{v}|/\tau+1=0. \tag{75}$$

More familiarly, this may be written

$$\partial|\boldsymbol{v}|/\partial\tau+|\boldsymbol{v}|/\tau+1=0.$$

Since neither θ nor any derivative with respect to θ occurs in this first order, linear equation it may be solved as an ordinary differential equation in τ, where only the arbitrary integration constant can depend on θ.

The solution is therefore

$$|\boldsymbol{v}|=\tfrac{1}{2}(T^2-\tau^2)/\tau, \tag{76}$$

where T^2 is the constant mentioned. It is written as a square because this facilitates the interpretation. In what follows we regard the region as a unit disk. When this is so, $\boldsymbol{v}$, having the direction of a straight line from ξ,η inside the disk, cannot be perpendicular to the boundary normal. If the boundary condition $\boldsymbol{v}\cdot\boldsymbol{n}=0$ is satisfied then the modulus $|\boldsymbol{v}|$ must be zero on the boundary. But then, due to (76), T can be interpreted as the distance from ξ,η in the direction θ to the boundary circle.

We have now arrived at an expression for the *partial* local intensity of traffic. The total local intensity can now in principle be obtained from (76) according to (19) but, in general, the calculation becomes extremely complicated. For the simple case considered, where the region is a unit disk centered around the origin, we can, however, obtain the solution quite easily.

From (19) $i(x,y)=\iint|\boldsymbol{v}|\mathrm{d}\xi\,\mathrm{d}\eta$. As $\xi=x-\tau\cos\theta$ and $\eta=y-\tau\sin\theta$, we get the Jacobian $\partial(\xi,\eta)/\partial(\tau,\theta)=\tau$. Hence, we have $\mathrm{d}\xi\,\mathrm{d}\eta=\tau\,\mathrm{d}\tau\,\mathrm{d}\theta$. We can use this coordinate change together with (76) to obtain $i(x,y)=\frac{1}{2}\iint(T^2-\tau^2)\mathrm{d}\tau\,\mathrm{d}\theta$. If the evaluation of the innermost integral is carried out we arrive at

$$i(x,y)=\tfrac{1}{6}\int_0^{2\pi}((T'+T'')^3-T'^3-T''^3)\,\mathrm{d}\theta, \tag{77}$$

where

$$T'=\surd(1-r^2\sin^2\theta)-r\cos\theta \quad\text{and}\quad T''=\surd(1-r^2\sin^2\theta)+r\cos\theta \tag{78}$$

denote the lengths of the two segments of the chord through x,y, falling on either side of the point x,y. Here r is the perpendicular distance from the origin to the chord, and θ is its inclination.

But, the integrand is $((T'+T'')^3-T'^3-T''^3)=3T'T''(T'+T'')$. However, as $T'T''=(1-r^2)$, we can factor this out before the integration sign, and behind it remains $(T'+T'')=2\surd(1-r^2\sin^2\theta)$. Hence, we get

$$i(x,y)=(1-r^2)\int_0^{2\pi}\surd(1-r^2\sin^2\theta)\,\mathrm{d}\theta, \tag{79}$$

where the remaining integral obviously has a perfect periodicity of $\pi/2$. For the integral we could then take four times the integral between the limits 0 and $\pi/2$. However, the latter is, by definition, the complete elliptic integral of the second kind, conventionally written $E(r)$ and evaluated by the series

$$E(r)=\pi/2(1-(1/2)^2r^2/1-(3/8)^2r^4/3-\ldots). \tag{80}$$

Hence,

$$i(r)=4(1-r^2)E(r). \tag{81}$$

We see that i is a circularly symmetric function that uniformly decreases with the distance r from the origin.

We may also calculate total traffic $\iint i\,\mathrm{d}x\,\mathrm{d}y$, but proceeding from (81) is awkward as we only obtain an interminable series of integrals after substitution for $E(r)$. It is better to use the following procedure.

In the present case $n=0$ in (54). Hence, transportation cost I equals distance, which we have been using as the natural parameter for the linear paths, i.e. $I=\tau$. Substituting $I=\tau$ together with $\bar{p}p=1$ and $f=1$, into (10) and (17), and equating, we get

$$\int\int_S |v| \mathrm{d}x\,\mathrm{d}y = \int\int_S \tau\,\mathrm{d}x\,\mathrm{d}y, \tag{82}$$

where $\tau = \sqrt{((x-\xi)^2+(y-\eta)^2)}$. Relation (82) has the interpretation that total traffic caused by transports having a common starting point at ξ, η equals all the transportation work done from this point of origin. Obviously, the same holds true for total traffic and total transportation work, as already seen in (22), i.e.

$$\int\int_S i\,\mathrm{d}x\,\mathrm{d}y = \int\int_S\int\int_S \tau\,\mathrm{d}x\,\mathrm{d}y\,\mathrm{d}\xi\,\mathrm{d}\eta. \tag{83}$$

The right-hand integral is relatively easy to evaluate directly. For the evaluation it is, however, wise to introduce the following coordinate transformations

$$\begin{aligned} \xi &= \rho\cos\phi - a\sin\phi; \qquad & x &= \rho\cos\phi - b\sin\phi, \\ \eta &= \rho\sin\phi + a\cos\phi; \qquad & y &= \rho\sin\phi + b\cos\phi, \end{aligned} \tag{84}$$

where ρ is the normal distance from the origin to the chord on which the endpoints are situated, ϕ is the angle of the normal (perpendicular to the angle θ of the path), and a, b fix the endpoints in relation to the intersection of the chord and the normal, so that $(b-a)=\tau$. Note that the Jacobian of the transformation is $\partial(x,y,\xi,\eta)/\partial(b,a,\rho,\phi)=(b-a)=\tau$.

Changing the variables therefore yields the integrand τ^2, and we have to evaluate $2\int\int\int\int(b-a)^2\,\mathrm{d}b\,\mathrm{d}a\,\mathrm{d}\rho\,\mathrm{d}\phi$, where the factor 2 occurs because by the following specification of the integration limits we only catch counterclockwise trips. The limits are $0 \leqslant \phi \leqslant 2\pi$, $0 \leqslant \rho \leqslant 1$, $a \leqslant b \leqslant \sqrt{(1-r^2)}$, and $-\sqrt{(1-r^2)} \leqslant a \leqslant \sqrt{(1-r^2)}$.

First, we note that since nothing in the integrand or in the other integration limits is dependent on ϕ, the integration with respect to this variable results in a multiplication by 2π. Next, the integrations with respect to a, b are straightforward and yield $\int\int i\,\mathrm{d}x\,\mathrm{d}y = 16\pi/3\int(1-\rho^2)^2\,\mathrm{d}\rho$, where still $0 \leqslant \rho \leqslant 1$.

As we could now simply expand the quadratic, integration would be straightforward, but because later we encounter powers other than the second, even such that we cannot expand into a sum of finitely many terms, it is appropriate to make a change so that the evaluation is possible with all powers. This is done simply by putting $\rho^2 = t$, so that $\mathrm{d}\rho = \mathrm{d}t/(2\sqrt{t})$. By this, $2(1-\rho^2)^2\,\mathrm{d}\rho = t^{-1/2}(1-t)^2\,\mathrm{d}t$ and hence the remaining integral equals by definition the "beta"-function

$$B\left(\tfrac{1}{2},3\right) = \int_0^1 t^{-1/2}(1-t)^2\,\mathrm{d}t = \tfrac{16}{15}, \tag{85}$$

because $B(m,n)=\Gamma(m)\Gamma(n)/\Gamma(m+n)$ with $\Gamma\left(\frac{1}{2}\right)=\sqrt{\pi}$, $\Gamma(3)=2$, and $\Gamma(3.5)=15\sqrt{\pi}/8$. Hence we multiply $16\pi/3$ by half of $\frac{16}{15}$ to get

$$\int\int_S i\,\mathrm{d}x\,\mathrm{d}y = 128\pi/45,$$

which approximately equals 8.94.

It is interesting to notice that this total, divided by π^2, which is the total number of trips, is the measure from integral geometry for a set of segments cut off from the set of all straight lines intersecting the unit disk or, in terms of geometric probability, the average length of a segment.

In summary, with an equal distribution of population over the unit disk and with a constant transfer cost function (leading to linear transportation paths) the total intensity of traffic always *increases as we move towards the center of the disk*. This may be interpreted as a *pure* influence of the bounded two-dimensional region, causing the most intense communications to take place in the central parts of the region, because this occurs in the absence of the two factors that might otherwise give rise to the same result, namely concentration of population to the central parts and concentration of traffic (by convex paths) due to lower transfer cost.

5.2. Radial paths

We may solve the problem completely for one more case, namely that of radial transports. Suppose that population is still constant but that the transports are all radial instead of linear, i.e. they go from one endpoint right into the center and right out again to the other endpoint.

We have already seen that some of the transports generated with the function $f=r^n$ are of this kind. The radial transports radiating *out from* the center go in the direction of the gradient of r. Hence, $\boldsymbol{v}=|\boldsymbol{v}|\nabla r$ and the differential equation corresponding to (75) above is

$$\nabla|\boldsymbol{v}|\cdot\nabla r+|\boldsymbol{v}|/r+1=0. \tag{86}$$

Its solution is

$$|\boldsymbol{v}|=\tfrac{1}{2}(1-r^2)/r. \tag{87}$$

This time it is very easy to obtain the total intensity according to (19). We see that the partial intensity is independent of the point of origin. Identical transports, in quantity and direction, radiate from the center for all ξ,η. Hence, i would simply be the product of expression (87) and the area of the disk, which is π. But, we have only considered transports radiating out from the center. There are as many transports that radiate *in to* the center, and thus we have to multiply the number obtained by 2. We have

$$i(x,y)=\pi(1-r^2)/r. \tag{88}$$

Total traffic in this case is

$$\int\int_S i(x,y)\,\mathrm{d}x\,\mathrm{d}y=4\pi^2/3, \tag{89}$$

which approximately equals 13.16. This means that 47 percent more traffic is created with radial paths than with linear paths (which represent the case of minimum possible total traffic).

5.3. Comparison

As compared with (81) this gives a distribution where the tendency for traffic to increase in intensity towards the center of the region is even more pronounced. Table 5.1 and the computer diagrams in figs. 5.1 and 5.2 show the traffic distributions with linear and radial paths. (Observe that in fig. 5.2 an infinitely high spire has been removed.)

Table 5.1
Traffic with linear and radial transports.

r	0.0	0.2	0.4	0.6	0.8	1.0	$\int\int i\,dx\,dy$
Linear	6.29	5.97	5.06	3.63	1.84	0.00	8.94
Radial	∞	15.08	6.60	3.35	1.45	0.00	13.16

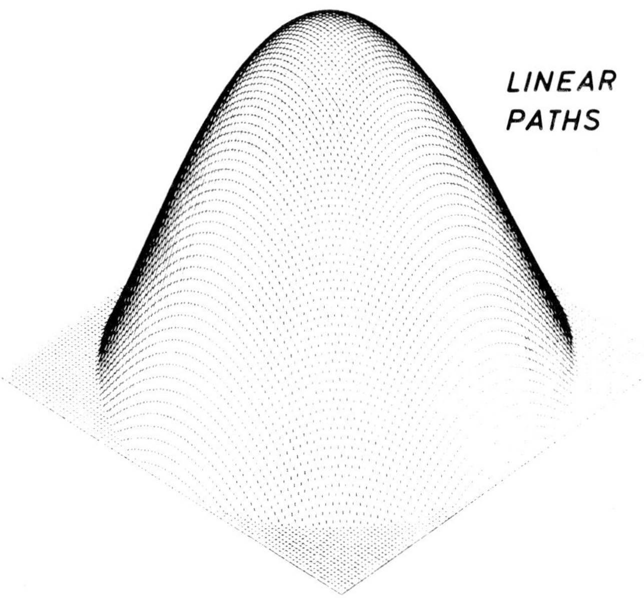

Figure 5.1. Traffic, linear paths.

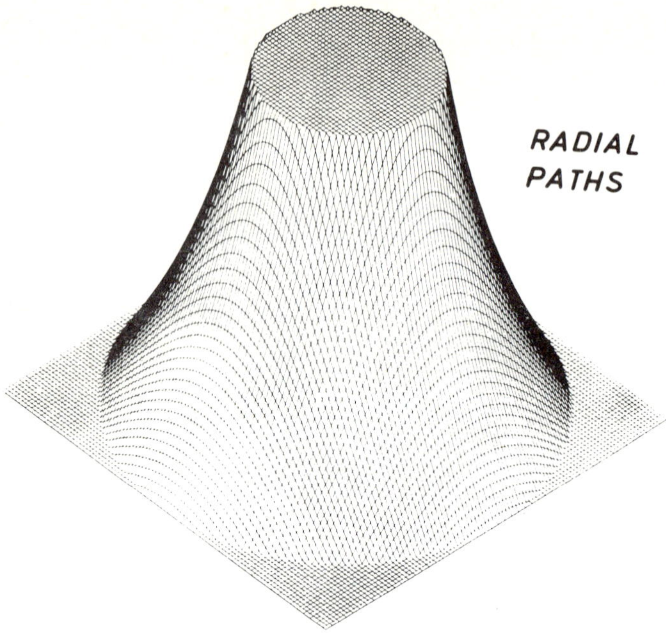

Figure 5.2. Traffic, radial paths.

The two cases compared are not just any two cases which are easy to treat analytically. They are also interesting in themselves as important limiting cases. The case of linear transports naturally is the limit between convex and concave paths.

Moreover, we saw in the preceding paragraph that with $f = r^n$ the transports in a sector which is $n/(n+1)$ of the unit disk are radial. As n increases, the portion of the disk where the paths are not radial rapidly approaches zero, and we see that the case with only radial transportation is the limiting case as n goes to infinity.

5.4. The general case

A moment of reflection reveals that radial transportation is a limiting case not only for this special type of transfer cost function. It represents in general the case of the "most convex possible" paths for a transfer cost function with circular symmetry $f(r)$, *provided that the paths are optimal*. This is so because, as can easily be seen, every path which is not wholly contained in the acute angle formed by joining the endpoints to the center is both longer and more expensive than the path formed by segments of the lines defining this angle.

Hence, linear transports are the least convex and radial transports are the most convex ones that may be optimal. It may be expected that the intensity distribution for any case of convex paths falls somewhere between the two limiting cases tabulated above (table 5.1). We could also guess that total traffic with any set of convex paths lies somewhere between the two figures (8.94 and 13.16) tabulated in the last column. This is so because the total amount of traffic generated is related to the length of the paths, and because radial paths are the longest possible and linear paths the shortest possible for each individual transport.

Since in both cases the intensity of traffic decreases with the distance from the center we can surmise that this behavior is typical of all types of sufficiently regular convex paths – including the limiting case of linearity – and that the paths must have a certain degree of concavity (due especially to good transportation facilities in the peripheral parts) in order for i to be constant or even increase with r.

Chapter 6

THE DETERMINANTS OF TRANSPORTATION DEMAND

So far we have assumed that the need for transportation between any two locations is proportionate to population densities there, and on nothing else. It is not difficult to defend this assumption of proportionality. At a very unsophisticated level it is natural to expect communication, whether by messages, transportation of goods or travellers, to be in proportion to the number of potential senders at the origin as well as to the number of potential receivers at the destination. As a first approximation one could take these potentials as proportionate to population densities, and then the model actually used is the obvious consequence.

It is harder to defend the abstraction from other possible determinants of transportation demand, above all distance, communication time or travel cost between the locations concerned — whichever seems most relevant. For this reason we take into consideration the effect of an explicit consideration of a sensitivity of transportation demand to cost. It should, however, be stressed that traffic distributions are the only elements in the model that are affected by this. The rest of the analysis works however transportation demand is determined, provided it is ultimately a given function of the geographical coordinates of origin and destination.

There are no difficulties in finding reasons why transportation demand displays a sensitivity to cost (or distance, or time) of communication. It seems appropriate to distinguish between two different types of sensitivity.

6.1. General reasons for cost sensitivity

First, it is well known that people and institutions that need numerous contacts agglomerate closely in space. Employees live close to their working places, shops locate in population clusters, factories are close to markets or suppliers, etc. All this is related to the spatial structure of the economy, and ultimately to a multitude of locational choices by individual subjects. This spatial structure is, of course, dependent upon the facility of communication over various distances and therefore changes as the allocation of road capital is altered. This dependence, however, is a long-term effect. Because of the fixed costs of relocation it is defensible to regard the spatial structure of the economy as sufficiently inert to be taken as a given datum in the present context. We are concerned with discovering the appropriate allocation of roads in space for a given spatial organization of the economy. The analysis turns out to be so complicated that we have to leave a multitude of loose ends even with this simplification. If in addition we tried to consider the effects of road capital allocation on locational patterns, we would end up in an enormously complicated general equilibrium system. At present this seems almost insurmountable.

Secondly, there is also a short-term sensitivity of transportation demand to cost. Each individual subject always has a multitude of possible ways of satisfying his various needs at different locations. As distance to a facility in itself is a disadvantage, because of high costs and waste of time, any optimization to maximize some preference function subject to financial constraints leads to a choice where second-best solutions that are close in space are preferred to first-best solutions that are distant in space. A rearrangement of road capital that makes communication at distance easier or more difficult may thus lead to changes in communication patterns. As such alterations are not connected with fixed costs like proper relocations, we may expect a dependence of transportation demand on cost that is sensitive to short-term relocations of road capital. Hence, in addition to the structural distance dependence we can speak of a nonstructural one.

As we are going to introduce an explicit dependence on distance in the next chapter, we concentrate on the nonstructural type. The reason is that the structural type, being invariant due to assumption, does not present anything new in terms of analytically interesting general conclusions.

Strictly speaking, the reflections above should be sufficient to formulate a transportation demand function. In addition to the proportionality to population densities at two locations, the number of transports, communications or trips should be a decreasing function of communication cost, time or distance between the locations. For simplicity of analytic treatment or econometric specification the dependence could be taken as a power function or an exponential. Such a specification is sufficiently appealing to the intuition, and there are a multitude of empirical studies in existence supporting such relationships for various spatial interaction, such as telephonic communication, aviation traffic between cities, and migration flows. These empirical studies do not discriminate between various forms of the cost (distance or time) dependence. In some cases the power function works best, while in others the exponential function works best.

In addition it should be stressed that there is a consensus among the regional scientists working on the theoretical foundations for such transportation demand patterns as are outlined above about the type of empirical generalization they want to derive. The consensus is surprising, because there is little general agreement about why such transportation demand, or interaction, patterns arise.

For this reason, because there are a multitude of alternative, very elaborate theories about spatial interaction, the picture would be incomplete if we said nothing about these theories themselves, even though the summary has to be very brief and fragmentary in view of the volume of accumulated literature. It should be emphasized, however, that we make a distinction between the theories on the one hand and their almost identical implication for interaction behavior on the other. As the latter is empirically well supported, it is possible to accept the conclusion as a building block without choosing any of the theories excluding all the others.

6.2. Gravity and entropy models

There is one interesting feature in interaction theories, namely that the most influential of them have been based on physical analogies. The field has sometimes been called "social physics", and in the evaluations of various models very general discussions about whether social and physical phenomena are sufficiently similar are almost as common as attempts to base the theories on intuitively acceptable assumptions about the behavior of individual subjects.

There are two physical prototypes, namely Newtonian gravitation theory and the Maxwell–Boltzmann theory concerning the distribution of kinetic energy among the molecules in a dilute gas. Models of the first type are designated "gravity models" and those of the latter type "entropy models". This is so because one of the derivations of the Maxwell–Boltzmann distribution is based on picking out the most probable frequency distribution of molecules in different states of kinetic energy, provided that the total kinetic energy is given. As the objective is reached by combinatorics under the basic a priori assumption that it is equiprobable for each molecule to be in each possible state and that the states of the molecules do not influence each other (provided the given total energy is not exceeded), we can say that the derivation is based on a principle of minimum information, or maximum "disorder", i.e. entropy.

Historically, the gravity model precedes the entropy model. Newtonian gravity makes the attraction of two point masses proportionate to their masses and reciprocal to the square of their Euclidean distance. Regarding a two-dimensional plane, instead of three-dimensional space, and disregarding the vectorial property of the attractive force so that we only speak of its magnitude, it is convenient to identify population densities with masses and to let the demand for transportation be $\bar{p}p/\tau^2$ in our symbolism, where $\bar{p}=p(\xi,\eta)$, $p=p(x,y)$, $\tau^2=(x-\xi)^2+(y-\eta)^2$. Stewart (1947) is responsible for the first complete application of this type to geographical interaction, even though there seem to be much earlier attempts. For historical facts and a more complete survey the reader is referred to the articles by Nijkamp (1975, 1978).

Later writers thought it unnecessary to take just the square of distance. Because the transportation of bulky goods, for example, should be more sensitive to distance than telephonic communication, it is natural to let the exponent vary from one application to another, determining it in each case from empirical data. There have also been other changes in the model, such as taking powers of population densities, or taking measures of distance other than the Euclidean. However, whatever the exact formulation, the model was successfully applied to a number of situations where it fitted empirical data well. For examples of this the reader is referred to Lloyd and Dicken (1972).

The feature common to these applications, to telephonic communication or to passenger air traffic for example, was that they dealt with multipurpose communications. When the model was applied to specific, single-purpose communications, such as trips to work, a difficulty emerged. When one studies an urban region where working places are concentrated in the central parts, whereas workers live in suburbs, it is obvious that the origin and destination densities can no longer be equally distributed. Thus, the possibility of using population density as a proxy for everything relevant for generating trips is lost, and one must ask which distributions should replace the population density.

A most natural choice is to take the number of workers as the origin distribution and the number of working places as the destination distribution. These (different) densities being denoted by $O(\xi,\eta)$ and $D(x,y)$, respectively, we can specify the number of trips to work from ξ,η to x,y as $T=OD/\tau^{\varepsilon}$. But, because of this choice of origin and destination densities certain compatibility conditions emerge. We must have $\iint T\,d\xi\,d\eta=D$ and likewise $\iint T\,dx\,dy=O$, since the number of trips to work for each destination must equal the number of working places, whereas for each origin it must equal the number of workers. As T is itself determined by O,D according to the specified formula, it is easy to see that the integral constraints need not be satisfied. It should be observed that generally there is no problem with such nonspecific communication as telephone calls. There is no reason whatever why the number of calls to or from a location should equal population there.

Returning to the one-purpose case of trips to work, the oddity could also be put another way. Consider the number of trips from a given residential area to a given industrial center, and suppose that suddenly the number of workers in the former area and the number of working places in the latter area are doubled. The model would then predict a fourfold increase in the number of trips to work for the pair of locations considered, but this is absurd since only a doubling would be warranted for trips as well.

To remove the oddities a "calibration" by means of balancing factors $A(\xi,\eta)$ associated with the origin and $B(x,y)$ associated with the destination were introduced. Putting then $T=AOBD/\tau^{\varepsilon}$ sufficient degrees of freedom have been introduced to fulfill the integral constraints. When

$$A\iint BD\,\mathrm{d}x\,\mathrm{d}y/\tau^{\varepsilon}=B\iint AO\,\mathrm{d}\xi\,\mathrm{d}\eta/\tau^{\varepsilon}=1,$$

it is easy to see that the integral constraints are fulfilled. Also, supposing O,D to be doubled everywhere, we can by dividing the original A,B everywhere by $\sqrt{2}$ still have the integral constraints fulfilled and T doubled everywhere, as is reasonable. Hence, the calibration eliminates the inherent oddities. The introduction of weights, however, is an ad hoc procedure of a type generally considered as unsatisfactory in the philosophy of science. Therefore, it has been a constant challenge to find a theoretical reason for these weights or, even better, by deriving them *within* some acceptable theory.

Before continuing the review, we can stop to emphasize that the more specific is the purpose of communications studied, the more pronounced are the oddities calling for calibration. The problems dealt with in this book concern the most general, multipurpose type of communication. In view of the fact that a more densely populated location not only displays a greater number of agents within a fixed set of facilities, but also a greater variety of the set itself, the oddities are not so prominent. A quadrupling of communications in general in a doubled population is not so unreasonable and, after all, the uncalibrated model has worked well in a number of applications. To avoid complicating our model no balancing factors are introduced.

Apart from the challenge of needing to explain the balancing factors, there was uneasiness over the fact that the whole gravity model lacked an explanation. The reductionist instinct of scientists calls for a formal derivation of the transportation demand function and regards it as inadequate that a model merely fits empirical data and is intuitively plausible by general arguments such as those supplied above. This is a little odd because there is no "reason" for Newton's law of gravity either. It merely fits data well for astronomical observations and physical experiments. (Modern, relativist physics even rejects the idea of action at distance, dissolving the concept of gravity by the intrinsic curvature of space–time.)

The most influential response to the challenge was the entropy model proposed by Wilson (1967, 1970). As mentioned above, it was modelled on the Maxwell–Boltzmann energy distribution for the molecules of a dilute gas. The typical problem dealt with in Wilson's treatment is a one-purpose communication, such as trips to work. The model is discontinuous, considering a finite number of locations within the region. Even though it is possible to put the theory in a continuous form, we describe it in its original form because the description is thereby simplified.

In each of these locations there is a number of workers and working places. In location i there are O_i workers and in location j there are D_j working places. The number of work trips from i to j is designated T_{ij}. We immediately get some summation constraints, $\Sigma_j T_{ij} = O_i$ and $\Sigma_i T_{ij} = D_j$, corresponding to the integral constraints written above. The matrix $[T_{ij}]$ provides a complete description of the communication pattern. We define $T = \Sigma_i O_i = \Sigma_j D_j$ as the total number of trips that also equals the totals of workers and working places. This naturally requires full employment and no vacancies.

Now, the trip matrix $[T_{ij}]$ can be considered as a *macro* characteristic of the system, as distinct from the micro characteristic of a complete assignment of individual workers to individual working places. A given trip matrix may arise from many micro assignments of individuals. In fact, the individuals represented by the entry T_{ij} in any cell of the trip matrix may be permutated among themselves in $T_{ij}!$ different ways, and these permutations can be made independently for all cells, leading to a total of $\Pi_i \Pi_j T_{ij}!$ permutations that do not change one entry of the trip matrix. The total of distinct micro states being $T!$ we know that the number of different ways in which a given trip matrix can arise is given by the multinomial coefficient $T!/(\Pi_i \Pi_j T_{ij}!)$.

If we regard all these different ways, i.e. all the micro states, as a priori equiprobable, then we can interpret the multinomial coefficient as a "probability", or rather an absolute frequency easily convertible to a probability. We can see how this works from an example. With ten locations and ten workers as well as ten working places in each location, there are (among many others) two different trip matrices that satisfy the summation constraints. One is the matrix with a unit entry in all of its hundred cells. The multinomial coefficient associates the frequency $100!/(1!)^{100}$ approximately equal to 10^{157}. The other matrix has tens in its main diagonal and zeros everywhere else. Its frequency is $100!/(10!)^{10}$, approximately equal to 10^{100}. Even though both frequencies are enormous, in view of the fact that a relatively small problem was considered, we should not disregard the fact that the ratio of these frequencies is enormous also (amounting to 57 zeros). The two matrices actually represent the most probable and the least probable matrices that are in agreement with the summation constraints. They also represent extremes in the sense that the diagonal matrix means a minimum of communication with everybody working at his own location, whereas the matrix of unit constants represents a communication pattern completely without dependence on distance between the locations.

The property that a matrix of equal elements in all the cells is the most probable one has general applicability, provided it is admitted by the constraints. Anyhow, the measure assigns the larger probability to a matrix the more equal are its elements.

It is interesting to note another general feature at this stage, namely that the multinomial coefficient assigns the same frequency to all matrices obtained from each other by reshuffling the elements. Hence, the probability has to do not so much with the matrix as an ordered structure arranged in rows and columns, as with the unordered set of its elements.

The matrix character of the set is, however, of importance when the summation constraints are considered. A given set of elements of an $N \times N$ matrix can be arranged in matrix shape in $N^2!$ different ways, different not necessarily meaning indistinguishable when there are equal elements, but the constraints on the row and column sums of the elements eliminate many of these matrices.

In addition a cost constraint that Wilson (1976, 1970) introduces makes the set of admissible matrices even smaller. If we denote the cost of communication between locations i and j by $c_{ij} = c_{ji}$, then we can compute the total cost of communication as the expression $C = \Sigma_i \Sigma_j c_{ij} T_{ij}$.

By taking all micro assignments as equiprobable, we can associate a probability to each matrix of trips. On the other hand, we can delimit a set of admissible matrices by stipulating that the summation constraints on rows and columns are satisfied and by stipulating that a given cost should not be exceeded. This opens the road for an optimization problem. Given the distributions of origins and destinations and assuming that a total travel budget is not exceeded, which is the most probable trip matrix? In the absence of any detailed information we may simply ask for the matrix which can arise in the greatest number of ways that (due to the absence of information) are considered equiprobable.

Wilson (1967, 1970) is able to solve the problem by maximizing the logarithm of the multinomial frequency measure, approximated by a simplified version of Stirling's formula, subject to the summation and the cost constraints. The maximand is

$$\ln\left(T!/\left(\prod_i \prod_j T_{ij}!\right)\right) \approx T(\ln T - 1) - \sum_i \sum_j T_{ij}(\ln T_{ij} - 1),$$

and the constraints are

$$O_i - \sum_j T_{ij} = D_j - \sum_i T_{ij} = 0, \qquad i,j = 1, \ldots, N,$$

$$C - \sum_i \sum_j c_{ij} T_{ij} \geqslant 0.$$

The maximization can be made by a straightforward Lagrangian method that presents no details of particular interest. Hence, we do not reproduce the details. The result is

$$T_{ij} = A_i O_i B_j D_j \exp(-\beta c_{ij}),$$

with

$$A_i \sum_j B_j D_j \exp(-\beta c_{ij}) = B_j \sum_i A_i O_i \exp(-\beta c_{ij}), \qquad i,j = 1, \ldots, N.$$

Hence, Wilson (1967, 1970) is able to derive a model of the gravity type, with the distance dependence taken as exponential instead of a power function, where balancing factors are built in so that fulfillment of the summation constraints is guaranteed. This latter fact is not surprising, because the summation constraints were actually used in the derivation.

Formally the derivation is neat, and Wilson manages to demonstrate that the probability maximum is very sharp. As a matter of fact, a maximum probability would not be so interesting if it were not so sharp that it is almost the only state worth consideration. This is the point of statistical mechanics from which the analogy is borrowed.

6.3. Critical remarks

In evaluating the model two questions may be posed: is the derived behavior rule in accordance with empirical experience, and are the assumptions appealing to intuition of what idealized reality is like?

As to the first question, it is possible to refer to a multitude of successful applications of the entropy model. However, the same could be said about the gravity model, and thus the entropy model cannot claim to be superior on empirical grounds. Actually, Wilson's claim is based on reductionist advantages and, referring to logical positivist philosophy, he regards the derivation as a scientific improvement because the constraints are "unrestrictive", probably in comparison to some other alternative derivation of gravity-like models. Before considering the interesting question of whether the assumptions really can be considered as unrestrictive, we will stress one fact concerning the trip matrix derived.

We have already mentioned that there is one matrix that is more probable than any other, namely the one with equal elements in all cells. Suppose that this matrix is admitted by the summation constraints. Assume also that the budget C is increased beyond that critical value, proportionate to $\Sigma_i \Sigma_j c_{ij}$, that admits equal communication between all locations. Then the cost constraint becomes a slack constraint, β becomes zero, and communication becomes independent of distance. If all communication for various purposes is explained by a set of entropy models, then it becomes more and more insensitive to distance as the travel budget increases. And, if the population can afford to spend a sufficiently large amount on travelling, communication is completely insensitive to travel cost.

Referring to our introductory discussion about structural and nonstructural cost dependence, we can conclude that the entropy model is only relevant to the nonstructural case provided there is no implication that location structure readjusts so fast to any increase in the money people can spend on travelling that the locational structure too becomes independent of communication cost. Otherwise, the need for more contacts between institutions closer in space than for those more distant remains even if people can afford to travel more.

Beckmann (1974) has criticized the entropy theory because it solves the trip distribution problem independently of individual workers' locational choices of places to work and places to live. In Beckmann's view the distribution of trips to work is simply the residual of the locational decisions, which therefore should be explicitly introduced into the model. To this we could add that these primary factors are not only missing explicitly. They *cannot* be even implicit parts of the picture because the communication structure becomes insensitive to cost when the budget is increased.

As to the acceptability of the assumptions made, both the procedure of maximizing the frequency measure and the constraints could be questioned. Personally, I find the concept of maximum entropy or minimum information a valuable complement to the preference maximization of traditional economics. The entropy approach may become a powerful tool particularly in solving aggregation problems where many individuals are involved about whose tastes we know very little. This alternative is especially welcome if one dislikes introducing interpersonal utility comparisons or social welfare functions. Moreover, recent interpretations of the model as being similar to a geometric programming model where the objective function *is* a kind of social welfare function, makes it possible to dispense with entropy altogether. For a detailed discussion the reader is referred to Nijkamp (1975, 1978).

I find it much more difficult to accept one of the constraints, namely the cost constraint as something reflecting even idealized reality. Taken literally it implies either that there is some supreme authority that can control the system so that one worker can change the location of his work only if he can arrange a series of changes involving other workers so that total travel expenditure is unchanged, or that the system works as if there were such an authority.

For illumination on this issue, we can look at the corresponding constraint in statistical mechanics from which the paradigm is borrowed. This is the constraint of a given total energy. In the world of molecules the changes of state of the individuals are due to binary collisions among themselves, or to collisions with the walls of the vessel that defines the system. Because of the fundamental principle of energy conservation, the elastic collisions leave the sum of the kinetic energies of the molecules unchanged even if they constantly change their kinetic energies. Through the walls of the vessel a change may be introduced in total energy for the system if the vessel is cooled or heated. However, this change is slow in relation to the changes of state of colliding molecules, and hence it is meaningful to take the system as "quasistatic", treating total energy as if it were constant and asking if there is a frequency distribution for kinetic energy that is much more probable than any other distribution. In fact there is one – the Maxwell - Boltzmann distribution. It is a macro characteristic, like Wilson's trip matrix, and has the property that it arises from an overwhelming number of equiprobable micro assignments of energy to the individual molecules.

To this we should add that the combinatoric way of deriving the Maxwell-Boltzmann distribution is by no means the only possible one. It can equally well be derived within the framework of a deterministic scattering model as the limit in infinite time of the solution to Boltzmann's integro-differential "transport equation". This demonstrates the equilibrium character of the distribution. In order that such an equilibrium may be attained, the macro characteristic must remain constant. This refers to total kinetic energy, i.e. temperature.

Hence, we must conclude that the constancy of total kinetic energy must be assumed for the validity of the derivation. To my knowledge there is as yet nothing in modern statistical mechanics that is increasingly concerned with open systems to allow us to dispense with the validity of the constraint.

Looking now at the "social physics" of trips to work, we must conclude that there is nothing to allow us to base the derivation on fixed total trip expenditure. There is nothing corresponding to the principle of energy conservation for two colliding molecules. The point is that it is not sufficient that for some period total travel expenditure in fact has a certain value and even changes slowly for the derivation to be valid. It must be assumed that no changes of individual state are possible if the cost constraint is not fulfilled. This seems to be the main weakness of an otherwise very appealing theory.

To illustrate the importance of the assumption that micro state changes are in fact impossible if they do not fulfill the cost constraint, we can take an example with another constraint. Take any number that can be associated with a pair of locations, such as the difference in their elevation above sea level. For any trip matrix we can compute the total "vertical transportation work" over a period. We may even conclude that this total changes relatively little, owing to the same inertia that makes total travel expenditures vary relatively little. Now, impose constancy of total vertical transportation work as a constraint to replace the cost constraint. What is the result? Obviously a trip matrix that displays an exponential dependence on differences in elevation above sea level. This is certainly nonsense. But the reason it is nonsensical is because it leads to a matrix that is not in agreement with empirical data.

It should be emphasized that I do not mean that using aggregate communication costs in a model is inadmissible if it can be interpreted as a result of individual decisions. To exemplify, we can take the linear programming model by Nijkamp and Paelinck (1974). They minimize $\Sigma_i \Sigma_j c_{ij} T_{ij}$ subject to $\Sigma_j T_{ij} = O_i$, $\Sigma_i T_{ij} = D_j$ and a non-negativity constraint on all T_{ij}. The idea seems to be that all needs may be equally well satisfied at any location and that the least expensive communication pattern is chosen. But, here the minimization of aggregate cost is equivalent to minimizations of private costs for each individual traveller.

In my opinion such a simple theory in conjunction with Beckmann's idea that communication is a result of primary locational choices is all that is needed to make a communication pattern of the gravity or entropy type intuitively plausible. Since empirical data support patterns of this type, there is no difficulty in choosing a hypothesis for use in the present book. For analytical simplicity the original gravity type has been preferred, without balancing factors, since we do not deal with single-purpose communication.

This far from complete review of the literature has been concerned with the mainstream on gravity and entropy models. This means that important contributions like the very elaborate axiomatic theory by Smith (1975) leading to gravity-like models as special cases have not been mentioned. However, this review is parenthetical in the book. The most important conclusion to be drawn from it is that all the different theories lead to almost the same interaction hypothesis, and this, in simplified form, is all we need.

Chapter 7

DISTANCE-DEPENDENT INTERACTION

So far we have employed the gravity hypothesis for interaction in a form where the assumption that transports are generated in proportion to population densities in the two points considered was retained, but the assumption of an inverse proportionality to their distance or some power of it was discarded. It is now time to take the latter dependence into explicit account. For simplicity we still assume the case of linear paths and unitary population density.

7.1. The distribution of traffic

The number of transports between the points x,y and ξ,η would now be $\bar{p}p/\tau^{\varepsilon}$. Eq. (9) above would have to be modified and written

$$\nabla \cdot v = -\bar{p}p/\tau^{\varepsilon}. \tag{90}$$

Viewed superficially, there may be a suspicion that this would create problems at the minimization of the counterpart of (24) above, since τ depends on the transportation path followed, which is an outcome of the minimization problem itself. But it is obvious that τ should be considered as a constant at the minimization because the transporters want to find the optimal routes for their transports, no matter how numerous these are, and not to make the minimization by finding such long paths that they abstain from undertaking the transports. It is easy to see that the solutions (25) and the following derivations based on them in Chapter 4 are independent of which constant value τ has.

The difference appears with the differential equation (75) above, where $1/\tau^{\varepsilon}$ replaces the constant 1. This variant of the differential equation is only slightly more complicated than (75) and has the solution

$$|v| = (1/\alpha)(T^{\alpha} - \tau^{\alpha})/\tau, \tag{91}$$

where we define $\alpha = 2 - \varepsilon$.

The integration of this expression, according to (19), to obtain the total intensity of traffic may only be carried out analytically for specific values of ε. For $\varepsilon = 0$ we have already obtained expression (81) above. For $\varepsilon = 1$, we even

Table 7.1
Traffic with different distance elasticities.

r	0.00	0.20	0.40	0.60	0.80	1.00
$\varepsilon=2.5$	14.70	14.50	13.88	12.64	10.26	0.00
$\varepsilon=2.0$	8.73	8.50	7.83	6.62	4.56	0.00
$\varepsilon=1.5$	6.92	6.72	6.02	4.78	2.94	0.00
$\varepsilon=1.0$	6.28	6.03	5.28	4.02	2.26	0.00
$\varepsilon=0.5$	6.13	5.85	5.03	3.70	1.96	0.00
$\varepsilon=0.0$	6.29	5.97	5.06	3.63	1.84	0.00

more easily obtain

$$i(x,y)=2\pi(1-r^2).$$

The cases for demand elasticities other than zero and unity may be obtained by numerical quadrature from[1]

$$i(x,y)=\int_0^{2\pi}((T'+T'')^\beta-T'^\beta-T''^\beta)/(\alpha\beta)\,\mathrm{d}\theta, \tag{92}$$

where we define $\beta=3-\varepsilon$, and where

$$T'=\surd(1-r^2\sin^2\theta)-r\cos\theta,$$

$$T''=\surd(1-r^2\sin^2\theta)+r\cos\theta.$$

The results of the calculations are given in table 7.1. We see that with any elasticity of transportation demand traffic is still a decreasing function of the distance from the center. Apart from this a highly elastic demand tends to increase total traffic by encouraging very numerous short trips.

7.2. Total traffic and total communication

A measure of total traffic can be obtained analytically. With $f=1$, we have because of (11), (17) and (19), that

$$\int\int i\,\mathrm{d}x\,\mathrm{d}y=\int\int\int\int|v|\,\mathrm{d}x\,\mathrm{d}y\,\mathrm{d}\xi\,\mathrm{d}\eta=-\int\int\int\int I\nabla\cdot v\,\mathrm{d}x\,\mathrm{d}y\,\mathrm{d}\xi\,\mathrm{d}\eta.$$

With unitary transfer cost and linear paths, transportation cost equals distance, $I=\tau$. Using this together with (90) and putting $p=1$, we get

$$\int\int_S i\,\mathrm{d}x\,\mathrm{d}y=\int\int_S\int\int_S 1/\tau^{\varepsilon-1}\,\mathrm{d}x\,\mathrm{d}y\,\mathrm{d}\xi\,\mathrm{d}\eta. \tag{93}$$

By the same method as in the derivation (83)–(85) this integral is easily evaluated. Using $J=\int\int i\,\mathrm{d}x\,\mathrm{d}y$ for total traffic

$$J(\varepsilon)=32\pi B(\tfrac{1}{2},3-\varepsilon/2)/((3-\varepsilon)(4-\varepsilon)2^\varepsilon), \tag{94}$$

[1]These formulae are only valid when ε is different from 2. For the special case a slightly different formula with the integrand $(T'+T'')\ln(T'+T'')-T'\ln T'-T''\ln T''$ is used at the numerical quadrature.

where B again denotes the "beta function". With $\varepsilon=0$ we have $B(\frac{1}{2},3)=\frac{16}{15}$ and hence $J(0)=128\pi/45$ as already obtained.

We see that J becomes infinite as ε approaches 3. From table 7.1 we also notice that, with a high elasticity, traffic is much more uniformly distributed over the region and drops sharply only very close to the boundary. This is intuitively understandable since with a high elasticity only local transports are important in number. Thus, it does not matter whether a small "isolated" local traffic area is close to the boundary or not, unless it comes very close to it.

In addition to the measure of total traffic (=total transportation work, which is the same as total cost with $f=1$) another total is of interest. We might want to obtain a measure of total communication or a total "number of trips". As, obviously, $-\nabla\cdot\boldsymbol{v}=\bar{p}p/\tau^{\varepsilon}$ is the number of trips between two locations, the total number of trips is the integral $N(\varepsilon)=\int\int\int\int 1/\tau^{\varepsilon}\,\mathrm{d}x\,\mathrm{d}y\,\mathrm{d}\xi\,\mathrm{d}\eta$. This means that

$$N(\varepsilon)=J(\varepsilon+1). \tag{95}$$

With $\varepsilon=0$, $B(\frac{1}{2},\frac{5}{2})=3\pi/8$, and hence $N(0)=\pi^2$ which is intuitively appealing because the number of trips, when one trip connects any two locations, is equal to the square of the area of the region.

There is one oddity, namely that total communication goes to infinity faster than total traffic. As with linear paths total traffic measures cost; this means that if ε approaches the value 2 then total communication becomes infinite whereas total cost is still finite. Put in another way, any finite total communication may be obtained at zero cost as ε goes to 2. This is an inherent oddity in the gravity model.

We could now argue that the costs (=traffic) tabulated should not be compared as they are, because they represent cases of very different total communication. It may seem reasonable to compare costs for a pattern of long distance communication with one of communication confined to the neighborhood, but where the total number of trips is the same. It is easy to do this. We can assume that there is a proportionality factor for the distribution of sinks, to which both total traffic and total communication become proportional. We can then prescribe that total communication be, say, π^2 in all cases. This means that we can solve for the proportionality constant in each case, and obtain the traffic distribution from the corresponding entries in the previous table by multiplication with $N(0)/N(\varepsilon)$. As $N(0)=9.87$, $N(0.5)=11.83$, $N(1)=16.76$ and $N(1.5)=34.07$, we get table 7.2.

Table 7.2

Traffic distribution with different distance elasticities and with given total communication.

r	0.00	0.20	0.40	0.60	0.80	1.00
$\varepsilon=1.5$	2.01	1.95	1.75	1.39	0.85	0.00
$\varepsilon=1.0$	3.71	3.56	3.12	2.37	1.33	0.00
$\varepsilon=0.5$	5.09	4.86	4.17	3.07	1.63	0.00
$\varepsilon=0.0$	6.29	5.97	5.06	3.63	1.84	0.00

Chapter 8

DIRECT DERIVATION OF TRAFFIC DISTRIBUTIONS

If we want to derive traffic distributions in cases other than those treated, i.e. with linear and radial paths, the matter becomes much more difficult, even with transfer cost functions as simple as those of the power variety. We may then want to avoid having to carry out the successive steps of solving the two differential equations and taking a double integral.

A direct method, which may be used at Monte Carlo simulation or numerical quadrature, is illustrated below for the cases $f = r^n$. We have seen that traffic is then a result of two different categories of paths: curved if the acute angle of the radii vectors of the endpoints does *not* exceed $\pi/(n+1)$ and radial if the critical angle *is* exceeded.

Computation of traffic resulting from radial paths does not present any difficulty. Obviously, the fraction $n/(n+1)$ of all transports being radial, we only need to take this fraction of traffic when *all* trips are radial. So

$$i_{\text{rad}} = (n/(n+1))\pi(1-r^2)/r. \tag{96}$$

The contribution i_{crv}, due to curved paths, is harder to calculate. However, in the special case illustrated we receive great help from the conformal mapping introduced earlier.

8.1. "Cordon crossings" and weighting

Let the unit disk S be divided into two disjoint parts by a circle with radius r (less than unity) and concentric with the boundary circle. Let S' denote the small disk inside the r-circle and S'' the ring outside it.

Consider an arbitrary vector field with its source point ξ, η inside S'. Then, take its divergence $\nabla \cdot \boldsymbol{v} = -1$ and integrate with respect to x, y over S''. Since no transports cross the outer boundary of this ring, we have from Gauss's theorem

$$\int\int_{S''} \mathrm{d}x\,\mathrm{d}y = \int \boldsymbol{v} \cdot \boldsymbol{n}\,\mathrm{d}\sigma.$$

The minus signs have been cancelled because the line integral in the right-hand member is taken counterclockwise along the r-circle (i.e. in negative direction in relation to the interior of S'').

But, the unit outward normal to the r-circle is $\boldsymbol{n}=\nabla r=(\cos\omega, \sin\omega)$. As $\boldsymbol{v}=|\boldsymbol{v}|(\cos\theta, \sin\theta)$ and as arc length $\mathrm{d}\sigma=r\,\mathrm{d}\omega$ we get

$$\iint_{S''} \mathrm{d}x\,\mathrm{d}y = r\int_0^{2\pi} |\boldsymbol{v}|\cos(\theta-\omega)\,\mathrm{d}\omega.$$

Provided that from the outset we had divided the divergence by $\cos(\theta-\omega)$, we would have

$$\iint_{S''} \sec(\theta-\omega)\,\mathrm{d}x\,\mathrm{d}y = r\int_0^{2\pi} |\boldsymbol{v}|\,\mathrm{d}\omega.$$

As $|\boldsymbol{v}|$ varies, at first sight this seems no more interesting than the preceding formula. However, if we integrate once more, now with respect to ξ,η over S', we obtain

$$\iint_{S'}\iint_{S''} \sec(\theta-\omega)\,\mathrm{d}x\,\mathrm{d}y\,\mathrm{d}\xi\,\mathrm{d}\eta = 2\pi r i_o \tag{97}$$

as circular symmetry and invariance of $\iint|\boldsymbol{v}|\,\mathrm{d}\xi\,\mathrm{d}\eta = i_o$ with respect to ω results from integration on the disk S'. The integral denoted i_o is a component of traffic through any point at distance r from the center. The context makes it clear that outward traffic from S' to S'' is concerned, hence the index o. Observe that in the right-hand member the traffic component is multiplied by the perimeter of the r-circle.

Outward trips were chosen for illustration. The same derivation could be made for inward trips or for throughgoing trips cutting the r-circle twice.

The integration in (97) over all starting points in S' and all endpoints in S'' parallels the Angel and Hyman procedure of counting "cordon crossings". Two features that Angel and Hyman (1976) forget should, however, be noticed. First, the intersections are not simply "counted", but *weighted* by the reciprocals of $\cos(\theta-\omega)$, i.e. by $\sec(\theta-\omega)$, which are the secants of the angles of incidence formed between tangents to the paths and normals to the r-circle. Secondly, the traffic component is obtained only after division by the perimeter $2\pi r$.

There are good intuitive reasons for both operations. To begin with the latter, the same number of intersections means a greater intersection *density* the shorter the perimeter. This is taken care of by the division by $2\pi r$. As to the weighting, we may imagine the r-circle as a very thin ring. A path segment cutting this ring will then be almost linear with an approximate length of $\sec(\theta-\omega)$, provided that the length of a path segment in the normal direction is standardized to unity. As the weight of traffic put on the ring by an intersecting path should be proportional to the length of the cutting segment, the weighting procedure in (97) is appealing to the intuition. Only radial paths receive unit weights; all other weights exceed unity, going to infinity for tangential paths.

8.2. Weights in general

We can easily obtain a formula for the weights in the general case of a circularly symmetric transfer cost function. This demonstrates that the procedure is not limited to the cases where conformal mappings make the calculations especially simple. From (38) we can solve

$$\mathrm{d}r/\mathrm{d}\omega = r\surd\left((fr/c)^2 - 1\right). \tag{98}$$

If we regard $x = r(\omega)\cos\omega$ and $y = r(\omega)\sin\omega$ as curves parameterized by ω, we obtain the derivatives

$$\mathrm{d}x/\mathrm{d}\omega = -r\sin\omega + r\cos\omega\surd\left((fr/c)^2 - 1\right),$$

$$\mathrm{d}y/\mathrm{d}\omega = r\cos\omega + r\sin\omega\surd\left((fr/c)^2 - 1\right). \tag{99}$$

The length of the tangent vector is

$$|\mathrm{d}x/\mathrm{d}\omega, \mathrm{d}y/\mathrm{d}\omega| = (fr/c)r. \tag{100}$$

On the other hand, the unit normal to a circle with radius r is $(\cos\omega, \sin\omega)$. From the formula for the dot product of this normal and the tangent vector to the path (in direction θ) $(\mathrm{d}x/\mathrm{d}\omega, \mathrm{d}y/\mathrm{d}\omega) = (fr/c)r(\cos\theta, \sin\theta)$, we get

$$\cos(\theta - \omega)(fr/c)r = r\surd\left((fr/c)^2 - 1\right) \tag{101}$$

or

$$\sec(\theta - \omega) = fr/\surd\left((fr)^2 - c^2\right). \tag{102}$$

Obviously, if $fr = c$, the weight is infinite and we have a case of tangency. If $c = 0$, the weight is always unitary and the paths are radial. For $f = r^n$ we get, again putting $R = r^{n+1}$, $\sec(\theta - \omega) = R/\surd(R^2 - c^2)$.

8.3. Traffic distributions for power functions

The way is now open for deriving a formula for i_{crv} in the case we are illustrating. However, we cannot proceed to integration directly because of difficulties in sorting out throughgoing paths with both endpoints in the outer ring from those with endpoints in this ring that do not cross the r-circle at all. Only by a judicious choice of integration variables can we fix the integration limits nicely. As a matter of fact we need two different coordinate transformations.

One is readily at hand, namely from x,y to X, Y. This mapping has two advantages. First, all the wedges where the optimal paths are curved are magnified to complete unit disks. At present we need not bother with the complicated spiral-shaped Riemann surfaces, only with their projections onto a unit disk. All angles will then be referred to the principal branch, i.e. the interval

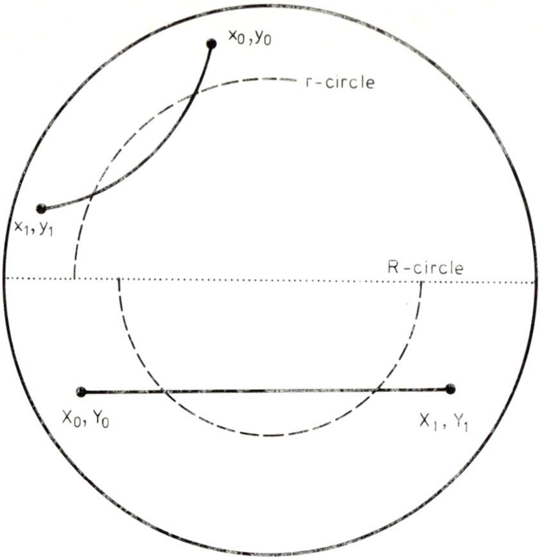

Figure 8.1

$(0, 2\pi)$, but as long as circular symmetry is preserved this causes no trouble. We should only remember that just one $(n+1)$th of i_{crv} will be computed from a unit disk by this procedure. Secondly, all the curved paths are, as we have seen, mapped onto straight-line segments. Both properties are helpful in simplifying calculations.

Fortunately, a conformal mapping, such as from x,y to X, Y, does not change angles between intersecting curves. Hence, the incidence angles and the weights are not changed. The nature of the mapping is shown in fig. 8.1, drawn for the case of $n=1$. The curve is mapped onto the straight line, whereas the upper half of the disk is mapped onto the whole disk. For convenience, the r-circle as well as its image under the mapping, a circle with radius $R=r^{n+1}$, have been drawn. Observe in particular that the intersection angles between the paths and the circles are not altered. Notice also the change of symbols for the endpoints.

Let $r_0=\sqrt{(x_0^2+y_0^2)}$ and $r_1=\sqrt{(x_1^2+y_1^2)}$. Then, as we have seen above, the Jacobians of the mappings from x_0,y_0 to X_0, Y_0 and from x_1,y_1 to X_1, Y_1 are $((n+1)r_0^n)^{-2}$ and $((n+1)r_1^n)^{-2}$, respectively. Using the variables $R_0=r_0^{n+1}$ and $R_1=r_1^{n+1}$, we must divide the integrand by the product of the Jacobians $(n+1)^4$ $(R_0^2 R_1^2)^{n/(n+1)}$.

As was said we need another coordinate transformation. Hence, put

$$X_0=\rho\cos\phi-A\sin\phi; \qquad Y_0=\rho\sin\phi+A\cos\phi,$$

$$X_1=\rho\cos\phi-B\sin\phi; \qquad Y_1=\rho\sin\phi+B\cos\phi. \tag{103}$$

The geometry of this second transformation is shown in fig. 8.2.

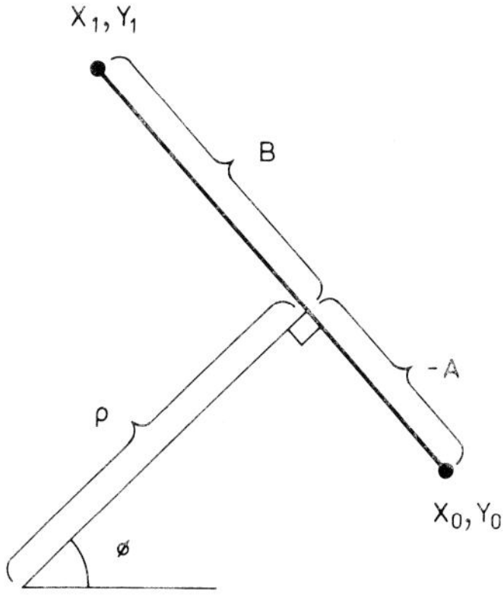

Figure 8.2

The limits of integration may now be determined as follows. Considering only counterclockwise trips, we catch inward trips by integrating with respect to A between $-\sqrt{(1-\rho^2)}$ and $-\sqrt{(R^2-\rho^2)}$ and with respect to B between $-\sqrt{(R^2-\rho^2)}$ and $\sqrt{(R^2-\rho^2)}$. Likewise, we obtain outward trips by integrating with respect to A between $-\sqrt{(R^2-\rho^2)}$ and $\sqrt{(R^2-\rho^2)}$ and with respect to B between $\sqrt{(R^2-\rho^2)}$ and $\sqrt{(1-\rho^2)}$. Owing to symmetry these two integrals for inward and outward trips are equal. Throughgoing trips are caught by integrating with respect to A between $-\sqrt{(1-\rho^2)}$ and $-\sqrt{(R^2-\rho^2)}$ and with respect to B between $\sqrt{(R^2-\rho^2)}$ and $\sqrt{(1-\rho^2)}$. Because of the double intersections they must be counted twice.

It then remains to integrate with respect to ρ and to ϕ. The proper interval for ρ is from 0 to R, since no intersections can occur for a ρ that exceeds R. Otherwise the whole extension of the line joining the two endpoints would be completely outside the R-circle. Finally, integration with respect to ϕ, between 0 and 2π, rotates the whole system of parallel paths. Because of the circular symmetry this last integration simply amounts to a multiplication by 2π.

We have noticed that this procedure only takes care of counterclockwise curved trips in one $(n+1)$th sector of the unit disk. To catch all the traffic due to curved trips, we must finally multiply by $2(n+1)$.

The integrand is the product of the Jacobians (and the weight, but because the latter is independent of A and B we can leave it until integration with respect to ρ is performed). The Jacobian of the mapping $A, B, \rho, \phi \Rightarrow X_0, Y_0, X_1, Y_1$ can easily be calculated as $(B-A)$. Since, from Pythagoras's theorem, $R_0^2=\rho^2+A^2$ and $R_1^2=\rho^2+B^2$, the Jacobians for the conformal mappings are $(n+1)^{-2}(\rho^2+A^2)^{-n/(n+1)}$ for $X_0, Y_0 \Rightarrow x_0, y_0$ and $(n+1)^{-2}(\rho^2+B^2)^{-n/(n+1)}$ for $X_1, Y_1 \Rightarrow x_1, y_1$. The integrand is accordingly

$$\frac{(B-A)}{(n+1)^4((\rho^2+A^2)(\rho^2+B^2))^{n/(n+1)}}. \tag{104}$$

Before integration with respect to ρ, the weight, which equals $\sec(\theta-\omega)=R/\surd(R^2-\rho^2)$, must be multiplied into the integrand. Finally, the measure must, as just noted, be multiplied by $2(n+1)$ and divided by the perimeter $2\pi r$. These operations can, however, wait until all the integrations have been performed.

After lengthy, but elementary, calculations, the result of the integrations with respect to A and B is obtained as

$$\frac{(1-r^2)\int_{-\surd(1-\rho^2)}^{\surd(1-\rho^2)}(\rho^2+u^2)^{-n/(n+1)}\mathrm{d}u}{(n+1)^3}. \tag{105}$$

Next, we have to multiply by the weight $R/\surd(R^2-\rho^2)$ and integrate with respect to ρ from 0 to R. The formula is simplified, however, if we first put $\rho=R\sin\gamma$, and integrate with respect to γ. As γ varies on the interval $(0,\pi/2)$, ρ varies on the interval $(0,R)$. Because we now have $\mathrm{d}\rho=R\cos\gamma\,\mathrm{d}\gamma=\surd(R^2-\rho^2)\mathrm{d}\gamma$, we can cancel this square root against the one in the denominator of the weight.

Thus, taking consideration of the weight, integrating with respect to γ, multiplying by $2(n+1)$, and by 2π, and dividing by $2\pi r$, we get the final result:

$$i_{\mathrm{crv}}=\frac{2(1-r^2)r^n\int_0^{\pi/2}\int_{-\surd(1-R^2\sin^2\gamma)}^{\surd(1-R^2\sin^2\gamma)}(R^2\sin^2\gamma+u^2)^{-n/(n+1)}\mathrm{d}u\,\mathrm{d}\gamma}{(n+1)^2}. \tag{106}$$

We can check the formula by letting $n=0$. Then the integrand is unitary, and hence the inner integral can be evaluated as $2\surd(1-R^2\sin^2\gamma)$. Accordingly $i_{\mathrm{crv}}=4(1-r^2)E(r)$. In this case there are no radial paths, all paths being "curved" (i.e. straight lines). The measure of traffic thus obtained is in perfect agreement with the one obtained by different methods.

8.4. Quadrature and simulation

For other n, explicit solutions generally are not obtainable. Instead, we can use numerical quadrature of the double integral. This procedure is particularly simple when one integration can be made analytically. We can exemplify by putting $n=1$. Then we get

$$\int_{-\surd(1-R^2\sin^2\gamma)}^{\surd(1-R^2\sin^2\gamma)}(R^2\sin^2\gamma+u^2)^{-0.5}\mathrm{d}u$$

$$=\ln(u+\surd(R^2\sin^2\gamma+u^2))\Big|_{-\surd(1-R^2\sin^2\gamma)}^{\surd(1-R^2\sin^2\gamma)}$$

$$=\ln((1+\surd(1-R^2\sin^2\gamma))/(1-\surd(1-R^2\sin^2\gamma))).$$

Table 8.1
Traffic distributions with different power functions.

r	0.00	0.20	0.40	0.60	0.80	1.00
$n=0.0$	6.29	5.97	5.06	3.63	1.84	0.00
$n=0.4$	∞	6.58	4.48	3.08	1.60	0.00
$n=1.0$	∞	8.92	5.00	3.12	1.53	0.00
$n=\infty$	∞	15.08	6.60	3.35	1.45	0.00

Hence, we have only to evaluate

$$i_{\text{crv}}=0.5(1-r^2)r\int_0^{\pi/2}\ln((1+\sqrt{(1-r^4\sin^2\gamma)})/(1-\sqrt{(1-r^4\sin^2\gamma)}))\,\mathrm{d}\gamma, \tag{107}$$

which can be done numerically by Simpson's rule. Doing this and adding traffic $i_{\text{rad}}=0.5\pi(1-r^2)/r$ provides the entries for $n=1$ shown in table 8.1.

We can use simulation as an equivalent method. This means that we generate endpoints at random. We then decide the character of the curve, and whether it cuts the circle twice, once, or not at all. All the intersections are weighted by the incidence angle secants, and the average intersection weight is calculated. This is multiplied by the measure of the total number of trips, and the result is divided by the perimeter of the circle.

This procedure is illustrated in the program TRAFFIC that is appended. We have taken $n=0.4$. (This value will, in Chapter 11, become optimal within a specific class of transfer cost functions. Therefore we have a specific interest in knowing what the traffic distribution looks like in this case.) We assume constant population density, so that the probability for each point of falling within any subregion of unit area must be equal. With a random number generator, producing random numbers with equal density on the unit interval, the best way to proceed is to generate polar coordinates for the endpoints. For the unit disk the random number itself can be taken as a radial coordinate, whereas the angular coordinate must be multiplied by 2π. But, in doing this the density of points would increase towards the center because the areas $\mathrm{d}r\,\mathrm{d}\omega = r\,\mathrm{d}x\,\mathrm{d}y$ increase with r, if we are discussing areas in the original rectangular coordinates. To correct for this we have taken the square root of the random numbers as radial coordinates. This obviously makes the area probability equal.

After generating random endpoints, the program converts the coordinates to those of the conformal mapping that takes curved paths to straight lines, determines the character of the path (linear versus radial after transformation), the number of intersections, and the weight. The sum of weights is cumulated until the prescribed number of iterations has been performed. Then the average intersection weight is calculated, and the total is obtained after multiplication by π^2, and other final adjustments.

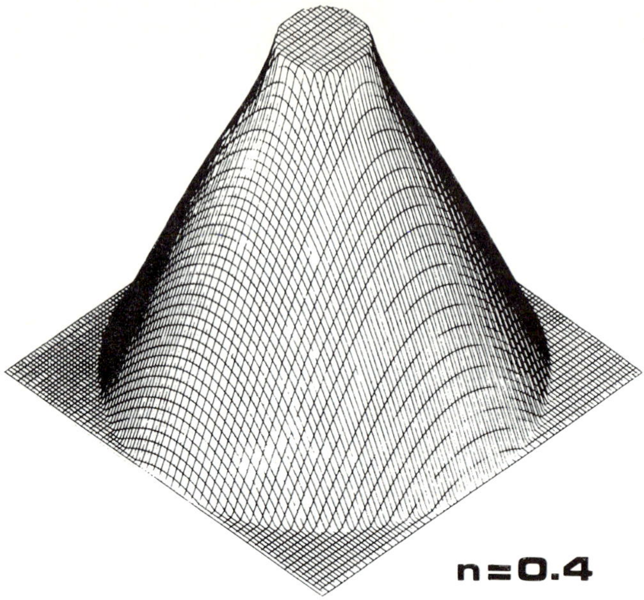

Figure 8.3. Traffic, $n=0.4$.

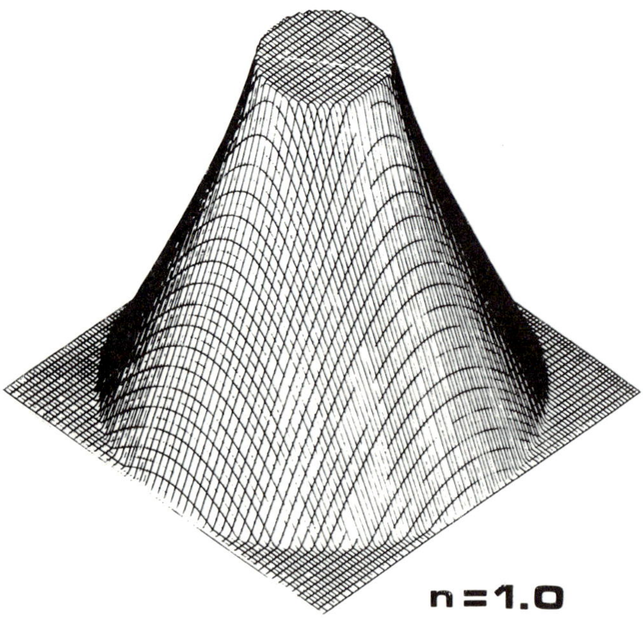

Figure 8.4. Traffic, $n=1.0$.

The convergence for small r was very slow, so that 500 000 iterations were needed. The computations therefore turned out to be very expensive. But the efficiency in computation could certainly be improved. The results of the simulation, together with the results from the case solved by numerical quadrature, are presented in table 8.1. In the table we also repeat the results obtained from pure analysis, with n zero and infinity, respectively. As the reader may see the conjecture holds true that traffic distributions for power functions have shapes inbetween the linear and radial distributions. A visual impression of this can be obtained from the computer diagrams (figs. 8.3 and 8.4), and these may be compared with the two diagrams already presented (figs. 5.1 and 5.2).

8.5. A rough graphic method

Finally, we can construct a simple practical way to get a very rough estimate of any traffic distribution when the transfer cost function is circularly symmetric and the solution curves are known. As mentioned by Angel and Hyman (1976) the paths too may be obtained by graphical construction. This means that we can deal with any case of transfer cost function with circular symmetry.

The idea is to take the sector in which the solutions are nonradial, and put a family of optimal paths at various distances from the center within it. They are all put in a symmetric position, so that they have the same symmetry axis and so that the curves do not intersect. Then the sector is divided into several strips. From the fact that their boundaries are solution curves for the paths, we infer that all communication takes place *within* these strips. The subdivision can be made as refined as desired.

Now, draw a circle of given radius with its center at the center of the disk. The circle intersects some of these strips and leaves others unaffected. If we now take the areas of a strip that lie on either side of the circle and multiply we get a measure of the number of communications starting inside the circle and ending outside it (or in the opposite direction). To catch both ingoing and outgoing trips, we have to double the measure. By taking the square of the area outside the circle we catch throughgoing trips (in both directions), but we have to double this measure too because throughgoing trips account for two intersections. By adding the measures we get a density of trips crossing the small segments of the circle into which it is divided by the solution curves defining the strips. To avoid the measure going to zero with increasing refinement of the subdivision, we divide it by the fraction that the strip in question represents of the area of the whole disk.

Hence, we can associate an intersection density with each segment of the circle. In addition we need a weight. This can be approximated as the incidence angle secant somewhere near the midpoint of the segment. We can multiply the

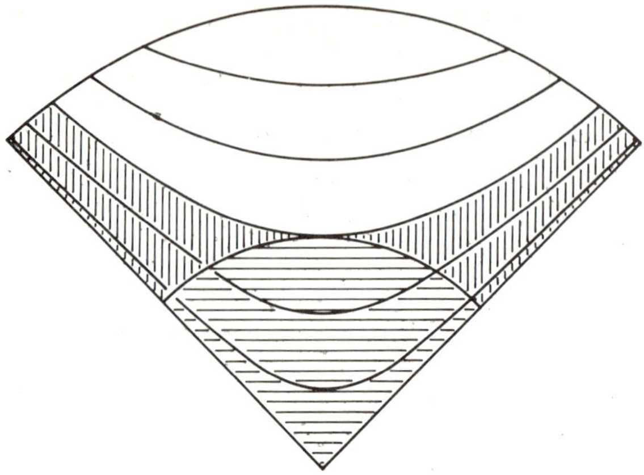

Figure 8.5. Geometrical construction for approximate calculation of a traffic distribution.

intersection densities with the weights and add for all relevant strips. Then we multiply by π^2 and by the reciprocal of the fraction of the whole disk that the area of the sector represents. The first constant is a measure of the total number of communications and the latter is a correction for the fact that only a sector of the solution curve space is taken into account. Finally, we divide by the perimeter of the circle and add traffic due to radial paths. The geometry of the construction is illustrated in fig. 8.5.

8.6. Spiral paths and unitary elasticity

The above analysis of power functions does not cover the case $n=-1$, where the optimal paths are logarithmic spirals. This is because even though we can still use a conformal map to transform the spirals into straight lines, the disk will be mapped onto an infinite strip. Thus, the following discussion can illustrate how the method can be used in cases where the circular symmetry no longer remains on the map.

With $f=1/r$, we have seen that the optimal paths are given in polar coordinates by $r=a\mathrm{e}^{b\omega}$. With regard to the parameter ω, we can write $x=a\mathrm{e}^{b\omega}\cos\omega$, $y=a\mathrm{e}^{b\omega}\sin\omega$. The tangent vector in terms of the parameter ω is therefore $(x',y')=(bx-y,x+by)$, with length $\surd(1+b^2)r$. Consequently, we can also write the unit tangent vector $(\cos\theta,\sin\theta)=(bx/r-y/r,x/r+by/r)/\surd(1+b^2)$.

On the other hand, the normal to a circle of radius r is $(\cos\omega,\sin\omega)=(x/r,y/r)$. If we now take the dot product of the unit tangent vector and the normal vector, we obtain, because of definition, $\cos(\theta-\omega)=b/\surd(1+b^2)$ or

$$\sec(\theta-\omega)=\surd(1+b^2)/b. \tag{108}$$

Suppose now that we have constant population density but that there is a distance dependence so that the number of trips between a pair of points is reciprocal to the distance between them (along the actual spiral paths). We get arc length

$$\tau=\int\sqrt{(r^2+r'^2)}\,\mathrm{d}\omega$$

$$=\sqrt{(1+b^2)}\int r\,\mathrm{d}\omega=\sqrt{(1+b^2)}a\int \mathrm{e}^{b\omega}\,\mathrm{d}\omega=a\,\mathrm{e}^{b\omega}\sqrt{(1+b^2)}/b,$$

i.e.

$$\tau=(r_1-r_0)\sqrt{(1+b^2)}/b. \tag{109}$$

Since $\nabla\cdot\boldsymbol{v}=-1/\tau$, we get the integrand as

$$\nabla\cdot\boldsymbol{v}\sec(\theta-\omega)=1/(r_1-r_0). \tag{110}$$

We can therefore evaluate the integral

$$\int\int_{S'}\int\int_{S''}1/(r_1-r_0)\,\mathrm{d}x_1\,\mathrm{d}y_1\,\mathrm{d}x_0\,\mathrm{d}y_0, \tag{111}$$

where S' and S'' are again the inner disk and the outer ring defined by the separating r-circle. By evaluating this integral we catch outgoing trips. Ingoing trips simply double the measure of traffic. In this case there are no throughgoing paths. This fact is obvious because the incidence angle cosines are constants for each path. Outward paths continue to be outward, and inward paths continue to be inward.

The integral is easiest to evaluate if we use polar coordinates. As the Jacobian is r_0r_1, we get

$$\int_0^{2\pi}\int_0^{\pi}\int_0^{r}\int_r^{1}r_1r_0/(r_1-r_0)\,\mathrm{d}r_1\,\mathrm{d}r_0\,\mathrm{d}\omega_1\,\mathrm{d}\omega_0. \tag{112}$$

By this procedure we catch outward and counterclockwise trips. The number obtained must therefore be multiplied by 4. Finally, to get a measure of traffic we must divide by the perimeter $2\pi r$.

Integration with respect to the angular coordinates results in a simple multiplication by $2\pi^2$ because the integrand is independent of these coordinates. Hence

$$i=(4\pi/r)\int_0^{r}\int_r^{1}r_1r_0/(r_1-r_0)\,\mathrm{d}r_1\,\mathrm{d}r_0, \tag{113}$$

which, after some trouble, can be evaluated as

$$i=(4\pi/3)(r^3-r-1+r^3\ln(r-r^2))/r. \tag{114}$$

The resulting distribution is given in table 8.2 and shown in fig. 8.6. Owing to the spiral paths which avoid the center, traffic is obviously concentrated to the

Table 8.2
Traffic with spiral paths and unitary distance elasticity.

r	0.00	0.20	0.40	0.60	0.80	1.00
i	0.00	1.02	1.88	2.57	2.68	0.00

periphery. We can also calculate

$$\int\int_S i\,\mathrm{d}x\,\mathrm{d}y = 2\pi^2/3. \qquad (115)$$

In Chapter 5 we found that total traffic with linear paths and (as presently) unitary distance elasticity was π^2. Hence, even though the paths become longer with spirals instead of straight lines, total traffic is reduced by one-third due to the distance elasticity which causes numerous trips to be cancelled.

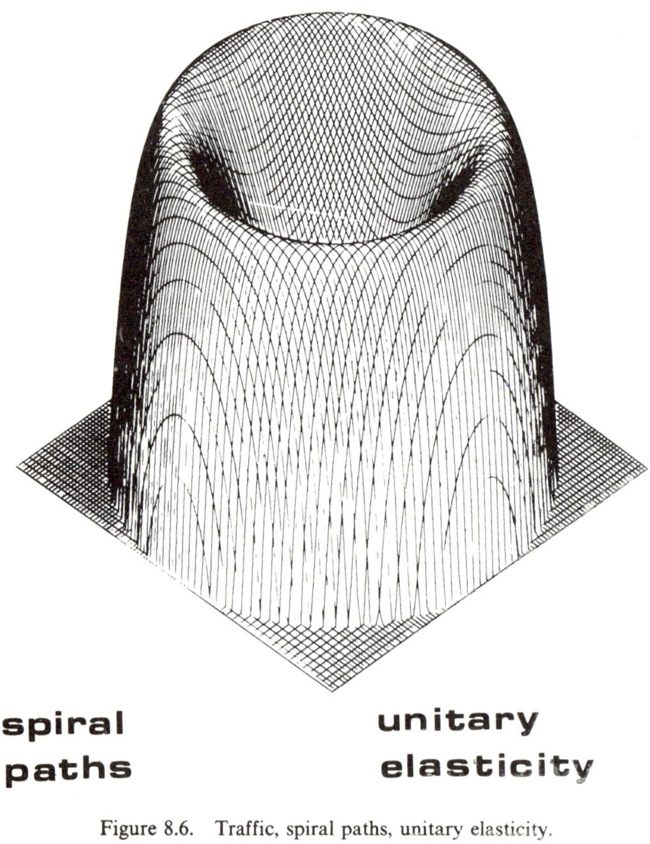

Figure 8.6. Traffic, spiral paths, unitary elasticity.

8.7. Program TRAFFIC

```
100 N=500000
110 M=0
120 T=0
130 PRINT "EXPONENT";
140 INPUT A
150 A=A+1
160 PRINT "RADIUS";
170 INPUT S
180 R=S↑A
190 L=4*ATN(1)
200 H=(2*A-1)*L
210 R0=SQR(RND(0))↑A
220 R1=SQR(RND(0))↑A
230 V0=RND(0)
240 V1=RND(0)
250 V=2*A*L*ABS(V1-V0)
260 IF V<L THEN 330
270 IF V>H THEN 330
280 IF R0<R THEN 300
290 T=T+1
300 IF R1<R THEN 320
310 T=T+1
320 GO TO 440
330 D=SQR(R0*R0+R1*R1-2*R0*R1*COS(V))
340 E=R0*R1*ABS(SIN(V))/D
350 IF E>=R THEN 440
360 B=R/SQR(R*R-E*E)
370 IF (R0-R)*(R1-R)>0 THEN 400
380 T=T+B
390 GO TO 440
400 IF R0<R THEN 440
410 IF R0*R0-E*E>D*D THEN 440
420 IF R1*R1-E*E>D*D THEN 440
430 T=T+2*B
440 M=M+1
450 IF M<N THEN 210
460 T=L*T/N/2/S
470 PRINT "TRAFFIC=";T
480 END
```

Chapter 9

TRAFFIC WITH NONCONSTANT POPULATION – ILLUSTRATION OF THE DIRECT METHOD

The direct method can be used advantageously to compute traffic distributions with nonconstant, but circularly symmetric, population density functions. The procedure of solving two differential equations in sequence followed by integration twice is more awkward than necessary since the simplifications, because of circular symmetry, can only be brought into the picture at the very last stage of taking the final double integral. Simplification could be expected if the symmetry were taken into account at an earlier stage. A course which is possible with the direct method outlined in Chapter 8.

Let population be distributed by

$$p(x,y)=(m+2)r^m/2. \tag{116}$$

The reader may convince himself that the double integral of this on the unit disk, i.e. total population P, equals π, no matter what value m takes (provided of course that the integral does converge). We suppose that transfer costs are everywhere unitary, so that all optimal paths are straight lines. It is implicit in the comments above that the region is assumed to be a circular unit disk.

The population density expressions at the points of origin and destination now take the place of the Jacobians in Chapter 8. Both are of the same type, i.e. power functions in the distance from the center. We no longer need the Jacobians because the paths are straight lines in the original solution space and need not be transformed into this shape. (Of course, we could have combined the case of a general power function for transfer cost with a power function for population density, but this generalization is obvious.)

Now, by exact analogy to the case treated in the preceding chapter, we arrive at the formula

$$i=(m+2)(1-r^{m+2})\int_0^{\pi/2}\int_{-\sqrt{(1-r^2\sin^2\gamma)}}^{\sqrt{(1-r^2\sin^2\gamma)}}\sqrt{(r^2\sin^2\gamma+u^2)^m}\,\mathrm{d}u\,\mathrm{d}\gamma. \tag{117}$$

Computations with this expression can be carried out exactly as in the case where transfer cost is a power function.

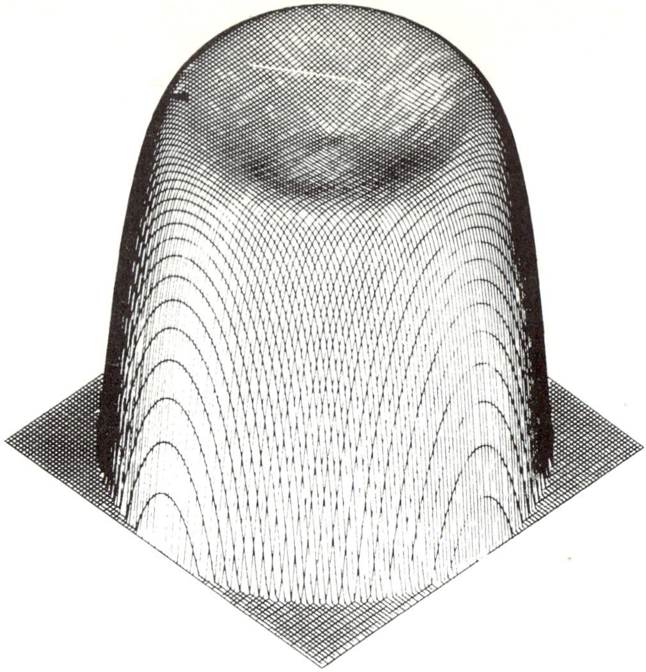

Figure 9.1. Traffic, centrifuged population, $m=2$.

With integral m we can make one integration analytically, so that we only need to make one numerical quadrature by Simpson's rule. For $m=1$, we have

$$i=\frac{3(1-r^3)}{2}\int_0^{\pi/2}\left\{2\sqrt{(1-r^2\sin^2\gamma)}+r^2\sin^2\gamma\ln\left(\frac{1+\sqrt{(1-r^2\sin^2\gamma)}}{1-\sqrt{(1-r^2\sin^2\gamma)}}\right)\right\}\mathrm{d}\gamma; \tag{118}$$

for $m=2$

$$i=\frac{8(1-r^4)}{3}\int_0^{\pi/2}\sqrt{(1-r^2\sin^2\gamma)}(1+2r^2\sin^2\gamma)\mathrm{d}\gamma; \tag{119}$$

for $m=3$

$$i=\frac{5(1-r^5)}{8}\int_0^{\pi/2}\left\{\sqrt{(1-r^2\sin^2\gamma)}(4+6r^2\sin^2\gamma)\right.$$

$$\left.+3r^4\sin^4\gamma\ln\left(\frac{1+\sqrt{(1-r^2\sin^2\gamma)}}{1-\sqrt{(1-r^2\sin^2\gamma)}}\right)\right\}\mathrm{d}\gamma; \tag{120}$$

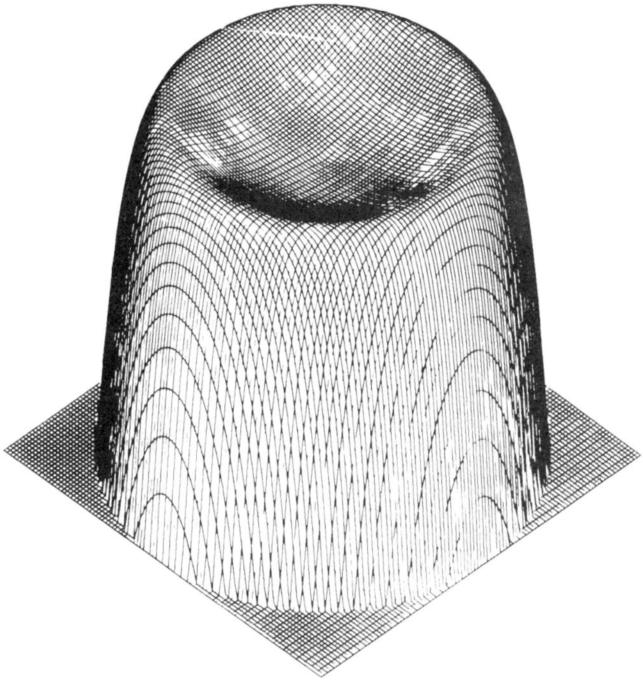

Figure 9.2. Traffic, centrifuged population, $m=4$.

and finally for $m=4$

$$i=\frac{4(1-r^6)}{5}\int_0^{\pi/2}\surd(1-r^2\sin^2\gamma)(3+4r^2\sin^2\gamma+8r^4\sin^4\gamma)\mathrm{d}\gamma. \tag{121}$$

These four integrals have been evaluated numerically and the results are given in table 9.1. It can be seen that with positive exponents, as population is "centrifuged" to the outskirts of the region traffic is redistributed so that it takes on its highest value somewhere between the center and the extreme periphery, but it is still considerable in the center. This is so because numerous transports, even between points close to the boundary, still pass the center of the disk. A visual

Table 9.1
Traffic with nonconstant population.

r	0.00	0.20	0.40	0.60	0.80	1.00
$m=4$	3.77	3.84	4.06	4.37	3.88	0.00
$m=3$	3.93	4.01	4.25	4.42	3.57	0.00
$m=2$	4.19	4.30	4.53	4.41	4.14	0.00
$m=1$	4.71	4.86	4.86	4.21	2.57	0.00
$m=0$	6.28	5.97	5.06	3.63	1.84	0.00
$m=-1$	∞	7.59	4.36	2.35	0.97	0.00

impression of this can be obtained from the two computer diagrams (figs. 9.1 and 9.2).

If we take the exponent as negative we get traffic concentrated even more to the central part than we do with a constant population. We can give an example of this using one case, namely when $n = -1$. Then

$$i=(1-r)\int_0^{\pi/2}\ln\left(\frac{1+\sqrt{(1-r^2\sin^2\gamma)}}{1-\sqrt{(1-r^2\sin^2\gamma)}}\right)\mathrm{d}\gamma. \tag{122}$$

The results of the evaluation of this integral are shown in table 9.1 together with those for the case of constant population.

Chapter 10

THE RELATION BETWEEN TRANSFER COST AND ROAD CAPITAL

It was argued in Chapter 1 that there is an obvious connection between transfer cost in terms of actual transfer distance along the existing network and the amount of road capital invested, at least as far as its general properties are concerned. As long as the whole surface of the region is not completely paved with roads, going through every point in every imaginable direction, it is not possible to go along a straight line between any pair of points. Because of the detailed nature – above all the density – of the network, it is in general necessary to take shorter or longer detours, i.e. deviations from the straight-line path. The more ramified the network, i.e. the more road capital that is invested, the more like a straight line an "average" path can be.

Obviously, it is always necessary to traverse at least the straight-line distance. No amount of road capital can reduce distances below that. Moreover, there must be "decreasing returns" from successive additions of new road segments to an existing network. The more ramified the network already is, the fewer detours can on average be saved by adding another shortcut and, as already observed, only an infinite amount of road capital can bring the average distance traversed down to the linear distance.

Taking such factors into consideration, it was suggested in Chapter 1 that the relation between average transfer cost f (i.e. the actual transfer distance including detours per unit of linear distance) and road capital l (i.e. the total length of roads in the microscopic network per unit area contained in a "point") should be specified as the hyperbola $f = a + b/l$, where a and b are some constants.

The aim of the present section is to give some theoretical support to this relation by deriving it explicitly for a class of networks.

10.1. Hexagonal cells and various network densities

We start by imagining a Christaller–Lösch space subdivided into regular hexagonal cells, where the roads go in six different (oriented) directions, intersecting at 60° angles. For this paradigm we discuss various "states" for the cells, representing different network densities. In the 0-state, the roads are the six boundary segments of the hexagonal cells and, in addition, the three diameters joining pairs of opposite vertices.

If we normalize distance by taking the diameter of the circles inscribing the cells as unity, then we can count the total length of the network belonging to a cell as equal to 6 units. But this is correct only if we consider an isolated cell. If we take into consideration the whole tesellation, we must make a correction for the fact that each road along the boundary actually belongs to two cells, and hence only half of these should be counted as belonging to one cell. As the total of 6 units is divided into 3 units of boundary roads and 3 units of diametrical roads, we end up with 4.5 units per cell in the 0-state.

Let us now turn to the average transfer distance. The shortest distance straight across a cell, going along a diameter in the 0-state is 1 unit. The longest distance across the cell by passage from one boundary point to the opposite one is incurred when one wants to go from the midpoint of one boundary segment to the midpoint of the opposite one, and amounts to 1.5 units. The average distance for a diametrical passage then is 1.25 units in the 0-state.

In the 1-state the density of the network is doubled, so that a new road is placed midway between each pair of roads in the 0-state network. These new roads are parallel to the former ones and thus also go in six different, oriented directions. Measuring the additional road segments we find that road capital per cell is increased by another 4.5 units, to 9 units in all.

As to transfer distance in the 1-state network, it is now also possible to take a minimum distance route between the midpoints of opposite boundary segments, as well as between opposite vertices. The minimum is, of course, still 1 unit. The maximum diametrical passage distance is incurred when one travels between opposite points each one-quarter of a boundary segment distant from opposite vertices. This maximum is 1.25 units, and hence the average diametrical transfer distance is 1.125 units in the 1-state.

We can now generalize the results to new states, each obtained from the previous one by doubling the density of the network in the way mentioned. Three different states are illustrated in fig. 10.1. It is important to observe that we can interpret the three states in various ways. Either we can regard cell size as given and road density as doubled in the next state, or we could just as well consider the diameter of the cells as halved, whereas the unit building blocks of the tesellation, although of different size, all look like the fundamental 0-state cell. In fig. 10.1 this is emphasized by the heavy lines. We can now see that in each new state the variable detour part of the transfer distance is halved, so that in the n-state

$$f_n = 1 + 0.25/2^n, \tag{123}$$

which is valid for $n = 0, 1, 2,$ etc.

We can also easily arrive at a general formula as regards road capital in the n-state. We first observe that all the new roads added in each step can be

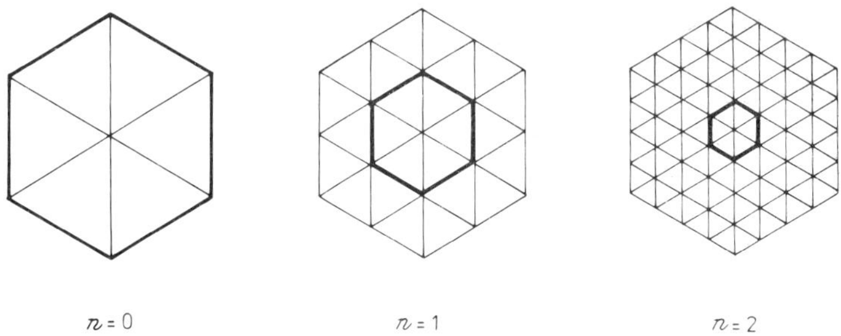

Figure 10.1.

regarded as the sides of equilateral triangles, inscribed in each of the triangles from the previous state, into which the cells are subdivided by the network. In each step the number of triangles is quadrupled because each triangle is divided into four by the process of inscription. On the other hand, the sides of the triangles are halved in each step.

Hence, in the n-state there are initially 1.5×4^n triangles. In each of them a new triangle with three sides $0.5/2^n$ long is inscribed, which makes an addition of 2.25×2^n units of new roads. To obtain total road capital per cell in the n-state we have to evaluate the series

$$l_n = 4.5 + 2.25\times(2^1+2^2+\ldots+2^n), \tag{124}$$

which equals

$$l_n = 4.5\times 2^n, \tag{125}$$

again valid for $n=0,1,2$, etc.

From the expressions for f_n and l_n we can eliminate the power function 2^n and get

$$f = 1 + 1.125/l, \tag{126}$$

deleting the subscripts since the relation holds for all integral n.

It is remarkable that the relation, which indeed is the hyperbola suggested, is independent, not only of the state, but also of the measurement unit (the cell diameter). Hence, it still holds true when we let the diameter go to zero.

The cells then shrink to points and the diametrical passage, which is arbitrary with finite cells, becomes the only interesting possibility. There is obviously no sense in talking about whether a path cuts a point diametrically or only passes through a part of its "area". Nor is there any sense in talking about the angle under which a point, "hexagonal" or whatever its "shape", is intersected. The paths that are actually sequences of line segments turn into smooth curves in the limiting process. Strictly speaking they would have discontinuous tangents everywhere but there is no harm in approximating them with smooth curves. The actual length of the microscopic path contained in a point, including all the kinks that make the detours, has been summed up already in the transfer cost (=distance) function.

We must now take note that we have only been speaking of individual cells and their states. The ensuing question is: How can we join such cells to a continuous network of roads, extending over the whole region? One possibility is obvious, namely to take only cells that are in the same state. But this is trivial for then road capital could only be constant. The derivation of (126) would be without interest since it could be applied only to l=constant, and we could just as well have taken f=constant as an assumption.

10.2. Conformal transformation of the network

Fortunately, there is the possibility of putting the cells together in another, nontrivial, way with continuous roads and a *nonconstant* distribution of road capital. Let us again consider the regular network of uniform density, obtained from cells of equal size and in the same state, and ask if there are any deformations of the network such that its density varies in space, but that the derivation of (126) still holds true. The answer is that there is actually a class of such transformations that make the derivation hold true in the limiting process of shrinking a cell size to nothing.

This class of transformations is that of conformal mappings, obtained by any analytic complex function of a complex variable with a nonvanishing derivative. The reason that this works is that angles of intersecting curves are not altered while the linear magnification factor is equal in all directions from a point. Hence, "infinitesimal" equilateral triangles are mapped onto smaller or larger equilateral triangles, and regular hexagons are mapped onto regular hexagons. Only the areas of the hexagons differ – by the magnification factor. For areas this is the squared modulus of the derivative of the complex function used, whereas for distances it is the modulus. One might ask how it is possible to join regular hexagons of unequal areas to a continuous network. The answer is that it is not possible with finite hexagons. But, if they are drawn sufficiently small, one can see how they gradually change shape and size, even though each of them looks almost like a regular hexagon. To be precise, this holds true only in the limiting process.

We can now profit from the observation that a passage to the next state is equivalent to a halving of cell diameter. As the measure of road capital was seen to double in each passage to a new state, we can regard road capital as reciprocal to cell diameter, i.e. to the linear magnification factor.

Formally, with the conformal mapping $z \Rightarrow Z$, where $z=x+\mathrm{i}y$ and $Z=X+\mathrm{i}Y$ are points in the original and the transformed complex planes, the magnification factor is $|\mathrm{d}Z/\mathrm{d}z|$, and we can take l proportionate to $|\mathrm{d}z/\mathrm{d}Z|$. In the original z-plane, the picture of the network is that of a regular hexagonal tesellation,

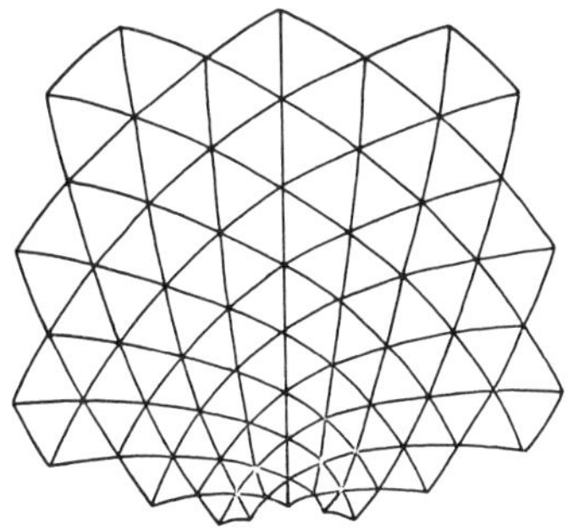

Figure 10.2. Network conformal to triangular.

whereas in the Z-plane the roads of the network become curved arcs and the density varies over the plane.

Fig. 10.2 illustrates a special case, $Z=z^2$, or $X=x^2-y^2$ and $Y=2xy$, where $l=1/(X^2+Y^2)^{1/4}$ measures road capital. This is one of many possible transformations, but we should notice that conformal mappings are the only ones that keep (126) valid.

10.3. Regular network types

Before proceeding we must say something about the choice of shape for the basic network that was transformed by means of conformal mappings. We termed it "hexagonal". At every junction six roads met at 60° angles and this was seen to constitute cells of a hexagonal shape. But this could cause confusion because by deleting the diagonals in the hexagonal cells we would obtain another network where the smallest building blocks are the hexagons themselves. In this case all junctions join three roads instead of six. In our case the hexagonal cells were actually not the smallest building blocks of the network. Rather, the six equilateral triangles that together composed the cell would deserve this name. They, however, must be tilted at different angles, and not only translated, to assemble the puzzle.

To avoid confusion we will follow Mosler (1976) and denote the two types "triangular" and "hexagonal", respectively, thus changing terminology and calling the basic network used at the conformal transformation above "triangular", whereas the case with the three diagonals deleted is called "hexagonal". The equivalent would be to speak of six-road junctions, instead of triangular networks, and three-road junctions instead of hexagonal networks.

In addition there is the interesting case of a quadratic network, where at every junction four roads meet at 90° angles. The smallest building blocks are quadrats. Strictly speaking the possibilities of filling the plane with regular polygons end here, since there are no polygons except the equilateral triangle, the quadrat and the hexagon, by which the plane can be tiled without overlapping and without leaving empty corners.

However, there is yet another type of network that has been discussed extensively and that we shall have to take into consideration. It is obtained in the following manner. As the triangular network can be obtained from the hexagonal by adding the diagonals, so can a new type be obtained from the quadratic by adding the diagonals. Following Mosler (1976), this case will be called "quadratic with diagonals". This case is much more irregular than the others. We have already mentioned that the three previous cases exhaust all the possibilities of covering the plane with regular polygons. Hence, the smallest building blocks can no longer be regular polygons. In fact they turn out to be right-angled isosceles triangles. We can also note that the network is no longer characterized by a definite number of roads meeting at each junction. Eight-road junctions and four-road junctions occur with equal density, eight-road junctions being completely surrounded by a ring of four-road junctions and vice versa.

Finally, as Werner (1966, 1968) has demonstrated, the basic triangles can be put together in several different ways, thus generating quite different network patterns. These allow six-road junctions together with those of four and eight roads, but as the six-road junctions, from geometrical necessity, join roads at different angles (alternately 90° and 45°), we will disregard these configurations, and only discuss the quadrat with diagonals where all roads meet at 90° or at 45°, depending on the type of junction.

In fact this last observation leads us to the basic reason why we consider just these regular networks. Launhardt (1869) has already observed that roads with equal travelling cost, i.e. of equal quality and load, must meet at equal angles in order for the network to minimize the total cost for all traffic flowing between the vertices. This is why we confine the discussion to these regular shapes.

Of course, the matter is not as simple as that. If the population using the network is not located at the nodes or vertices, but is continuously dispersed in the plane, and if the density of the population – as well as the facility for getting from one's original location to the closest road, and from the closest road to the point of destination – varies, then other solutions may be warranted.

However, if we assume that population density is constant, as well as the facility for moving outside the network, and that the cost of moving outside the network is of a higher order of magnitude than the cost of moving along it, so that the paths to and from the network become orthogonal straight lines, then the Launhardt conjecture seems relevant. To assume a constant population density and equal facility of movement may seem contradictory to the basic model of the present book, but we must not forget that we are at present dealing with a microstructure in which we may well assume constancy. The microstructure determines the shape of the network, whereas at the macro level its density can vary. There is no contradiction because the conformal mapping can change the mesh size gradually without changing the basic shape of the microscopic network.

10.4. Efficiency measures from graph theory

If we can accept this, we still have to compare and evaluate the "efficiency" of the various regular network types. Some measures proposed emanate from the theory of graphs. They may be illustrated by just one instance, i.e. the first of the Betti numbers, also called nullity or cyclomatic number for a graph. If we denote the number of vertices by v, the number of edges by e, and the number of components (i.e. the number of disjoint subgraphs) by k, then the cyclomatic number is $(e-v+k)$. If we have a network made in one piece, which is reasonable for a transportation network, then $k=1$. If, moreover, the network represents a so-called polygonal decomposition of a plane region then we know, by a very simple application of the Gauss–Bonnet theorem, that the Euler–Poincaré characteristic $(v-e+p)$, where p is the number of polygons into which the region is divided, is unitary. From this it follows that the cyclomatic number simply equals the number of polygons of which the network is built. As a measure of the efficiency of a network *shape* it is quite uninteresting.

Kansky (1963) has proposed several of these criteria for the characterization of transportation networks, and Werner (1966, 1968) has employed them to discriminate between network types. However, all these topological measures lack economic significance, and we will therefore leave them.

10.5. Accessibility to the network

Instead, we will take a measure proposed by Mosler (1976b) as the criterion of comparison. Or, to be more exact, a closely related criterion, namely the average orthogonal distance to the closest segment of a network. This distance is relevant if we again imagine the cost of moving outside the network to be so high in comparison to the cost of moving along it that the trajectories outside the network intersect it orthogonally along the segments. The average distance is then a good proxy for the total (or rather average) transportation cost outside the network. A network shape that minimizes this distance would be efficient.

However, for the comparisons to be relevant we must normalize relative mesh size for the networks compared, so that the density of roads is the same. Otherwise we would be comparing transportation costs for networks which represent different investment costs for road capital. The density of the network can easily be measured by taking the semiperimeter of the elementary building block in each case and dividing by its area. We take the semiperimeter because, considering the whole network, boundaries are shared by two adjacent building blocks. Hence, only half the perimeter belongs to each. We then get the density dependent on an arbitrary side length parameter, s. More exactly it is reciprocal to side length since the perimeter is proportional and the area is proportional to the square. By specifying density to one unit, the side lengths for all the building blocks at unit density can be calculated.

On the other hand, the average orthogonal distance is proportional to s, and hence substitution of the proper side length in each case is algebraically equivalent to the elimination of s. If we multiply the average orthogonal distance by the measure of density then the side length is obviously eliminated, and we obtain a measure of average distance given the unit density for the network. Multiplication by a price ratio gives the transportation cost at unitary investment cost. As shown by Mosler (1976b), the measure is unable to discriminate among the regular network types. We now formally demonstrate this.

The areas for an equilateral triangle, a quadrat, a regular hexagon with sides s, and for a right-angled isosceles triangle with the hypotenuse s, are $\sqrt{3}s^2/4$, s^2, $3\sqrt{3}s^2/2$ and $s^2/4$, respectively, and the semiperimeters are $3s/2$, $2s$, $3s$ and $(1+\sqrt{2})s/2$. The measures of network density are thus in order $2\sqrt{3}/s$, $2/s$, $2\sqrt{3}/(3s)$ and $2(1+\sqrt{2})/s$. These measures come in the first column of table 10.1. We can also equate the measures to unity in each case and solve for s. We obtain $2\sqrt{3}$, 2, $2/\sqrt{3}$ and $2(1+\sqrt{2})$. These side lengths have been used in figs. 10.3–10.6, which are drawn to proper scale so that they all represent equal road density.

In the figures one elementary building block is filled with thin lines, representing the orthogonal trajectories to the closest segment. As can be seen, each building block is split into three, four or six different parts that communicate with the different sides of the blocks. It is the average distance along these capillary trajectories that is calculated. The averages are obtained through straightforward integration. When, as in all cases except the last one, all the communication regions are alike we only have to evaluate the integral for one of them, or even for half of it since they have a symmetry axis. In the last case the communication regions into which the elementary building block is split, are

Table 10.1
Efficiency of different lattice networks.

Type	Network density	Average distance	Normalized measure
Triangular	$2\sqrt{3}/s$	$\sqrt{3}s/18$	$\frac{1}{3}$
Quadratic	$2/s$	$s/6$	$\frac{1}{3}$
Hexagonal	$2\sqrt{3}/(3s)$	$\sqrt{3}s/6$	$\frac{1}{3}$
Quadratic with diagonal	$2(1+\sqrt{2})/s$	$(\sqrt{2}-1)s/6$	$\frac{1}{3}$

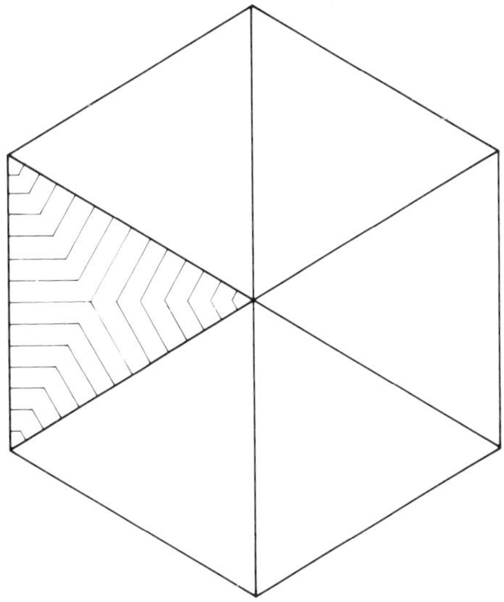

Figure 10.3. Network built by triangular blocks.

unequal. We have to evaluate two integrals and take their average, weighted by the respective areal parts.

The average distance for the triangular network is

$$\frac{\displaystyle\int_0^{s/2}\int_0^{x/\sqrt{3}} y\,\mathrm{d}y\,\mathrm{d}x}{\displaystyle\int_0^{s/2}\int_0^{x/\sqrt{3}} \mathrm{d}y\,\mathrm{d}x} = \frac{\sqrt{3}s}{18}; \tag{127}$$

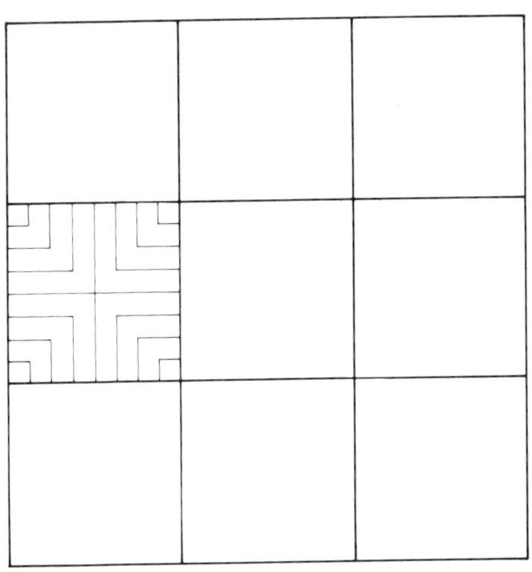

Figure 10.4. Network built by rectangular blocks.

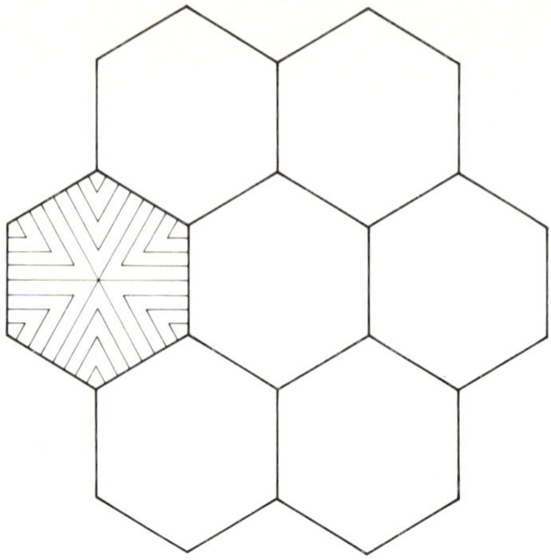

Figure 10.5. Network built by hexagonal blocks.

for the quadratic it is

$$\frac{\int_0^{s/2}\int_0^{x} y\,dy\,dx}{\int_0^{s/2}\int_0^{x} dy\,dx} = \frac{s}{6}; \tag{128}$$

for the hexagonal it is

$$\frac{\int_0^{s/2}\int_0^{x\sqrt{3}} y\,dy\,dx}{\int_0^{s/2}\int_0^{x\sqrt{3}} dy\,dx} = \frac{\sqrt{3}s}{6}; \tag{129}$$

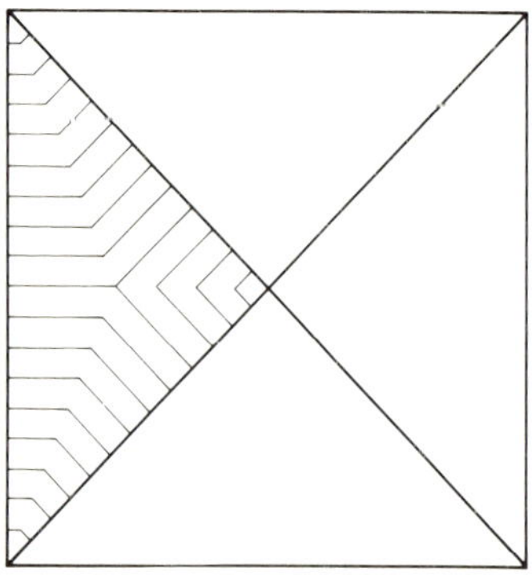

Figure 10.6. Quadratic network element with diagonals.

and finally for the quadratic with diagonals

$$\frac{\int_0^{s/2}\int_0^{x(\sqrt{2}-1)} y\,\mathrm{d}y\,\mathrm{d}x}{\int_0^{s/2}\int_0^{x(\sqrt{2}-1)} \mathrm{d}y\,\mathrm{d}x}\frac{4}{6}+\frac{\int_0^{s(\sqrt{2}-1)/2}\int_0^{x} y\,\mathrm{d}y\,\mathrm{d}x}{\int_0^{s(\sqrt{2}-1)/2}\int_0^{x} \mathrm{d}y\,\mathrm{d}x}\frac{2}{6}=\frac{(\sqrt{2}-1)s}{6}. \tag{130}$$

These measures come in the second column in table 10.1. As mentioned above, they are proportionate to the side length parameter, whereas the network density measures were reciprocal. But when in the third column we take the product of the two preceding ones in order to get rid of s and obtain an *average orthogonal distance with unit network density*, we end up with the same constant in all four cases. Hence, the measure cannot discriminate between the network types. With unit density the average distance is always $\frac{1}{3}$ regardless of the type of network we consider.

10.6. The detour factor

However, even if the different networks are equivalent from the point of view of best average access to the roads, they may involve different detour requirements. Even if the cost for each transport across a distance unit along the network is negligible as compared to the cost across a point in the plane, it is quite logical to bring into the picture travel distances along the network when the cost for travelling outside the network does not discriminate between the different types. Since our whole reasoning has been based on the idea of detours it is natural to investigate the extent to which the different network types require the taking of detours. Mosler (1976b) has defined a quite ingenious measure for just this.

Let imaginary travellers move from one point of origin, a junction, in all possible directions and mark their positions after they have traversed a distance of one edge-length, two edge-lengths, etc. Every time the travellers come to a junction they part and go in all possible directions. At each stage we mark their positions and join the most advanced positions by line segments. It is seen that they constitute regular polygons.

If we now take the number of edge-lengths travelled, denoted by n, as very large then – looking at a side of the isotravel-distance polygon – the points become more and more densely packed. In fact, the distance between two adjacent points in relation to the whole side goes to zero when n goes to infinity. As Mosler (1976b) says, we can then identify the side of the polygon with the set of points. Before continuing, we note that letting n go to infinity is equivalent to the already familiar process of shrinking the cell size to zero while keeping finite the distances compared.

Having the set of points, or the polygon itself, we can determine the average distance from the starting point by simple integration. This distance turns out in

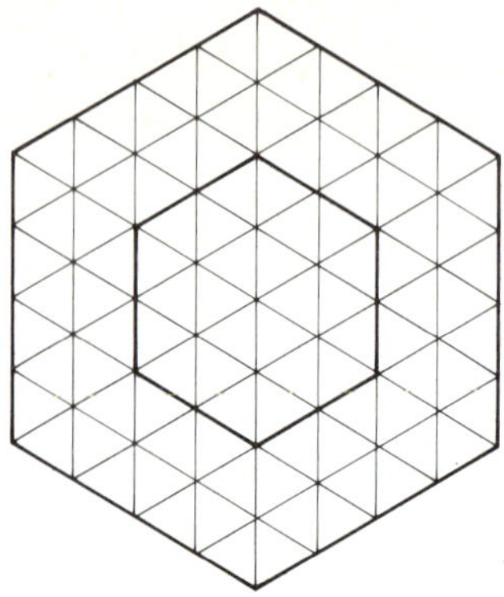

Figure 10.7. Detour factor for triangular network.

each case to be in constant proportion to the number of edges traversed, i.e. the distance traversed along the network. Since the Euclidean distance and the distance traversed along the network, for each type of network, are in a characteristic constant proportion, we can let this proportionality factor express an inherent property of the network type, namely its average necessity for detour-taking.

In fig. 10.7 we see the case of a triangular network. Obviously, the isodistance (actual travel distance) points are regularly spaced on the hexagons. The side length of the equilateral triangles is taken as unity. Hence, for $n=1$ the side of the hexagonal locus is 1 as well, for $n=2$ it is 2, and so on. In general the side is n. The perpendicular distance to the side from the point of origin is $\sqrt{3}n/2$.

To evaluate the average distance, a, to the hexagon we only need to evaluate the average distance to one of its sides, or even only half of one side, since symmetry again makes this sufficient. Recalling that half the side is $n/2$ and the orthogonal distance is $\sqrt{3}n/2$ we get

$$a=\frac{\int_0^{n/2}\sqrt{(3n^2/4+x^2)}\,\mathrm{d}x}{\int_0^{n/2}\mathrm{d}x}=\frac{(2+3\ln\sqrt{3})n}{4}. \tag{131}$$

We see that $a/n=(2+3\ln\sqrt{3})/4=0.91$. Hence, 91 percent of the network distance from the origin, reached on average along a triangular network, is the Euclidean distance. Only 9 percent is due to detours.

The case of a quadratic network is as simple as the preceding one. The locus of points is a quadrat. Again we only need to calculate the average distance to half of one of its sides. If the quadratic network has unit sides, then both the half side of a locus quadrat and its orthogonal distance from the origin are

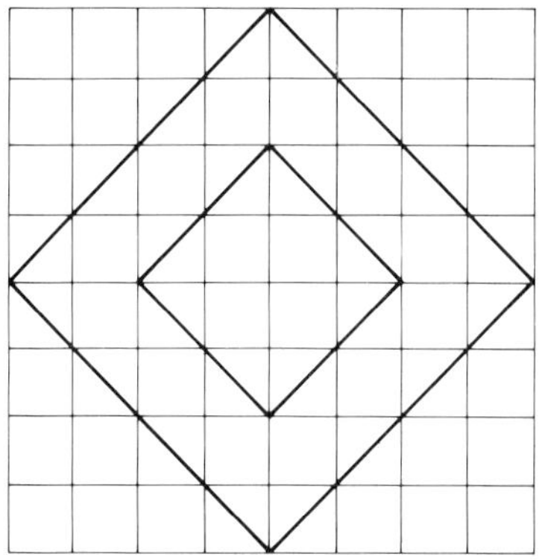

Figure 10.8. Detour factor for quadratic network.

$n/\sqrt{2}$. Hence, for this case

$$a=\frac{\int_0^{n/\sqrt{2}}\sqrt{(n^2/2+x^2)}\,\mathrm{d}x}{\int_0^{n/\sqrt{2}}\mathrm{d}x}=\frac{(2+\sqrt{2}\ln(1+\sqrt{2}))n}{4}. \tag{132}$$

Accordingly, $a/n=(2+\sqrt{2}\ln(1+\sqrt{2}))/4=0.81$. This means that, with a quadratic network, 81 percent of the distance traversed is on average the Euclidean distance, whereas 19 percent is due to detours. This network type is obviously inferior to the triangular one, where only 9 percent of the distance was due to detours. The case is illustrated in fig. 10.8.

As may be seen in fig. 10.9, the isodistance loci for the hexagonal network are hexagons, as they were for the triangular case. But only with even numbers of n is the locus always a regular hexagon. With odd n the loci are something between a hexagon and an equilateral triangle. However, this irregularity decreases with increasing n, and may be expected to disappear as n goes to infinity. In this case half the side is $\sqrt{3}n/4$, and the orthogonal distance $3n/4$. Accordingly, we get

$$a=\frac{\int_0^{\sqrt{3}n/4}\sqrt{(9n^2/16+x^2)}\,\mathrm{d}x}{\int_0^{\sqrt{3}n/4}\mathrm{d}x}=\frac{\sqrt{3}(2+3\ln\sqrt{3})n}{8}. \tag{133}$$

Obviously, $a/n=\sqrt{3}(2+3\ln\sqrt{3})/8=0.79$. Hence, with a hexagonal network 79 percent of distances traversed are Euclidean distances, whereas 21 percent are due to detours. This network type is accordingly the least efficient of those considered.

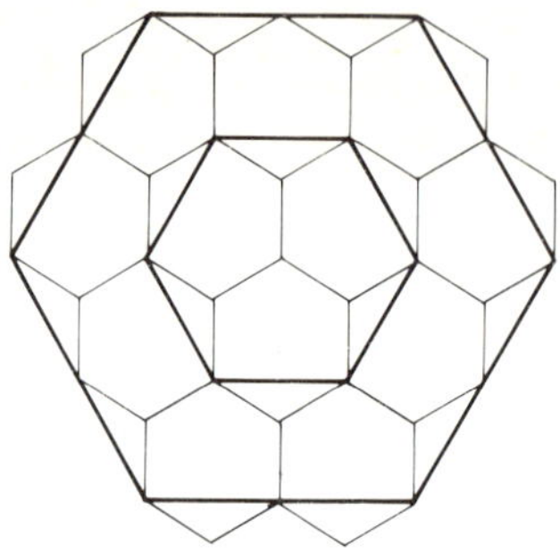

Figure 10.9. Detour factor for hexagonal network.

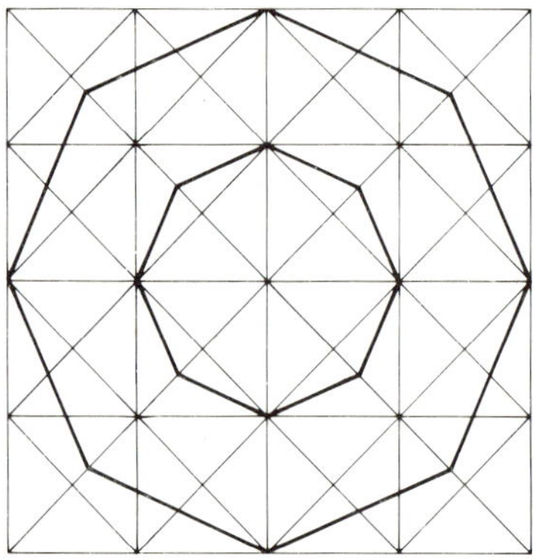

Figure 10.10. Travel distance loci with quadratic network complemented by diagonals, when the starting point is an eight-road junction.

The triangular network that we have used is thus the most efficient regular network from the point of view of saving detours. It is definitely better than the quadratic or the hexagonal, and therefore is the best of the regular polygonal networks.[1]

The quadratic networks with diagonals remain to be discussed. Mosler suggests that the locus of points is a quadrat, as in the case of quadratic network without diagonals. But, this is not true. If one starts from an eight-road junction, then the locus is a regular octagon, as shown in fig. 10.10. If one starts from a

[1]But the story can of course be made more complicated by using measures for the facility of access other than average distance. Mosler (1976b) proposes several. If the relation of travelling costs on the network to those in the plane is not so extreme that the first one is practically zero, as compared to the latter, then the communication paths issuing from and ending on the network segments need not cross them orthogonally. The computations become more complicated and the result can be different. For such complications the reader is referred to Mosler.

four-road junction then the locus becomes octagonal only with large n. But it is not worthwhile to push the investigations further at this point. After all, this case does not belong to the strictly regular ones.

10.7. Isotropic approximation and Minkowski-like distance

We argued above that when a network was shrunk in the mesh, then in the limit it was not interesting to know whether the path crossed a vanishingly small cell diametrically or only passed through a "part" of its area, neither was it interesting to know the direction in which the point cell was cut. This reasoning is a bit too vague and, as a matter of fact, it is not completely true.

In fig. 10.7 we can see that there are six directions (to the vertices of the hexagons drawn with heavy line) in which the ratio Euclidean distance to network distance is unitary. On the other hand, if we regard the six directions that halve the angles between the six aforementioned directions, then the ratio is $\sqrt{3}/2$. These directions are to the midpoints of the sides of the hexagon. The ratio is minimal in these directions and maximal in the aforementioned directions. It changes continuously with the direction.

Hence, if we let the direction of passage rotate a full turn, then the reciprocal ratio (our f = *network distance / Euclidean distance*) varies continuously between twelve minimum and maximum directions, where it alternately takes the values 1 and $2/\sqrt{3} = 1.15$.

This structure is not affected by shrinking the mesh. Hence, we conclude that it is not possible to pass from a network model to a continuous model by a limiting process, if we require the latter to be isotropic (i.e. direction-independent). This is the exact truth: the continuous transportation problem corresponding to an actual network is anisotropic.

But, we have seen that the difference between maximum and minimum f was only the difference between 1.15 and 1.00, and that in a full turn there are as many as twelve alternations. In view of this the abstraction from the anisotropy seems to be defensible. But it should be emphasized that we have to make this abstraction. The error from this is greatest if the paths compared are straight lines in directions at 30° angles. As soon as the curves change direction an averaging process works, so that (due to the frequency of alternations) errors are evened out. And any pair of closed curves that are different must include at least one curve that is not a straight line. Such curves, however, are the only ones we compare when we derive optimal paths for a fixed pair of endpoints. It seems that we abstract from relatively uninteresting features of real networks by the isotropic approximation.[2]

[2]For networks that are conformal transformations of the regular one, the above discussion holds mutatis mutandis. We have to consider the curved images of straight lines and the fact that the maximum and minimum directions vary, being related to the curved images of the straight lines.

Comparing figs. 10.7 and 10.9 with fig. 10.8, we see that the abstraction needed to transform the limiting cases of triangular and hexagonal networks into isotropic transportation models is less questionable than the corresponding abstraction needed for a quadratic network. When the isodistance loci are hexagons, then f was seen to alternate twelve times between a minimum of 1.00 and a maximum of 1.15. This was seen for the triangular case. The hexagonal case is similar but, owing to the lower efficiency of the network form, both the minimum and the maximum would be altered by the same factor as compared to an equally dense triangular network.

If we take the quadratic case, then there are obviously only eight alternations between a minimum and a maximum of f. Provided we arbitrarily put the minimum equal to unity again, the range is 1.00 to $\sqrt{2}=1.41$. It is not only true that there are fewer alternations in a full turn, but the range of variation is much greater. Intuitively, this is obvious since a hexagon is much more like a circle than a quadrat, and because we can pass to an isotropic case without any abstraction at all if the isodistance loci are circles.

The quadratic case naturally leads to the question of whether it would not be possible to use the continuous approach with an exact representation of network form by introducing a Minkowski-like measure of distance instead of the Euclidean one. Such a Minkowski measure is $(|x|^a+|y|^a)^{1/a}$. For $a=2$, we get the usual Euclidean measure, whereas for $a=1$ the measure turns into the sum $|x|+|y|$ of the norms of the coordinates. The Minkowski circle for this case, in fact, is a quadrat like those in fig. 10.8. We leave this conjecture as a loose end.

Chapter 11

OPTIMALLY ALLOCATED ROAD CAPITAL

11.1. Independence of constraints

Up to now we have dealt exclusively with one of the partial optimization problems, namely to minimize total transportation costs,

$$\int\int_S f(x,y)\, i(x,y)\, \mathrm{d}x\, \mathrm{d}y, \tag{20}$$

by choosing the function $i(x,y)$ on S within some set Φ of functions. The set Φ is defined by the constraints $\nabla \cdot \boldsymbol{v} = -1$ on S and $\boldsymbol{v} \cdot \boldsymbol{n} = 0$ on G, and the definition $i = \int\int |\boldsymbol{v}|\, \mathrm{d}\xi\, \mathrm{d}\eta$. We have seen that the constraints were independent for different ξ, η. Since by the definition of i total cost was $\int\int\int\int f|\boldsymbol{v}|\, \mathrm{d}x\, \mathrm{d}y\, \mathrm{d}\xi\, \mathrm{d}\eta$, we have seen that we could decompose the problem in minimizing $\int\int |\boldsymbol{v}|\, \mathrm{d}x\, \mathrm{d}y$ subject to $\nabla \cdot \boldsymbol{v} = -1$ and $\boldsymbol{v} \cdot \boldsymbol{n} = 0$ for each ξ, η. We have seen that we could solve $\boldsymbol{v}/|\boldsymbol{v}|$ from the Euler equations $f\boldsymbol{v}/|\boldsymbol{v}| = \nabla\lambda$. A differential equation derived from this yielded a complete solution to $\boldsymbol{v}/|\boldsymbol{v}|$. Then by using the constraint $\nabla \cdot \boldsymbol{v} = -1$ we could obtain a differential equation in $|\boldsymbol{v}|$, after which the solution could be integrated to get $i = \int\int |\boldsymbol{v}|\, \mathrm{d}\xi\, \mathrm{d}\eta$.

To carry out all the different parts of the solution was not always so easy. Most of the preceding part of this book is devoted to it and to the development of a direct method by which the solution of two differential equations in sequence and double integration could be replaced by the evaluation of a fourfold integral. However, the idea to minimize total cost (20) at a given function $f(x,y)$ by choosing an appropriate function $i(x,y)$ within the admissible set Φ of functions is simple.

It is now time to turn to the converse partial minimization problem, namely to minimize (20) by the choice of an admissible function $f(x,y)$ within some set Ψ of functions when $i(x,y)$ is taken as given. We have not yet touched upon this problem, except in Chapter 2.

In Chapter 1 we used the term "an equilibrium" (in a Cournot sense) for the case where both partial optimizations were solved and i was optimal with respect to f at the same time as f was optimal with respect to i. For the sake of generality this equilibrium was distinguished from an overall optimum (in a Stackelberg sense), characterized by the choice of f under consideration of how i would be adjusted to each f. We pointed out that the concepts need not be equivalent. However, they obviously are equivalent if the sets Φ and Ψ are *independent*. And in the case dealt with presently they are.

The constraints on f are at hand, namely

$$f(x,y)=a+b/l(x,y) \tag{134}$$

derived in (126) above, and the requirement of a given total quantity of road capital, L, written

$$\int\int_S l(x,y)\,\mathrm{d}x\,\mathrm{d}y=L. \tag{135}$$

The constraints (134) and (135) are obviously independent of the constraints that define admissible traffic distributions. Hence, Φ and Ψ are independent. This is not the case when congestion is introduced into the picture. Then, f depends on i, and this is sufficient to destroy the independence. But at present the independence is there, and the equilibrium is an overall optimum.

11.2. The square root rule

Let us now solve the second partial minimization problem, i.e. to minimize (20) by choosing f in the set Ψ, which means, subject to the constraints (134) and (135), when i is taken as given. This is much simpler than the previous problem. It is an infinite-dimensional problem of constrained optimization. We obtain the first-order condition

$$l(x,y)=\gamma\sqrt{i(x,y)}, \tag{136}$$

where γ is a constant. Its value can be calculated from (135) and (136) to equal $L/\int\int\sqrt{i}\,\mathrm{d}x\,\mathrm{d}y$. The minimization is straightforward. We substitute for f from (134) into (20) and add the constraint (135) multiplied by a Lagrange multiplier. The Lagrange function thus obtained is differentiated with respect to l at all x,y, and the derivative is put equal to zero. This yields (136). We also note that the convexity of (134) yields sufficient conditions for (136) to render a minimum with a linear constraint.

The solution of the second partial optimization problem is thus that road capital should be distributed in proportion to the square root of traffic.

In Chapter 12 we will see that empirical data for Sweden support this square root relation. Hence, if we assume that the Swedish authorities have been reasonably efficient in allocating road capital (through their proper planning instruments) we have indirect evidence for the continuous approach and for the relation of transfer cost to road capital, derived above by theoretical reasoning. We are now ready to turn to the problem of identifying the equilibrium (=overall optimum).

11.3. The equilibrating process

We start with a general discussion of an imaginary process of successive adjustments that reduce total transportation cost at each step, and see where the process leads. We therefore choose as the starting step a case with which we are familiar.

Assume that initially road capital is distributed with constant density. Transfer cost is then constant, and travellers choose straight lines as paths. Supposing the region to be the unit disk and population to be constant, we have explicitly derived the symmetric traffic distribution $i=4(1-r^2)E(r)$ that results from this choice of routes. Traffic is most intense in the center and fades off towards the periphery down to zero on the boundary.

Next, assume that the authorities observe this traffic distribution and apply the square root rule. Then road capital would be distributed so that $l=2\gamma \sqrt{(1-r^2)}\sqrt{E(r)}$, which is by no means constant, and neither is $f=a+b/l$. We can no longer derive the optimal paths for such a complicated transfer cost function, and even less can we obtain the resulting traffic distribution when the individuals have chosen their paths. However, from the qualitative analysis we at least know that because the transfer cost is uniformly increasing with the distance from the center, all paths will become curved, with a curvature vector pointing away from the origin. Since the paths are all convex to the origin, we can conjecture that the concentration of traffic to the central parts is enhanced even further. We saw this explicitly for power functions. But as the traffic is even more concentrated than in the preceding step the authorities will, by again applying the square root rule, find an even greater concentration of road capital appropriate.

One may imagine the process continuing until nothing more is gained from centralization. The general characteristics of an equilibrium-optimum distribution of traffic seem to be that traffic and road capital decrease uniformly with the distance from the center. The transfer cost would increase with distance from the center and all paths would be convex to the center. Observe that all this is pure conjecture. Intuition, however, suggests that the equilibrium exists, since the adjustments seem to be smaller and smaller, and also because there is a limit to centralization. This is true because total cost for the case of the most extreme possible centralization and convexity of paths, i.e. when all transportation moves radially, is greater than in the initial case with linear paths. This will be demonstrated later.

11.4. Total traffic and its variability

We will now look somewhat more formally at the matter. Let us therefore see what total transportation cost (20) looks like when we substitute from (134) for f

and use $l = \gamma\sqrt{i}$ together with $\gamma = L/\int\int\sqrt{i}\,\mathrm{d}x\,\mathrm{d}y$. The total cost is

$$a\int\int_S i\,\mathrm{d}x\,\mathrm{d}y + b\left(\int\int_S \sqrt{i}\,\mathrm{d}x\,\mathrm{d}y\right)^2 / L. \tag{137}$$

Since a and b are constants and as L is the total road capital, the only factors that vary in the process of finding an equilibrium described are the two double integrals. They are completely determined by the distribution of traffic i. The first integral can be interpreted as total traffic and it is thus an advantage (ceteris paribus) to have a small total traffic. This must, however, be weighted against a small value for the second integral. We see that the importance of the second integral is smaller the more road capital is invested, i.e. the greater is L.

In fig. 11.1, eq. (137) provides us with a family of isototal-cost curves in the plane where the two double integrals are measured on the axes. They are a family of parabolas, and it is advantageous to get on a parabola as close to the origin as possible. If we were able to derive the tradeoff between the integrals from the constraints on the vector fields and the boundary constraints, which together prescribe the conditions for the total need for transportation to be satisfied, then the problem would be solved. However, unfortunately we cannot derive this tradeoff curve.

We can, however, specify a region where points cannot be found. First, we cannot get total traffic below the minimum value when all transports move along straight lines. With a unit disk and constant unitary population density this minimum total was seen to be $128\pi/45$. But, even with other population distributions and other region shapes there is a minimum total traffic obtained by linear paths. Secondly, if total traffic is given, the second integral in (137)

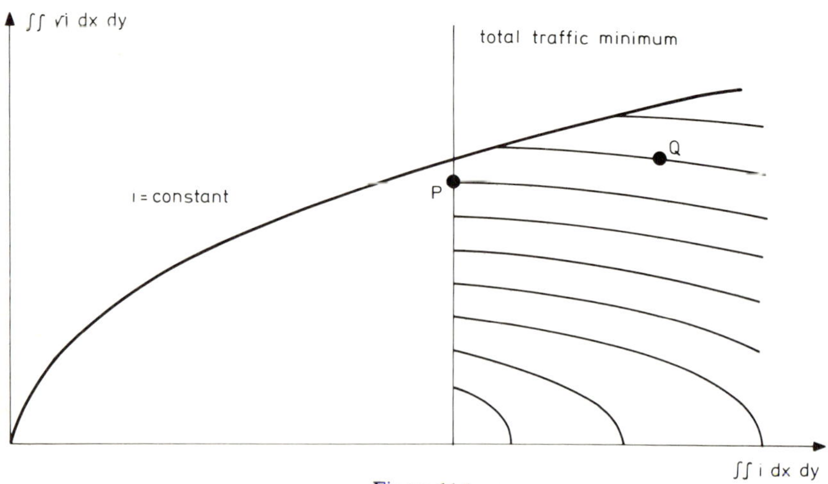

Figure 11.1

cannot rise above a certain value, related to total traffic. Observe that this is the case no matter what the specific constraints are, i.e. no matter what the demand for transportation.

This can be seen in the following manner. Let us formulate the problem of maximizing the second integral in (137) under the constraint that the first integral has a given constant value. The solution to the problem is obtained by a Lagrangean method and the obvious result is that the maximum is when $i=$constant in the region.

We can even strengthen the conclusion by directly interpreting the relation between the integrals in terms of the variability in the distribution of traffic. To be more exact, we deal with the distribution of the square root of traffic. Let us define the two first moments of the distribution surface for the square root of traffic in the region. Putting

$$A=\iint_S \mathrm{d}x\,\mathrm{d}y$$

for the area, we get

$$\mu=(1/A)\iint_S \sqrt{i}\,\mathrm{d}x\,\mathrm{d}y$$

and

$$\mu^2+\sigma^2=(1/A)\iint_S (\sqrt{i})^2\,\mathrm{d}x\,\mathrm{d}y.$$

Using these formulae, eq. (137) is transformed into

$$A\left(a(\mu^2+\sigma^2)+b\mu^2/\bar{l}\right), \tag{138}$$

where $l=L/A$ stands for average road capital. The first term is now proportionate to the second moment and the second term to the square of the first moment. Given total traffic, i.e. given $\mu^2+\sigma^2$, we conclude that the smaller is σ^2 the greater is μ^2. It is greatest when traffic is constant, i.e. when the variance is zero.

This knowledge can be used to calculate a maximum total cost when the square root rule is used. Making i constant we can factor out both itself and its square root before the integrals in (137) and thus obtain

$$\left(a+b/\bar{l}\right)\iint_S i\,\mathrm{d}x\,\mathrm{d}y \tag{139}$$

as the measure of cost. Hence, total cost cannot exceed the product of total traffic and the transfer cost that would result from a constant distribution of road capital within the region.

We can use the result in fig. 11.1 to draw the rising parabola, below which any distribution of traffic must be represented. There are also some points plotted in the diagram relevant for known traffic distributions, i.e. for linear and radial paths, respectively, denoted by P and Q. The values of the integrals of traffic have been tabulated. We simply recall that they were 8.94 and 13.16 for the linear and radial cases, respectively. The integrals for the square root of traffic are not difficult to evaluate because we know the explicit formulae. For the radial case I have made the evaluation analytically in terms of beta functions; for the linear case numerical quadrature by Simpson's rule was employed. As the calculations have no general interest, we simply record the values as 4.93 and 5.34, respectively.

What we lack is the whole set of possible points that could be confronted with the isocosts. Hence, we cannot determine the optimum.

11.5. On the existence of an equilibrium-optimum

There are, however, strong intuitive reasons for believing that an equilibrium-optimum exists. In fact, we confidently believe that for any distribution of traffic there is a distribution of road capital that makes total cost minimal, and that for any distribution of road capital there is a distribution of traffic that makes total cost minimal. As to the first, we have actually derived the square root relation. This obviously provides a minimum no matter what the distribution of traffic is. As to the second, we may first note that, in the absence of externalities, total cost would be minimized when each transport takes a minimum cost route. This does not interfere with the opportunities of others. Next, we recall from Chapter 4 that for the circularly symmetric case the Jacobi and Legendre conditions were satisfied. Hence, the only problem is the existence of solutions to the Euler equations for sufficient intervals. If they exist, then (43) and (44) show that they represent strong local minima. But, we have also seen that from (38) we could solve for ω' and hence obtain $\omega(r)$ by straightforward integration, except when the radial solution does the job.

A weak point is the assumption of circular symmetry. However, because the region is a unit disk we have strong reasons for believing that the equilibrium-optimum distributions must display circular symmetry.

Since the partial minimum of total cost exists both when we keep the allocation of roads constant and vary traffic, and when we keep traffic constant and vary the roads, there is no reason to think that a minimum does not exist if we let both traffic and road distribution vary. It must, however, be stressed that this does not provide any strict proof of existence.

11.6. Power functions

To shed more light on these matters we will discuss one example in some detail. Since we are already familiar with the power variety of transfer cost functions we will confine the discussion to this case. As we have specified $f=a+b/l$, we cannot make f proportionate to r^n unless a is zero. This is so because b is positive and r^n is zero (or infinite) in the center. This is in contradiction to our model as both constants had definite positive values. But let us forget this in the example and put $a=0$. If we then introduce a proportionality constant so that $f=2r^n/(2-n)$, we have $l=(1-n/2)r^{-n}$. It is easy to check that $\int\int l\,dx\,dy=\pi$, no matter what value (less than 2) the exponent n takes. Hence, the cases for different n represent different distributions, with different degrees of centralization, whereas aggregate road capital is fixed.

We know the transportation costs between any two points along optimal routes when the transfer cost is a power function. (The new multiplicative constant obviously has no influence on the choice of paths.) The costs are given by (54) and (55) above, depending on whether the angle between the endpoints exceeds a critical angle $\pi/(n+1)$ or not.

I have constructed a simulation program (COST, appended), that simulates 50 000 transports by choosing endpoints at random within the unit disk. The locational probabilities of the endpoints are taken as equal, since we assume constant density of population. The program evaluates the minimum cost for each transport (from the relevant expression) and calculates the average. This average, for which reasonable convergence is obtained by the number of runs, is multiplied by π^2, i.e. the square of the area of the disk, which is a measure of the total number of trips when the population density is unitary.

The results for different exponents are given in Table 11.1. We note that with $n=0$, so that $f=1$, the cost estimate equals total traffic with linear paths. This is reasonable because we have seen that total traffic equals total transportation work, and the latter equals cost when the transfer cost is unitary. If the exponent becomes negative, total cost only increases; if it becomes positive, then total cost decreases to an exponent of 0.4, and then rises again very rapidly to go to infinity with the exponent approaching the value 2. Thus, there is an optimal degree of capital concentration to the central parts. The traffic distribution with the exponent 0.4 has been calculated by another simulation program in Chapter 8, and is also shown in a computer diagram.

It must be emphasized that we have only been able to find the best one within a special class of functions, but we can take the traffic distribution, derived above for $n=0.4$, and tabulate it against the distribution of road capital $l=0.8\,r^{-0.4}$ (table 11.2).

Fitting a power curve to these data, we get $l=0.69\,i^{0.38}$, with $R^2=0.90$. This, of course, is not the square root curve. One can see this merely from inspection, since the amount of road capital at the boundary is 0.80 instead of 0.00 as it

Table 11.1
Total cost for power functions.

n	−0.80	−0.40	0.00	0.40	0.80	1.20	1.60
Total cost	14.07	11.76	8.94	7.80	8.17	9.24	14.84

Table 11.2
Road capital and traffic with $n=0.4$.

r	0.00	0.20	0.40	0.60	0.80	1.00
i	∞	6.58	4.48	3.08	1.60	0.00
l	∞	1.52	1.15	0.98	0.87	0.80

should be. However, the fit to the square root curve is close enough for us to suspect that within a more general class of admitted functions the degree of capital concentration is like the one for power curves in optimum.

11.7. Elastic transportation demand: cost versus communication

We have used total communication cost as a criterion by which to decide the best degree of capital concentration. Of course, this is reasonable only provided that communication is not sensitive to cost. For simplicity we assume that this is the case. In Chapters 6 and 7, however, we discussed the sensitivity of transportation demand to cost and the consequences of it for the traffic distributions. We now discuss the consequences in the present context. As before, we distinguish between two cost dependences: one due to the spatial structure of location, rendering a cost dependence that is inert with respect to short-run changes in communication possibilities, and one due to the possibility for people to choose better facilities located farther away as communications are facilitated. Again, we only take these latter dependences into consideration.

To illustrate the consequences of considering this latter type of distance dependence, we imagine that transportation demand has unitary elasticity. The cost of communication between any two points of the region is then constant and so is total communication cost, whichever paths are chosen and whichever transfer cost function they respond to. This is so because the number of communications is reciprocal to cost, so that cost per communication multiplied by the number of communications is constant. Hence, total communication cost cannot discriminate between different degrees of road capital concentration.

However, the individual transporters are certainly not indifferent to which paths they choose. Neither are they indifferent to the allocation of road capital. They naturally want each communication to be as inexpensive as possible. The question then is how to define an aggregate measure of efficiency instead of minimum cost. The most natural is a maximum number of communications. Since communication is reciprocal to the cost for each pair of locations, this automatically minimizes the cost for each transport. In aggregate, we can choose the total number of communications when total cost does not work. With unitary elasticity this measure is the total of all reciprocals of the costs for individual transports.

Table 11.3
Total costs with different elasticities of transportation demand and different degrees of road capital concentration.

n	−0.8	−0.4	0.0	0.4	0.8	1.2	1.6
$\varepsilon=0.0$	14.07	11.76	8.94	7.80	8.17	9.24	14.84
$\varepsilon=0.5$	10.03	9.57	9.07	8.66	8.62	9.23	11.56
$\varepsilon=1.0$	9.87	9.87	9.87	9.87	9.87	9.87	9.87
$\varepsilon=1.5$	10.96	11.36	11.85	12.34	12.46	11.83	9.69

In general, when the elasticity is not necessarily unitary, we should consider both total cost and total communication, wanting the first to be as small as possible and the latter to be as large as possible. If the criteria render different best solutions some balance between the two desideria must be struck. One possibility is to compute the ratio of average cost per communication.

If we denote the cost for an individual transport by I, population density by p, and the elasticity of transportation demand by ε, total cost is $\iint\iint \bar{p}p\, I^{1-\varepsilon}\, \mathrm{d}x\, \mathrm{d}y\, \mathrm{d}\xi\, \mathrm{d}\eta$ and total communication is $\iint\iint \bar{p}p\, I^{-\varepsilon}\, \mathrm{d}x\, \mathrm{d}y\, \mathrm{d}\xi\, \mathrm{d}\eta$.

By simulation we can compute the two measures for the case of power functions. To keep the total road capital constant we again put $f=2r^n/(2-n)$. The cost I for one transport can again be computed by (54) or (55), depending on which one is relevant for the pair of endpoints simulated. Again we take the region as the unit disk and put population density equal to unity everywhere. The program, COSTCOM, works in exactly the same way as the program COST, except that it calculates the number of communications together with the total cost. (There also is one computational change. To save computation time the simulation is made for half the disk because it has a symmetry axis. This saves one of the tests to decide whether the path is radial or curved.) The results are tabulated in tables 11.3 and 11.4. The entries for cost in the case of zero demand elasticity have simply been taken from table 11.2.

We can begin by checking the columns for $n=0.0$. For these cases we have analytic expressions derived in Chapter 7, namely the $J(\varepsilon)$ and $N(\varepsilon)$, respectively. The first measure is relevant for total traffic, as the reader may remember, but when the exponent in the transfer cost function is zero, the transfer cost is unitary and therefore total traffic equals total cost. By $J(\varepsilon)=32\pi B(\frac{1}{2},3-\varepsilon/2)/((3-\varepsilon)(4-\varepsilon)2^{\varepsilon})$ we obtain the sequence of values: 8.94, 9.08,

Table 11.4
Total communications with different elasticities of transportation demand and different degrees of road capital concentration.

n	−0.8	−0.4	0.0	0.4	0.8	1.2	1.6
$\varepsilon=0.0$	9.87	9.87	9.87	9.87	9.87	9.87	9.87
$\varepsilon=0.5$	10.96	11.36	11.85	12.34	12.46	11.83	9.69
$\varepsilon=1.0$	15.02	15.74	16.71	17.83	18.39	17.31	12.65
$\varepsilon=1.5$	30.27	30.95	32.46	35.26	39.14	42.75	37.80

9.87 and 11.83. By $N(\varepsilon)=16\pi B(\frac{1}{2},2.5-\varepsilon/2)/((2-\varepsilon)(3-\varepsilon)2^{\varepsilon})$ we likewise get 9.87, 11.83, 16.76 and 34.07. Except for the last entry, the agreement with the tables must be said to be good.

From the tables we notice that for elasticities less than unity total cost takes on a minimum for a degree of capital concentration of about 0.4–0.8. We also see that total communication for these elasticities takes on a maximum with approximately the same degree of capital concentration. With unitary elasticity communication still takes on a maximum at the degree 0.8 of capital concentration. If we compute the ratio of total cost to total communication we get a minimum for all the cases up to and including unitary elasticity. This minimum turns out to be at the same degree of capital concentration. However, when we come to the last rows, i.e. when the elasticity is 1.5, then we see that cost and communication change in the same direction (instead of the opposite as in the other cases), and computing the ratio of cost to communication we see that there is no longer a minimum. This anomaly is expected, but fortunately it only occurs wth extreme elasticities.

11.8. Program COST

```
100 N=50000
110 M=0
120 K=0
130 PRINT "EXPONENT";
140 INPUT A
150 A=A+1
160 L=4*ATN(1)
170 H=(2*A-1)*L
180 R0=SQR(RND(0))↑A
190 R1=SQR(RND(0))↑A
200 V0=RND(0)
210 V1=RND(0)
220 V=2*L*A*ABS(V1-V0)
230 IF V<L THEN 270
240 IF V>H THEN 270
250 T=R0+R1
260 GO TO 280
270 T=SQR(R0*R0+R1*R1-2*R0*R1*COS(V))
280 K=K+T
290 M=M+1
300 IF M<N THEN 180
310 K=2*L*L*K/N/A/(3-A)
320 PRINT "COST=";K
330 END
```

11.9 Program COSTCOM

```
100 N=10000
110 M=0
120 K=0
130 L=0
140 PRINT "ELASTICITY";
150 INPUT E
160 F=1-E
170 G=0-E
180 PRINT "EXPONENT";
190 INPUT A
200 A=A+1
210 P=4*ATN(1)
220 R=SQR(RND(0))↑A
230 S=SQR(RND(0))↑A
240 V=P*A*RND(0)
250 IF V>P THEN 280
260 X=SQR(R*R+S*S-2*R*S*COS(V))
270 GO TO 290
280 X=R+S
290 K=K+X↑F
300 L=L+X↑G
310 M=M+1
320 IF M<N THEN 220
330 K=((2/A/(3-A))↑F)*P*P*K/N
340 L=((2/A/(3-A))↑G)*P*P*L/N
350 PRINT "COST=";K,"COMMUNICATION=";L
360 END
```

Chapter 12

ON THE OPTIMALITY OF ROAD ALLOCATION IN SWEDEN, 1973

As was said above, in this chapter some empirical evidence in favor of the square root optimality rule will be presented. For Sweden in 1973 there are statistical data on total lengths of road networks in kilometers, L, and transportation work done in millions of vehicle kilometers, T, for a subdivision into 275 local districts (communes).

To obtain measures for i and l we have to take into consideration that the areas of the communes are very different. It is obvious that for any regular network of the types considered in Chapter 10 the length of the network for any part of the region is proportional to its area. The same is true for traffic that flows uniformly along the network, in the sense that during any given time period the same number of vehicles pass through any unit arc (in both directions). Thus, transportation work is proportional to area.

12.1. The fit of the square root rule

As we would say that both road capital and traffic are constant on a regular network with constant currents of vehicles, it is reasonable to divide L and T by areas in square kilometers, A, to obtain the measures for l and i. There is also some empirical support for this because a regression of $\ln L$ on $\ln A$ and $\ln T$ yields $L = 1.26A^{0.59}T^{0.35}$. The sum of the exponents being not so far from unity, i.e. the relation being almost homogeneous of the first degree, the definition of $i = T/A$ and $l = L/A$ is also suggested by the data.

Expecting a square root relation it is natural to try to fit a power curve for l as a function of i, or rather, a regression line after taking logarithms. The resulting curve and the scatter diagram are shown in fig. 12.1. The relation estimated is

$$l = 0.84 i^{0.40}, \qquad R^2 = 0.65. \tag{140}$$

The theoretical value of the exponent is 0.50. The standard error for the exponent is 0.02. Since there are 273 degrees of freedom, the t-distribution is virtually normal and a 99 percent confidence interval is ± 0.05. Thus, the theoretical value just fails to fall within the limits of confidence.

However, although the estimation is made in the logarithms of the variables and thus we have a multiplicative error specified, the spread away from the

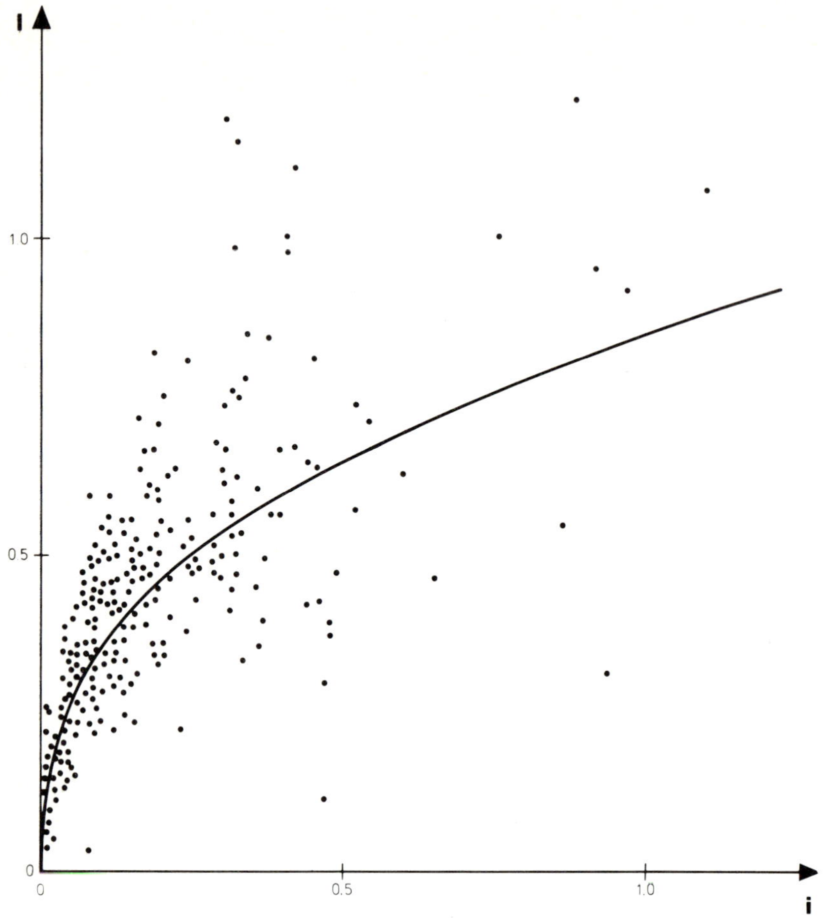

Figure 12.1

curve with increasing i is such that heteroscedasticity may be suspected. There are several tests available for heteroscedasticity. We use a method proposed by Glejser. According to Johnston (1972) it has some serious weaknesses, especially in that it is unable to distinguish between cases of pure and mixed heteroscedasticity, but the advantage of using this method for testing is that we simultaneously arrive at the proper weights to be used at generalized least square estimation.

The idea, in our case, is to take a regression of the absolute value of the residual, i.e. $|\ln \varepsilon|$, obtained from $l = 0.84 i^{0.40} \varepsilon$, on $\ln i$. The procedure yields

$$|\ln \varepsilon| = 0.33 + 0.03 \ln i. \tag{141}$$

The coefficient 0.03 is nonzero on a 99.5 percent level. Although the coefficient may seem tiny, the variation of $\ln i$, between -6.21 and 2.25, is such that the weights to be used vary considerably. Hence we cannot neglect the possibility of obtaining a better estimator by generalized least squares.

The weights are

$$\lambda = 1/(0.33 + 0.03 \ln i)^2 \tag{142}$$

and the renewed estimation yields

$$l = 0.95 i^{0.46}. \tag{143}$$

The exponent comes closer to the theoretical value of 0.50 but, as the standard error is reduced to 0.015, the confidence interval is reduced to ± 0.04. Hence, the theoretical value is now within 99 percent confidence limits.

12.2. "Benefit – cost analysis"

It could also be of some interest to use the data available to obtain a rough estimate of the gains from a redistribution of road capital, i.e. from moving all the points of the scatter to an exact square root curve while keeping the total road capital constant. The calculation can be done in the following way.

Assuming $i = T/A$ and $l = L/A$ to be constant within each commune, we can decompose the integrals in the left-hand members of the equations below into sums of 275 area integrals. In each of the latter the factors involving i and l can be moved outside the integration signs due to their constancy. The integrands remaining are unitary, and the remaining integrals become areas. Hence, the right-hand members

$$\iint i \; \mathrm{d}x\,\mathrm{d}y = \sum T = 35\,361,$$

$$\iint \sqrt{i} \; \mathrm{d}x\,\mathrm{d}y = \sum \sqrt{(TA)} = 94\,624,$$

$$\iint l \; \mathrm{d}x\,\mathrm{d}y = \sum L = 100\,269,$$

$$\iint i/l \; \mathrm{d}x\,\mathrm{d}y = \sum TA/L = 116\,384,$$

$$\iint i^2/l \, \mathrm{d}x\,\mathrm{d}y = \sum T^2/L = 35\,068.$$

These are operationalizations of the integrals occurring in the expressions for total costs. Using (134) in (20) and replacing the integrals by the sums we obtain a measure of *actual* cost as

$$a \sum T + b \sum TA/L. \tag{144}$$

To obtain a number we must specify the coefficients a and b. The natural assumption in this respect is to use the numbers obtained in Chapter 10 for the hexagonal case, i.e. $a=1$ and $b=1.125$. However, those figures were obtained by specifying unit diameters for the hexagonal cells, whereas the data are specified per unit area. The area of a hexagon with unit diameter being $\sqrt{27/8}$, we should adjust b by dividing by this number. Hence, $b=\sqrt{3}$. All this yields a measure of cost equal to 236909.

In a similar manner we may obtain *minimal* cost, when the square root relation is followed, by using the operationalizations made in (137). We get

$$a\sum T+b\left(\sum\sqrt{(TA)}\right)^2/\sum L, \tag{145}$$

which equals 190028. The reduction would equal 20 percent.

It must be stressed that the measures are not to be interpreted as costs in money, time, or transportation work. The unit makes no sense at all. What is interesting is the relation between different cost expressions. If desired we may use a normalizing factor 35361/236909=0.15 to convert the abstract cost measures to millions of vehicle kilometers.

This may be of use if one wants to make a rough "benefit–cost analysis" of increased road capital. Assuming road capital to be redistributed according to the square root rule we may differentiate the preceding equation with respect to $\sum L$ to obtain

$$-b\left(\sum\sqrt{(TA)}\right)^2/\left(\sum L\right)^2 \tag{146}$$

as a measure of the marginal cost of transportation saved by adding another road kilometer. According to the specifications used this equals -1.54. Now we may profit from the conversion factor 0.15 that translates the cost measures into millions of vehicle kilometers. Hencc, an additional road kilometer would save transportation work amounting to 230000 vehicle kilometers. Multiplying this by the average kilometer cost per vehicle and comparing with the cost of capital and maintenance for a new kilometer of road, we get a rough idea of costs and benefits. Of course, this underestimates the value of a new kilometer added at a strategic point to the actual network, since the calculation was made for an optimally redistributed network.

12.3. Maps transformed to represent actual communication distances

The statistical data may now also be used in another way, namely to draw a distorted map of Sweden such that linear distances are in proportion to average distances along road networks. The parts of the country where relatively little road capital is invested have to be inflated so that the linear magnification factor equals $f=1+\sqrt{3}/l$.

Using aggregate data for the 24 counties, instead of the very detailed data for the 275 districts, it is easy to see merely from inspection that the most important explanatory factor for the variation of f is the distance from the most southern part of the country. (Adding the next important factor, namely the distance from the capital, has relatively little additional explanatory power.) Observe that we speak of explanatory factors that specify geographical location only.

Denoting the distance from Malmö by r and normalizing distances so that the distance from Malmö to Stockholm is one unit, we can fit the curve

$$f = 7.25r, \qquad R^2 = 0.74. \tag{147}$$

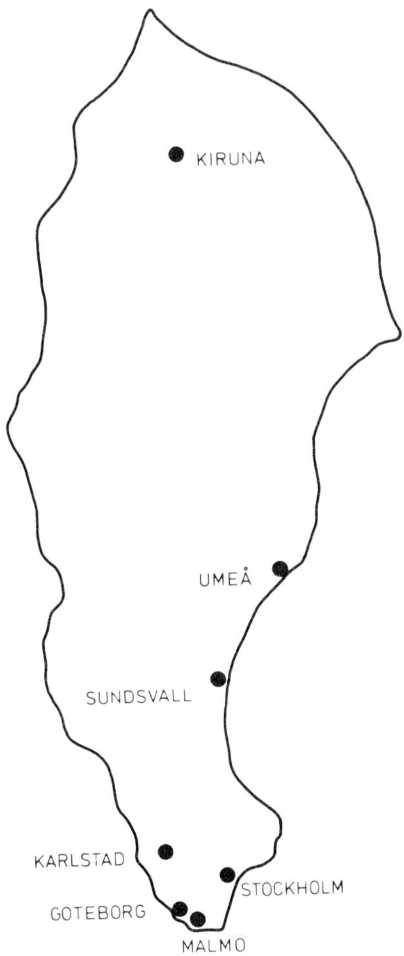

Figure 12.2

Of course, we could obtain a better fit by adding a constant, namely $f=1.66+5.97r$ with $R^2=0.78$. But, we cannot handle transfer cost functions with a constant, and lose relatively little in explanation by deleting the constant.

Hence we see that, following the discussion in Chapter 10, a conformal mapping by $w=z^2$ makes the average transfer distance, including detours, proportional to the linear distance on the map. The distorted map is shown in fig. 12.2. Actually, Malmö is a singular point because the derivative of the mapping is zero, and the southern coast of Sweden is folded into two overlapping sheets. But, because of the small scale in the extreme south this is not visible. The function fitted exaggerates the density of roads in the south since f in reality is not zero there (nor can it be according to the theory developed). This is the consequence of neglecting the constant term.

Appendix: the Swedish data for 1973

District (1)	A (km^2) (2)	T (10^6km) (3)	L (km) (4)	$T/A=i$ (5)	$L/A=l$ (6)
Stockholms län					
Upplands-Väsby	78.2	83	60	1.06	0.77
Vallentuna	359.6	87	169	0.24	0.47
Värmdö	438.5	71	178	0.16	0.41
Järfälla	55.7	111	38	1.99	0.68
Ekerö	216.0	69	132	0.32	0.61
Huddinge	129.4	238	79	1.84	0.61
Botkyrka	251.4	213	133	0.85	0.53
Haninge	454.0	150	148	0.33	0.33
Tyresö	68.9	32	20	0.46	0.29
Upplands-Bro	238.4	111	89	0.47	0.37
Täby	60.4	118	65	1.95	1.08
Danderyd	26.5	99	14	3.74	0.53
Sollentuna	52.0	231	67	4.44	1.29
Stockholm	184.5	958	86	5.19	0.47
Södertälje	675.9	435	301	0.64	0.45
Nacka	95.4	175	73	1.83	0.77
Sundbyberg	8.7	4	1	0.46	0.11
Solna	19.5	185	16	9.49	0.82
Lidingö	30.4	28	99	0.92	0.30
Växholm	367.1	142	202	0.39	0.55
Norrtälje	1999.4	269	859	0.13	0.43
Sigtuna	327.2	173	227	0.53	0.69
Nynäshamn	356.4	75	185	0.21	0.52
Uppsala län					
Håbo	140.0	61	57	0.44	0.41
Älvkarleby	208.4	73	72	0.36	0.35
Tierp	1542.5	154	538	0.10	0.35
Uppsala	2464.1	590	1138	0.24	0.46
Enköping	1179.8	238	637	0.20	0.54
Östhammar	1452.0	92	505	0.06	0.35

Södermanlands län					
Vingåker	368.0	42	203	0.11	0.55
Nyköping	2090.0	449	944	0.21	0.45
Oxelösund	33.2	17	18	0.51	0.54
Flen	715.4	110	341	0.15	0.48
Katrineholm	1018.9	151	456	0.15	0.49
Eskilstuna	1099.0	273	462	0.25	0.42
Strängnäs	735.7	176	270	0.24	0.37
Östergötlands län					
Ödeshög	431.6	110	209	0.25	0.48
Ydre	678.4	25	260	0.04	0.38
Kinda	1134.5	69	463	0.06	0.41
Boxholm	528.0	33	171	0.06	0.32
Åtvidaberg	683.5	48	315	0.07	0.46
Finspång	1059.7	76	265	0.07	0.25
Valdemarsvik	732.8	50	248	0.07	0.39
Linköping	1430.2	423	858	0.30	0.60
Norrköping	1492.2	468	645	0.31	0.43
Söderköping	670.8	67	290	0.10	0.43
Motala	1174.8	185	594	0.16	0.51
Mjölby	549.2	167	341	0.30	0.62
Jönköpings län					
Aneby	518.5	27	178	0.05	0.34
Gnosjö	422.0	37	189	0.09	0.45
Gislaved	1139.5	141	570	0.12	0.50
Vaggeryd	830.1	123	315	0.15	0.38
Jönköping	1484.2	534	719	0.36	0.48
Nässjö	916.0	119	416	0.13	0.45
Värnamo	1222.0	178	576	0.15	0.47
Sävsjö	679.0	69	283	0.10	0.42
Vetlanda	1525.5	126	62	0.08	0.40
Eksjö	802.2	92	382	0.11	0.48
Tranås	403.5	56	147	0.14	0.36
Kronobergs län					
Uppvidinge	1178.3	69	359	0.06	0.30
Lessebo	409.9	37	141	0.09	0.34
Tingsryd	1048.2	99	523	0.09	0.50
Alvesta	974.4	104	507	0.11	0.52
Älmhult	893.5	76	349	0.09	0.39
Markaryd	521.1	94	228	0.18	0.44
Växjö	1672.8	313	788	0.19	0.47
Ljungby	1760.8	209	756	0.12	0.43
Kalmar län					
Högsby	753.6	42	247	0.06	0.33
Torsås	469.2	44	185	0.09	0.39
Mörbylånga	667.1	94	257	0.14	0.39
Hultsfred	1125.4	108	384	0.10	0.34
Mönsterås	597.0	76	181	0.13	0.30
Emmaboda	689.2	60	264	0.09	0.38
Kalmar	955.5	205	377	0.21	0.39

District (1)	A (km^2) (2)	T (10^6km) (3)	L (km) (4)	$T/A=i$ (5)	$L/A=l$ (6)
Nybro	1181.9	91	360	0.08	0.30
Oskarshamn	1046.2	122	307	0.12	0.29
Västervik	1872.5	191	810	0.10	0.43
Vimmerby	1139.3	78	464	0.07	0.41
Borgholm	674.5	114	274	0.17	0.41
Gotlands län					
Gotland	3140.1	239	1498	0.08	0.48
Blekinge län					
Olofström	887.3	51	258	0.06	0.29
Karlskrona	1030.5	198	492	0.19	0.48
Ronneby	821.6	141	378	0.17	0.46
Karlshamn	485.1	145	317	0.30	0.65
Sölvesborg	184.1	81	145	0.44	0.79
Kristianstad län					
Östra Göinge	432.9	72	283	0.17	0.65
Örkelljunga	319.5	89	149	0.28	0.47
Tomelilla	396.1	71	256	0.18	0.65
Bromölla	160.7	63	89	0.39	0.55
Osby	576.3	64	277	0.11	0.48
Perstorp	158.7	32	72	0.20	0.45
Klippan	373.9	94	191	0.25	0.51
Åstorp	91.1	87	82	0.95	0.90
Båstad	217.4	75	181	0.34	0.83
Kristianstad	1238.1	355	811	0.29	0.66
Simrishamn	393.3	80	293	0.20	0.74
Ängelholm	419.0	213	303	0.51	0.72
Hässleholm	1270.8	269	770	0.21	0.61
Malmöhus län					
Svalöv	388.1	68	268	0.18	0.69
Staffanstorp	108.2	93	129	0.86	1.19
Vellinge	140.8	121	210	0.86	1.49
Bjuv	114.9	47	124	0.41	1.08
Kävlinge	153.9	114	151	0.74	0.98
Lomma	55.2	135	80	2.45	1.45
Skurup	193.9	58	225	0.30	1.16
Sjöbo	494.4	78	344	0.16	0.70
Hörby	421.0	81	336	0.19	0.80
Höör	292.7	96	222	0.33	0.76
Malmö	152.6	494	407	3.25	2.67
Lund	428.9	439	335	1.01	0.78
Landskrona	138.5	150	145	1.08	1.05
Helsingborg	343.3	309	318	0.90	0.93
Höganäs	142.9	59	140	0.41	0.98
Eslöv	418.6	155	346	0.37	0.83
Ystad	350.0	107	336	0.31	0.96
Trelleborg	338.1	108	382	0.32	1.13

Hallands län					
Hylte	943.1	74	446	0.08	0.47
Halmstad	1020.3	359	598	0.35	0.59
Laholm	887.1	146	430	0.16	0.48
Falkenberg	1114.5	217	655	0.19	0.59
Varberg	872.8	273	481	0.31	0.55
Kungsbacka	610.3	271	383	0.44	0.63
Göteborg och bohuslän					
Härryda	267.4	128	122	0.48	0.46
Partille	57.1	95	36	1.66	0.63
Öckerö	25.1	10	24	0.40	0.96
Stenungsund	250.5	145	153	0.58	0.61
Tjörn	166.3	54	122	0.32	0.73
Orust	386.0	65	238	0.17	0.62
Sotenäs	137.6	33	109	0.24	0.79
Munkedal	635.2	96	262	0.15	0.41
Tanum	918.6	92	487	0.10	0.53
Göteborg	443.7	727	256	1.64	0.58
Mölndal	147.2	201	78	1.37	0.53
Kungälv	361.0	140	233	0.39	0.65
Lysekil	208.4	62	150	0.30	0.72
Uddevalla	640.4	225	281	0.35	0.44
Strömstad	465.9	77	269	0.17	0.58
Älvsborgs län					
Dals-Ed	728.0	29	263	0.04	0.36
Färgelanda	591.9	40	267	0.07	0.45
Ale	318.2	143	130	0.45	0.41
Lerum	290.2	137	110	0.47	0.38
Vårgårda	428.5	101	215	0.24	0.50
Tranemo	747.7	53	321	0.07	0.43
Bengtsfors	891.4	61	364	0.07	0.41
Mellerud	512.6	69	269	0.13	0.52
Lilla Edet	318.1	78	149	0.25	0.47
Mark	939.2	137	212	0.15	0.23
Svenljunga	922.6	64	440	0.07	0.48
Herrljunga	499.9	41	289	0.08	0.58
Vänersborg	641.7	201	336	0.31	0.52
Trollhättan	411.6	131	202	0.32	0.49
Alingsås	445.1	126	221	0.28	0.50
Borås	1180.8	372	541	0.32	0.46
Ulricehamn	1046.3	139	558	0.13	0.53
Åmål	480.6	74	192	0.15	0.40
Skaraborgs län					
Grästorp	236.6	50	130	0.19	0.49
Mullsjö	202.0	34	119	0.17	0.59
Habo	330.1	45	151	0.14	0.46
Karlsborg	432.9	45	188	0.10	0.43
Gullspång	313.0	62	110	0.20	0.35
Vara	937.4	180	556	0.19	0.59
Götene	405.3	88	249	0.22	0.61

District	A (km^2)	T (10^6km)	L (km)	$T/A=i$	$L/A=l$
(1)	(2)	(3)	(4)	(5)	(6)
Tibro	219.5	33	98	0.15	0.45
Töreboda	545.4	47	234	0.09	0.43
Mariestad	602.9	167	329	0.28	0.55
Lidköping	689.1	133	356	0.19	0.52
Skara	439.5	138	249	0.31	0.57
Skövde	671.7	160	365	0.24	0.54
Hjo	299.0	37	145	0.12	0.48
Tidaholm	521.5	57	302	0.11	0.58
Falköping	1064.1	151	575	0.19	0.54
Värmlands län					
Kil	355.2	64	165	0.18	0.46
Eda	822.8	41	278	0.05	0.34
Torsby	4220.5	98	669	0.02	0.16
Storfors	380.1	24	127	0.06	0.33
Hammarö	54.2	17	40	0.31	0.74
Munkfors	140.3	15	62	0.11	0.44
Forshaga	346.7	49	141	0.14	0.41
Grums	382.6	64	145	0.17	0.38
Årjäng	1417.0	59	430	0.04	0.30
Sunne	1290.9	84	383	0.07	0.30
Karlstad	1157.9	331	517	0.29	0.45
Kristinehamn	740.3	149	253	0.20	0.34
Filipstad	1567.8	88	359	0.06	0.23
Hagfors	1833.9	95	417	0.05	0.23
Arvika	1654.9	135	555	0.08	0.34
Säffle	1219.0	98	378	0.08	0.31
Örebro län					
Laxå	564.6	74	156	0.13	0.28
Hallsberg	646.3	119	274	0.18	0.42
Degerfors	386.2	43	117	0.11	0.30
Hällefors	995.6	45	233	0.05	0.23
Ljunarsberg	579.2	49	157	0.08	0.27
Örebro	1835.9	519	837	0.28	0.46
Kumla	206.5	92	127	0.45	0.62
Åskersund	819.9	102	287	0.12	0.35
Karlskoga	470.9	88	165	0.19	0.35
Nora	622.3	54	160	0.09	0.26
Lindesberg	1386.4	124	456	0.09	0.33
Västmanlands län					
Skinnskatteberg	661.7	38	185	0.06	0.28
Surahammar	344.4	46	132	0.13	0.38
Heby	1169.5	97	385	0.08	0.33
Kungsör	202.8	74	79	0.36	0.39
Hallstahammar	171.4	71	112	0.41	0.65
Norberg	421.5	45	162	0.11	0.38
Västerås	953.3	308	500	0.32	0.52

Sala	1172.6	150	474	0.13	0.40
Fagersta	270.5	53	91	0.20	0.34
Köping	607.1	110	261	0.18	0.43
Arboga	324.2	95	154	0.29	0.48
Kopparbergs län					
Vansbro	1557.7	56	265	0.04	0.17
Malung	4153.3	80	563	0.02	0.14
Gagnef	776.3	67	160	0.09	0.21
Leksand	1224.0	84	329	0.07	0.27
Rättvik	1950.4	84	273	0.04	0.14
Orsa	1751.7	45	251	0.03	0.14
Älvdalen	6946.8	72	681	0.01	0.10
Smedjebacken	964.0	80	258	0.08	0.27
Mora	2839.6	118	372	0.04	0.13
Falun	2054.0	207	549	0.10	0.27
Borlänge	584.0	179	236	0.31	0.40
Säter	582.2	67	241	0.12	0.41
Hedemora	831.3	97	331	0.12	0.40
Avesta	613.3	107	281	0.17	0.46
Ludvika	152.9	119	385	0.78	2.52
Gävleborgs län					
Ockelbo	1070.5	40	166	0.04	0.16
Hofors	410.2	48	87	0.12	0.21
Ovanåker	945.5	33	159	0.03	0.17
Nordanstig	1378.8	106	302	0.08	0.22
Ljusdal	5294.5	144	727	0.03	0.13
Gävle	1603.3	369	346	0.23	0.22
Sandviken	1165.9	159	285	0.14	0.24
Söderhamn	1062.2	201	347	0.19	0.33
Bollnäs	2764.0	176	567	0.06	0.21
Hudiksvall	2496.4	229	549	0.09	0.22
Västernorrlands län					
Ånge	3090.6	94	561	0.03	0.18
Timrå	776.6	114	235	0.15	0.30
Härnösand	1064.7	125	353	0.12	0.33
Sundsvall	3218.6	414	936	0.13	0.29
Kramfors	1702.9	180	693	0.11	0.41
Sollefteå	5496.2	140	1061	0.03	0.19
Örnsköldsvik	6421.6	280	1435	0.04	0.22
Jämtlands län					
Ragunda	2539.6	57	432	0.02	0.17
Bräcke	3444.4	71	620	0.02	0.18
Krokom	6202.8	107	870	0.02	0.14
Strömsund	10632.6	107	1302	0.01	0.12
Åre	7587.5	78	611	0.01	0.08
Berg	5426.1	77	574	0.01	0.11
Härjedalen	11776.3	122	789	0.01	0.07
Östersund	2247.2	186	617	0.08	0.27

District (1)	A (km^2) (2)	T (10^6km) (3)	L (km) (4)	$T/A=i$ (5)	$L/A=l$ (6)
Västerbottens län					
Nordmaling	1240.5	68	358	0.05	0.29
Vindeln	2648.3	54	525	0.02	0.20
Robertsfors	1298.0	79	421	0.06	0.32
Norsjö	3390.1	75	715	0.02	0.21
Storuman	7484.5	75	881	0.01	0.12
Sorsele	7493.9	26	484	0.003	0.06
Vännäs	1843.7	58	446	0.03	0.24
Vilhelmina	8120.4	66	886	0.01	0.11
Åsele	7117.6	63	978	0.01	0.14
Umeå	2313.4	264	754	0.11	0.33
Lycksele	5635.8	80	963	0.01	0.17
Skellefteå	6842.8	355	1899	0.05	0.28
Norrbottens län					
Arvidsjaur	5708.3	59	843	0.01	0.15
Arjeplog	12945.0	31	663	0.002	0.06
Jokkmokk	18143.6	55	737	0.003	0.04
Överkalix	2778.4	61	433	0.02	0.16
Kalix	1802.9	126	543	0.07	0.30
Övertorneå	2366.6	42	419	0.02	0.18
Pajala	7897.2	65	814	0.01	0.10
Gällivare	15995.8	124	855	0.01	0.06
Älvsbyn	1712.1	53	425	0.03	0.25
Luleå	1808.9	244	601	0.13	0.33
Piteå	3086.9	183	760	0.06	0.25
Boden	4295.1	112	698	0.03	0.16
Haparanda	918.5	45	232	0.05	0.25
Kiruna	19447.0	76	516	0.004	0.03

$$\int\int i \, \mathrm{d}x \, \mathrm{d}y = \sum T = 35\,361,$$

$$\int\int \sqrt{i} \, \mathrm{d}x \, \mathrm{d}y = \sum \sqrt{TA} = 94\,624,$$

$$\int\int l \, \mathrm{d}x \, \mathrm{d}y = \sum L = 100\,269,$$

$$\int\int i/l \, \mathrm{d}x \, \mathrm{d}y = \sum TA/L = 116\,384,$$

$$\int\int i^2/l \, \mathrm{d}x \, \mathrm{d}y = \sum T^2/L = 35\,068,$$

$$\gamma = \frac{\sum L}{\sum \sqrt{TA}} = 1.06.$$

Chapter 13

COST AND COMMUNICATION FOR DIFFERENT LOCATIONS

13.1. Inelastic demand

In Chapter 11 we tried to discover which of the special class of functions $f=2r^n/(2-n)$ was the best in the sense that *the total transportation cost for all commuters* was minimized. It could also be of interest to know how this total is distributed among individuals living in different locations. Even though a minimum total cost could be the best alternative for all, through an appropriate transfer policy, as far as purely *pecuniary* costs are considered the "cost" in terms of travelling time cannot be redistributed by transfer policy. The question is whether a more equal distribution of communication costs could be obtained at the expense of a slightly increased total cost.

To find out I have made another series of simulations to evaluate $C(\xi,\eta)$ at various distances $\rho=\sqrt{(\xi^2+\eta^2)}$ from the center. As before, a constant population was assumed, so that equal probabilities for all possible endpoints were used at the random point generation. I was evaluated from (54) or (55), depending on which one was relevant. The costs were added and the average for 10 000 in each simulation was computed. Finally, the cost estimate was obtained by multiplication with the area π, which represents the number of transports to all destinations.

The result is shown in the computer diagrams, figs. 13.1–13.5, and in table 13.1. The diagrams are identified by the different values of n, ranging from -0.4 to 1.2. In table 13.1 two more cases are represented. They are not pictured because the cylinders would have to be so much higher than the rest. The program COSTDIST is appended.

It can be seen that with positive n communication costs increase uniformly with the distance from the center, as would be expected, because those located on the periphery have the longest communication routes and also have to travel through a high transfer cost region to get anywhere. If instead n is negative there is another tendency superimposed upon this increase of cost with distance. At the center there is a spire, due to the fact that persons located there have to get across points of high transfer cost just to get anywhere. In these cases the best location is somewhere between the center and the periphery.

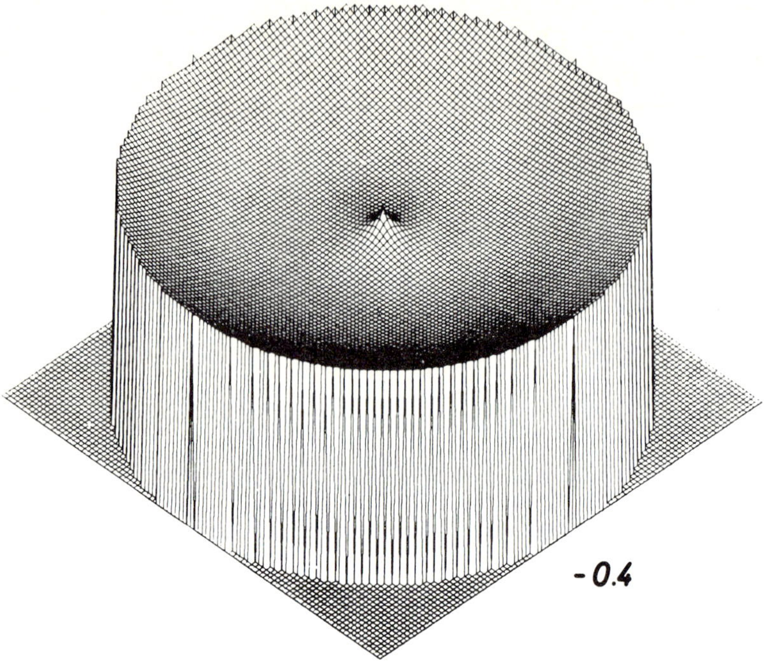

Figure 13.1. Cost and location, $n = -0.4$.

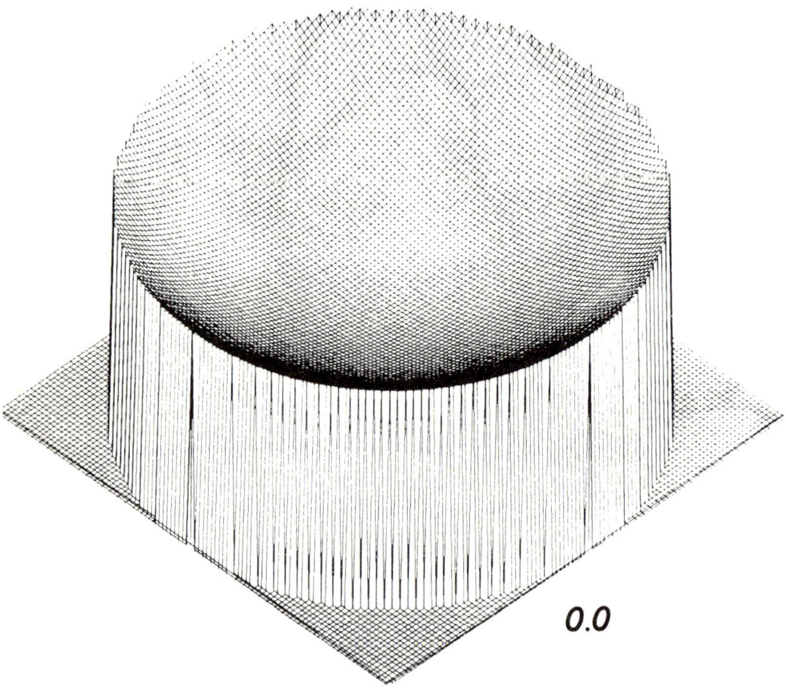

Figure 13.2. Cost and location, $n = 0.0$.

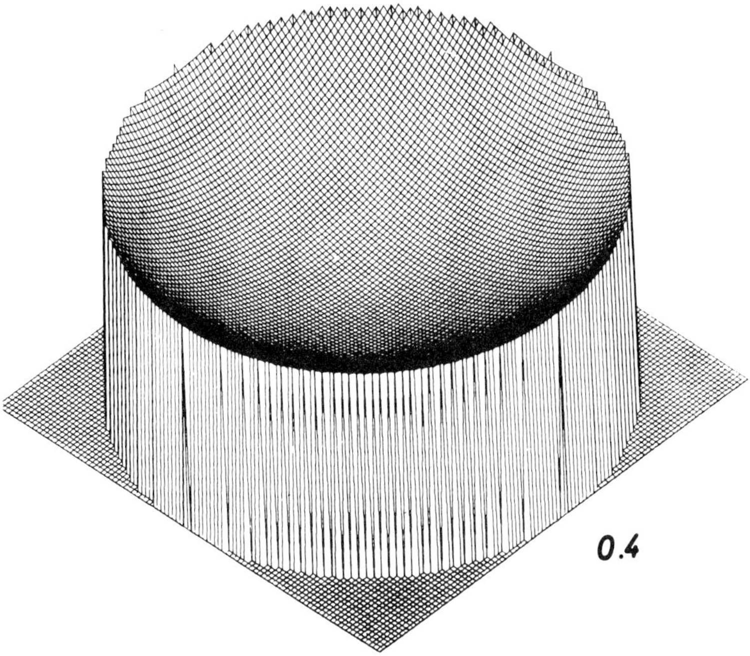

Figure 13.3. Cost and location, $n = 0.4$.

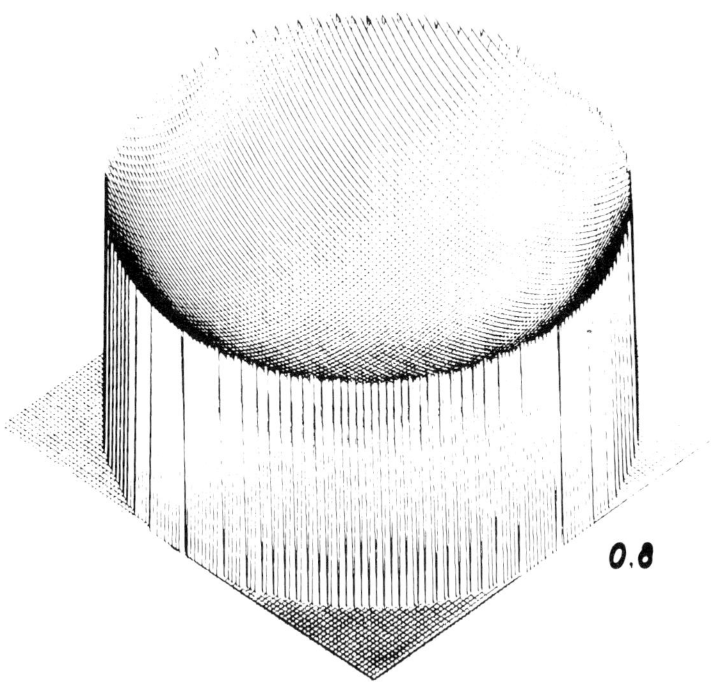

Figure 13.4. Cost and location, $n = 0.8$.

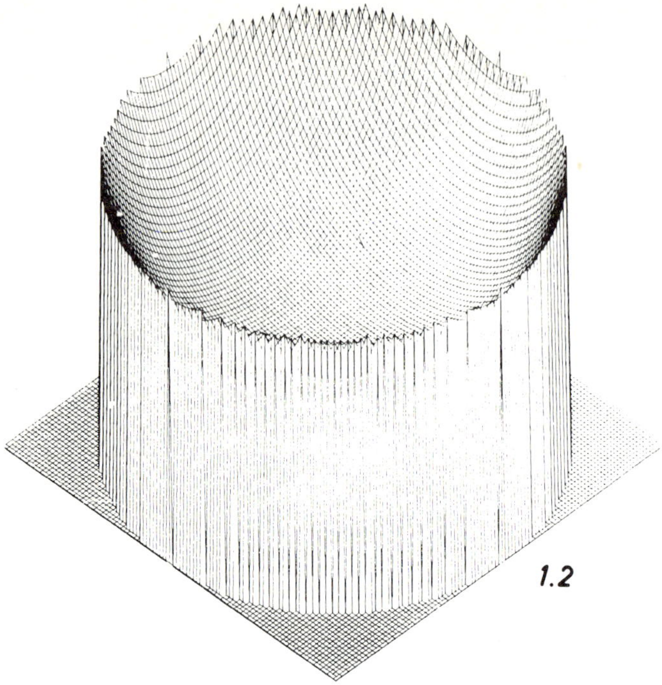

Figure 13.5. Cost and location, $n = 1.2$.

The most noteworthy thing, however, is that *the best degree of capital concentration* falls in a narrow interval between 0.40 and 0.80. *Hence, a social optimum is optimal for almost all individuals as well.*

13.2. Elastic demand

We can now ask whether this conclusion about the consensus does not wholly depend on the fact that transportation demand was taken as being independent of distance. As each location then has to communicate with every other location

Table 13.1
Commuting costs for different locations with various degrees of concentration of road capital.

ρ	Degree of capital concentration (n)						
	−0.80	−0.40	0.00	0.40	0.80	1.20	1.60
0.0	10.20	3.35	2.09	1.65	1.53	1.70	2.63
0.2	3.73	2.81	2.15	1.75	1.61	1.76	2.69
0.4	3.35	2.82	2.33	1.97	1.83	1.99	3.00
0.6	3.22	2.99	2.63	2.32	2.24	2.49	3.80
0.8	3.44	3.27	3.03	2.83	2.86	3.34	5.32
1.0	3.64	3.62	3.52	3.48	3.73	4.61	7.80

to the same extent, however distant it is, it is inavoidable that many transports from any origin have to pass over the center. Hence, it is natural that all more or less agree about the need for a concentration of road capital to the center.

However, we have seen that distance dependence tends to create isolated local communication areas, and then it is natural to expect the consensus to be destroyed because everybody would like a lot of road capital to be invested in his neighborhood where most of his communications take place.

Let us look somewhat more closely at the matter. Suppose we have a unitary elasticity of transportation demand with respect to cost. As we have already noticed, the criterion of minimum communication cost then runs into difficulties. The number of trips being reciprocal to the cost of each trip, the cost for communication between any two locations is the same, and hence the total communication cost is the same for all locations of origin. This, however, is irrelevant, because the individuals are certainly not indifferent to the cost of each trip. Even though their total transportation outlay is a given constant, the cheaper each communication is the more they can have. Thus, we are again led to the criterion of the number of communications instead of the criterion of communication cost.

We can easily obtain the number of communications by a simulation procedure, analogous to that of obtaining total cost. The only difference is that we now add reciprocals of transportation costs instead of the costs themselves. The generation of random points in the program COMDIST is exactly the same as in the program COSTDIST, and the cost is taken according to (54) or (55), whichever is relevant. The reciprocal is taken as a measure of the number of communications. One difference is that whereas in the preceding simulation we only simulated curved paths, adding a simple expression for the cost due to radial paths, we cannot now evaluate the cost due to the latter trips so readily by analytical means. So, all types of routes are simulated. As the number of runs is the same, the precision is a little diminished, but the tendency is clear nevertheless.

The class of transfer cost functions is again $f=2r^n/(2-n)$, the region is taken as the unit disk, and population density is supposed to be unitary. The results are shown in table 13.2. We see, in fact, that an exponent of -0.8 is best for people living at the periphery, whereas an exponent of 0.8 is best for those in the center (among the exponents simulated). Thus, as warranted, those living at the periphery want decentralization, and those in the center want centralization. But if we look at the last row, relevant for people living on the limiting circle of the unit disk, we see that the entries in fact vary very little. And this is true for all, except those living very centrally for which a high degree of capital concentration would be desirable. As a matter of fact, communication becomes infinite for people living in the center when the exponent approaches unity.

Apart from people living in the very center wanting to have heavily centralized road capital, we see that differences in communication possibilities (within the class of power functions discussed) are not important.

Table 13.2
Communication for different locations with various degrees of road capital concentration when transportation demand has unitary elasticity.

ρ	Degree of capital concentration (n)				
	−0.8	−0.4	0.0	0.4	0.8
0.0	1.0	3.2	6.3	11.7	33.9
0.2	3.3	4.6	6.3	8.7	11.3
0.4	4.2	5.0	5.9	7.0	7.8
0.6	4.9	5.2	5.5	5.9	5.9
0.8	5.5	5.9	5.3	5.2	4.8
1.0	4.7	4.4	4.1	3.8	3.3

13.3. A word on congestion

In Chapter 14 we find that the case of $n=0$, corresponding to fig. 13.2, can be optimal under pure congestion (i.e. when the detour-saving quality of road capital is neglected). This is true if land acquisition cost does not vary in the region. If it does vary, being highest in the center, then the optimum case may look like that shown in fig. 13.1. Disregarding congestion, fig. 13.3 represents the optimum, as we know from Chapter 11.

13.4. Program COSTDIST

```
100 DIM R(11),T(11),K(11),L(11)
110 P=4*ATN(1)
120 N=10000
130 M=0
140 MAT K=ZER
150 MAT L=ZER
160 PRINT "EXPONENT";
170 INPUT A
180 A=A+1
190 B=A/2
200 FOR I=1 TO 11
210 R(I)=(0.1*(I-1))↑A
220 NEXT I
230 IF A<1 THEN 270
240 FOR I=1 TO 11
250 L(I)=2*(A-1)*P*(R(I)+2/(A+2))/A/A/(3-A)
260 NEXT I
270 R=RND(0)↑B
280 V=P*RND(0)
290 IF A>1 THEN 310
```

```
300 V=A*V
310 C=COS(V)
320 FOR I=1 TO 11
330 T(I)=SQR(R(I)*R(I)+R*R-2*R(I)*R*C)
340 K(I)=K(I)+T(I)
350 NEXT I
360 M=M+1
370 IF M<N THEN 270
380 PRINT "DISTANCE COST",
390 FOR I=1 TO 11
400 K(I)=2*P*K(I)/N/A/(3-A)
410 IF A<1 THEN 430
420 K(I)=K(I)/A+L(I)
430 PRINT 0.1*(I-1);K(I)
440 NEXT I
450 END
```

13.5. Program COMDIST

```
100 P=4*ATN(1)
110 N=10000
120 PRINT "EXPONENT";
130 INPUT A
140 A=A+1
150 FOR I=1T06
160 R0=0.2*(I-1)
170 S=R0↑A
180 M=0
190 C=0
200 R=SQR(RND(0))↑A
210 V=P*A*RND(0)
220 IF V>P THEN 250
230 T=1/SQR(S*S+R*R-2*S*R*COS(V))
240 GO TO 260
250 T=1/(S+R)
260 C=C+T
270 M=M+1
280 IF M<N THEN 200
290 C=P*A*C*(3-A)/N/2
300 PRINT R0, C
310 NEXT I
320 END
```

Chapter 14

CONGESTION AND TOLLS

Congestion has been almost completely neglected in the discussion. We have given a reason for this, namely that the model concerned a large area, like a whole country, with few concentrated congestion nuclei. It was argued that for journeys of average length the path deviations necessary to avoid these congestion nuclei are so small as compared to the whole distance that the costs due to congestion as compared to total transportation costs are almost negligible. The result of this was that transfer cost could be regarded as independent of traffic. It only depended on road capital by the process of detour reduction specified in the hyperbola relation.

But congestion, at least in urban areas of limited size, is such an important factor that we cannot conclude this book without devoting some discussion to it. We must then make transfer cost dependent upon traffic. But to make transfer cost depend only on traffic is unsatisfactory. Rather, we need some measure of congestion like the ratio of traffic to capacity of carrying traffic. Hence, road capital twice enters the model: increasing it could save detours by increasing the density of the network and could increase the velocity of traffic flow by increasing the capacity of an existing network with given traffic.

We can distinguish between actual transfer *distance* (including detours) dependent on road capital as specified above, and transfer *time* (per unit distance actually traversed), dependent on the ratio of traffic to road capital. The use of this ratio is reasonable, because a denser network can do the same transportation work as a less dense one with fewer vechicles passing along each link per unit of time. Transfer cost could then be the product of transfer distance and transfer time.

We are not, however, going to pursue this generalized approach. It is, in fact, more illuminating to discuss a simplified pure case.

14.1. Optimum with constant congestion

As in the discussion above we disregrarded congestion and only considered the detour-saving quality of road capital, we now focus attention on congestion and only consider the capacity-increasing quality of road capital.

This would be quite realistic in a limited urban area where the density of the network of roads could, with sufficient realism, be taken as constant everywhere. From this case we obtain the result that road capital should be allocated in space so that it is proportionate to traffic. This is in contrast with the rule of proportionality to the square root already obtained.

We postulate a new transfer function, $g(i/l)$, to replace $f(l)$. A reasonable assumption would be to require that both g' and g'' be positive. Increasing congestion, i/l, then decreases the velocity of traffic flow and this effect increases in force so that flows may come to a total standstill with critical congestion. The reciprocal of velocity, transfer time, increases with congestion and goes to infinity at a critical limit. Wardrop (1966) has suggested the special relation $\sqrt{(1-i/l)}$ for velocity and also obtained some empirical evidence for it. Of course the unit of measurement for road capital must be in terms of the capacity for carrying traffic, and velocity would be measured in units so that it is unitary if there is no traffic at all. If we require conventional units, two constants can take care of the change needed. The reciprocal of Wardrop's function satisfies the requirements on the derivatives specified above.

Hence, transportation costs are now

$$\iint_S g(i/l)\, i\, \mathrm{d}x\, \mathrm{d}y. \tag{148}$$

These are to be minimized under the constraint of a given total road capital

$$\iint_S l\, \mathrm{d}x\, \mathrm{d}y = \text{constant}. \tag{149}$$

If we take the distribution of traffic as a given datum we can, exactly as in Chapter 11, obtain the condition

$$l(x,y) = \delta i(x,y), \tag{150}$$

where δ is a constant that can be calculated to equal the ratio $\iint l\, \mathrm{d}x\, \mathrm{d}y / \iint i\, \mathrm{d}x\, \mathrm{d}y$. As already mentioned, the proportionality to the square root is replaced by proportionality.

However, if this proportionality rule is satisfied then congestion and hence transfer time $g(i/l)$ is constant in the region. The consequence is that it can be factored out before the integration signs in (148), so that total cost equals the product of a constant transfer time and an integral that is simply total traffic.

Since we have taken the distribution of traffic as arbitrary, we must see how this product varies with different traffic distributions that satisfy the assumed need for transportation. First, we notice from (150) and the expression for δ as the ratio of total road capital to total traffic that $i/l = \iint i\, \mathrm{d}x\, \mathrm{d}y / \iint l\, \mathrm{d}x\, \mathrm{d}y$. Hence, the ratio of traffic to road capital at any point equals the ratio of total traffic to total road capital for the whole region. This implies that increasing total traffic – total road capital being constant due to assumption – increases congestion, and thus also transfer time at every point. Therefore the constant transfer time increases when total traffic increases and, for (148) to be minimal, we simply want minimum total traffic.

But we have already seen many times the choice of paths which minimizes total traffic, i.e. linear paths. We have already derived the relevant traffic distribution (for the unit disk with constant population density) in (81). Road capital should simply be distributed in proportion. We have been more fortunate in the present case than in Chapter 11 because we have actually found the optimum solution.

We now only need the additional information about whether it is an equilibrium that will be obtained by the actions of the individual transporters, or if congestion tolls are needed. The answer is at hand. With constant transfer time everywhere the transporters always choose straight line segments, because then the least time-consuming paths are the shortest ones. Hence, tolls turn out to be superfluous and we conclude that the presence of externalities does not always require tolls, if only road capital is adequately distributed in space. Admittedly, in reality road capital is more often not distributed optimally. Moreover, we have only considered the delaying effect of congestion on traffic flows. For the protection of health and property one might still want to redistribute traffic, or even cut its total below the minimum actually attained, so that the "need" for transportation is no longer satisfied.

14.2. Differential land acquisition costs

We can now ask whether the conclusion is not necessarily tied to the almost trivial case of a constant transfer cost and consequently linear paths. The triviality is obvious since tolls certainly cannot be required when congestion is equal everywhere in the region. If this is so, the introduction of a very realistic change in the present context, namely the assumption of varying land acquisition costs and building costs for roads, would invalidate the conclusion.

In the discussion in the previous chapters we could disregard differences in acquisition costs, for the same reason that we could abstract from congestion. This was that congestion, as well as especially high land value, is concentrated to relatively small nuclei in the vast region considered, so that avoiding these concentration nuclei would lead to almost unnoticeable deviations in transportation paths. The same could be said about putting a highway a few kilometers away from high land value nuclei, which would lead to an almost unnoticeable change in the distribution of road capital.

But at present we are no longer dealing with the vast region, but with a limited urban area. To introduce an assumption of land value decreasing with the distance from the town center seems fairly reasonable. We could then ask if we are not destroying the conclusion by introducing this change, so that after all congestion tolls turn out to be necessary. The answer is negative. The conclusion remains.

Assume that the acquisition cost for a piece of land for road-building is given by the function $c(x,y)$. This obviously changes the constraint (149) to

$$\iint_S cl\,\mathrm{d}x\,\mathrm{d}y = \text{constant}, \tag{151}$$

and condition (150) is no longer valid. As an outcome of minimizing (148) subject to the constraint (151) we have that $g'(i/l)(i/l)^2 = \delta c(x,y)$, where δ is again a constant. Since, however, c varies in the region, we can no longer conclude that i/l is constant. But, as c is a *given* function of the location, i.e. the space coordinates, we can *solve for* i/l as a function of c, and hence as a given function of the space coordinates. The same also holds true for transfer cost g which, being a function of congestion i/l, becomes a given function of the location.

Abbreviating all the substitutions by $f(x,y) = g(\phi(c(x,y)))$, where $i/l = \phi(c)$ is the solution of the first-order condition stated above, we end up minimizing

$$\iint_S f(x,y)\,i(x,y)\,\mathrm{d}x\,\mathrm{d}y \tag{20}$$

subject to the constraints of the model with respect to traffic. We can no longer factor out f before the integration signs, but note that we have ended up with our familiar expression (20). Even though we must interpret f in a different way than we did above, the fact that it is a given function remains. And the fact also remains that we have to minimize (20) with this given transfer cost function by choosing the best distribution of traffic to solve the need for transportation.

But, we have already seen that the necessary condition for (20) to be minimal, subject to $\nabla \cdot \boldsymbol{v} = -\bar{p}p$ and $\boldsymbol{v} \cdot \boldsymbol{n} = 0$, is that the paths are so chosen that

$$f\boldsymbol{v}/|\boldsymbol{v}| = \nabla\lambda. \tag{25}$$

It was also demonstrated that this agrees with the Euler equation for the individuals trying to find optimal paths by minimizing $I = \int f\,\mathrm{d}\tau$. *Hence, the individuals automatically choose socially optimal paths that minimize total transportation time (= cost). The conclusion holds even when congestion does vary in space dependent on varying land acquisition cost.* Therefore no tolls are needed when capital is properly allocated.

To find out something more about the equilibrium case with varying land acquisition cost functions $c(x,y)$, we use Wardrop's specification $g = 1/\sqrt{(1 - i/l)}$ that yields $g' = 0.5/(1 - i/l)^{3/2}$. This last expression can be substituted into the first-order condition $g'(i/l)(i/l)^2 = \delta c$ to yield $(i/l)^2/(1 - i/l)^{3/2} = 2\delta c(x,y)$.

For illustration, suppose that $g = ar^b$ so that we deal with the power functions with which we are familiar. Equating the two expressions for transfer cost we get $i/l = 1 - 1/(ar^b)^2$ which, substituted into the above equation, yields $2\delta c(r) = (ar^b)^3(1 - 1/(ar^b)^2)^2$. With b negative, as is the case when the center is congested, we see that the land value function is uniformly decreasing from an infinite value in the center. Supposing that a is unity, we can then represent the case where the cost of land falls to zero at the boundary of the region. Hence, if the cost of land falls uniformly from an infinite value at the center to zero on the boundary, then it is appropriate to let transfer velocity increase from unity at the boundary to zero in the center.

14.3. Temporal traffic variations

One interesting question is whether the conclusions must be altered if variations in traffic during the day between peak loads and excess capacity are introduced. The answer, of course, is positive under numerous circumstances. I am, however, going to specify a combination of conditions under which the conclusions still hold true.

Assume that the total demand for transportation is divided into two parts: one that must take place at certain moments of the day, and the rest that can be carried out equally well at any time. Assume, moreover, that the two fractions of trips of either category are the same for all pairs of points. Finally, assume that the trips that can be made at any time are carried out when they will take least time or, if several times of day are equivalent, that they are distributed among the various equivalent times with the same probabilities for all combinations of points. There may well be a preference for some of these trip duration-equivalent times. What is important is that any such preference is independent of the locations of origin and destination.

Let us begin by disregarding the trips that must be made at specified moments, and assume that all can equally well be made at any time of day, that they are undertaken when the trips are least time-consuming, and that if several times are equivalent then there is one given frequency distribution for the times of execution that is independent of origins and destinations.

It is obvious that we must let traffic, as well as the vector field representing traffic flows when an origin is given, be functions, not only of the space coordinates x,y, but of time t of the day as well. (Observe the change of notation, as t was formerly used for arc length.) Hence, we write $i(x,y,t)$ and $\mathbf{v}=(v_1(x,y,t),v_2(x,y,t))$.

Total communication cost is now

$$\int_0^{24}\int\int_S g(i/l)\,i\,\mathrm{d}x\,\mathrm{d}y\,\mathrm{d}t, \tag{152}$$

where we must remember that i and therefore g are functions of t. The fact that traffic depends on time is sufficient for transfer time to be dependent on time too, but what about l? In reality, of course, the capacity of a road does in general not vary throughout the day, but let us assume that it could be varied, so that roads are widened at rush hours and narrowed at other times. The reader can be assured that we are just making this assumption for derivational convenience. It will be removed again.

The constraint of given total road capital or capacity can therefore be written

$$\int_0^{24}\int\int_S l \,\mathrm{d}x\,\mathrm{d}y\,\mathrm{d}t = \text{constant}. \tag{153}$$

We can again carry out the minimization procedure of (152) subject to (153). The optimality condition is now

$$l(x,y,t) = \delta i(x,y,t). \tag{154}$$

Again the best solution is to let road capital be proportionate to traffic, at all locations as well as at all times, if this is possible. We can thus again factor out the constant transfer time $g(\delta)$ before the integration signs in (152) and obtain total communication cost as

$$g(\delta)\int_0^{24}\int\int_S i \,\mathrm{d}x\,\mathrm{d}y\,\mathrm{d}t. \tag{155}$$

But, integrating both members of (154) over all three independent variables we again obtain the constant δ as the ratio of total traffic to total capacity, where the totals are now taken by aggregation over time as well as over space. In view of the constraint (153), δ increases with the "grand total" of traffic, integrated over space and time, and hence (155) is obviously also minimal when this grand total of traffic is minimal.

Now, since there is a given total need for transportation, the grand total of traffic is obviously minimal when all the paths are straight lines. This is obvious, because the contribution to total traffic for each trip is independent of the contributions of the other trips. This contribution is smallest when the trip in question follows a straight-line path. From this it also follows that the contribution is the same, whenever the trip is made. Hence, the only thing that matters for the minimum of the grand total of traffic is the shape of the routes, not when the transports are undertaken. The same has been seen to hold true for total communication cost (=time) according to (155).

Summarizing the results, we have seen that with a given traffic distribution in space and time, communication cost is minimal when capacity is always and everywhere proportionate to traffic. Then transfer cost is constant in space and time. This constant depends only on total traffic, aggregated over space and time, and increases with it. Total cost then turns out to be the product of this total traffic and the constant transfer cost, being minimal when total traffic is minimal. Total traffic, on the other hand, turns out to depend only on the form of the paths and not on the times when the trips are made. When the paths are minimal total traffic is minimal.

Hence, total transportation cost is minimal when all paths are straight lines, but the trips can be distributed in time in any way. All such temporal distributions are equivalent. Now they are, of course, equivalent only provided that capacity is adjusted to proportionality to traffic everywhere and always. But, returning to reality, capacity can be distributed in different ways in space, but it must stay constant in time. Therefore only one of the equivalent optimal solutions is possible, namely when trips are equally distributed over time. Then traffic is distributed in space in a way that is unchanged over time, and the same, temporally constant, capacity distribution can be proportionate to the traffic distribution always and at every location.

The optimum is therefore found. Paths should be linear and trips equally spaced in time. But will this situation actually occur without tolls? To answer this, we first observe that linear paths are chosen if transfer cost is constant. The latter is in fact constant if trips are equally spaced in time and capacity is appropriately allocated in space. The remaining problem is then whether trips really are equally spaced. The fact that they are is assured by the two assumptions that each transporter chooses the time when the transport is quickest, and that if several times are equivalent preference is independent of the locations of origin and destination. These assumptions also ensure that the traffic distribution in space is the same at any time. The conclusion is that the optimum, in fact, is automatically attained.

To complete the picture, we must take into consideration the trips that must be made at certain times. Since they are assumed to be proportionate to the total trip distribution, they require the same spatial distribution of road capital. They may lead to peaks above the constant traffic load, but if they do it follows from the assumptions that no traffic of the other category will interfere with it.

Chapter 15

CONCLUSIONS AND CONJECTURES

In this final chapter we attempt to summarize the conclusions and point out some of the remaining loose ends. The latter are numerous, because we have tried in each chapter to take the problem as far as possible despite the fact that later on we should have to use such restrictive assumptions that much of the material developed in the book was not used at all in the final discussions on equilibrium and optimum.

The first main result is the demonstration that a measure of traffic could be defined with conservation properties. This was accomplished by transforming expressions of total transportation costs by partial integration in Chapter 2 and by Gauss's divergence theorem in Chapter 3. Apart from providing for conservation of traffic, the measure had the desirable property that total transportation costs could be obtained by taking the product of traffic and the cost of transfer for each location and aggregating over locations. This discussion was taken up again in Chapter 8, where it was shown that the measure of traffic could be obtained by a process of counting weighted "cordon crossings", which could be used in simulation by Monte Carlo methods. This implied that the unweighted counting of cordon crossings, employed by Angel and Hyman (1972a, 1972b, 1976), would not lead to a correct measure of traffic with the desirable conservation properties.

There is one obvious point at which the formal derivation should be strengthened, namely by taking into explicit consideration more singular points and whole curve segments, in addition to the singularities at the origin of each vector field. The cases treated in fig. 4.2 already call for this correction.

The main conclusion from Chapter 4 is that in the absence of external effects (i.e. congestion) total transportation costs for a given transfer cost function were minimized if each individual transporter had complete freedom to choose the cheapest route without any interference from the authorities. When we abstract from congestion the result is intuitively so obvious that it seems trivial. Its importance, however, was demonstrated in Chapter 14, where the given transfer cost received a new meaning, namely as the congestion-dependent transfer time that results from an optimal allocation of road capital to local traffic distribution and varying land acquisition costs. There it is shown that, in contrast to what is generally asserted by economists, tolls are not needed to make individuals behave in such a way that total transportation costs are minimized. If road capital is optimally spaced then the decreasing transfer velocity in congested areas, in fact, acts as the proper price or "signal". This makes tolls a "second-best" solution in cases of inoptimal allocations of roads which, admittedly, may be most frequently the case in reality.

Much of the material in Chapter 4 is well known from other studies. Optimal paths or routes were derived first by variational methods as solution curves to Euler equations in the original plane region discussed. After this it was shown that in certain cases a complex analytic function may be employed to transform the original region to another plane region where the optimal paths are mapped onto straight-line segments (or onto pairs of radials). From Wardrop's discussion (1969) we know that if the function has circular symmetry this works with transfer cost functions that belong to the power variety only.

Following Warntz (1967) and Angel and Hyman (1976), we also considered the possibility of mapping the original plane onto a curved surface on which distance equals transportation cost and the optimal paths are geodesics (i.e. the straightest curves that exist on a curved surface as well as the shortest connections between specified endpoints).

The Angel and Hyman construction, leading to surfaces of revolution, is however of limited applicability. Therefore, we employed Bonnet's fundamental theorem of surfaces to demonstrate that for any isotropic transportation problem there is in fact a local cost surface. Isotropy, i.e. independence of transfer cost on the direction of passage, was shown to lead to a cost surface that is conformal to the original plane, and which in turn led to a definite metric tensor. A definite metric tensor, however, is all that is needed to ensure the local existence of a cost surface. However, it must be emphasized that the existence of a global surface is a completely different matter. The difficulties of parameterizing a whole surface by the same set of regular coordinate functions are well known. Further research is necessary to produce more information on this point.

When dealing with the solutions to Euler equations in the original plane we demonstrate, by the Jacobi and Legendre conditions, that provided the transfer cost function is circularly symmetric the solutions to the Euler equations actually provide strong minima. As the solution curves in this case can be obtained by the quadrature of a simple integral, we know that minimum cost arcs exist. This is fortunate, because it is seldom clearly the case with variational problems. As has already been mentioned, total costs are minimal when each transport takes its minimum cost route with a given transfer cost function. Hence, given a transfer cost function with circular symmetry we know that a minimum total transportation cost always exists and – in association with it – a set of optimal paths between all pairs of locations as well as a distribution of traffic.

Chapters 5, 7 and 8 were devoted to the derivation and computation of traffic distributions. This, in fact, was the most difficult part of the whole matter. We have seen that although we solved the Euler equations to find optimal paths, we still have to solve a partial differential equation for the partial (directional) intensity of traffic and to perform a subsequent double integration to obtain total (local) traffic intensity. Alternatively, we found it possible to evaluate a fourfold integral directly.

This last method lends itself to simulation and it was also used for this purpose. As, with circularly symmetric transfer cost, the paths too may be calculated by numerical integration, the weights needed can be obtained. In principle, but only in principle, it is possible to construct simulation programs for the calculation of traffic with any transfer cost displaying circular symmetry. Unfortunately, the programs I have used for cases where we know the shape of the paths turn out to be complicated. Certainly, a lot more computational efficiency could be obtained by designing better programs.

Since the derivation of traffic distributions is the principal stumbling block preventing us from actually deriving equilibrium traffic distributions, a development of computations could prove most valuable.

Apart from this some general information about the connections between traffic distributions, the shapes of solution paths and the transfer cost function was obtained. Hence, we saw that linear paths and uniform population density within a disk-shaped region leads to a considerable concentration of traffic to the central parts of the region. Through exemplification it was conjectured that paths that are convex to the center imply an even greater degree of centralization of traffic and that the paths must have a certain degree of concavity to the center if traffic is to be constant or even increase towards the peripheral parts of the region. On the other hand, we were able to associate exclusively convex paths with monotonically increasing transfer cost and exclusively concave paths with monotonically decreasing transfer cost. If the former connection, i.e. between the shape of the traffic distribution and the shape of the paths, could be formally proved we could dispose of a whole qualitative theory that would enable us to draw formally safe conclusions about the character of equilibrium traffic distributions.

One of the main purposes of the book was to make more explicit the concept of transfer cost, its determinants and the exact form of the dependence on these determinants. In Chapter 14 we interpreted transfer cost as a reciprocal of velocity in a congested urban area. As such it should simply depend on a measure of congestion, for which we took the ratio of traffic to road capital. It was argued that the influence of road capital is twofold: besides reducing the load of traffic on roads an increase of road capital was seen to reduce the necessity to make detours and hence to make network distances on average more equal to Euclidean distances.

We decided to treat the two influences of road capital, that of reducing the load of traffic and that of eliminating detours, as two separate pure cases. The focus of interest in Chapter 14 was a congested urban area of limited size and there we concentrated on treating congestion and differential land acquisition costs, assuming the necessity for detour-taking to be constant for the region studied. This meant that the network of roads was taken as a quadratic grid of equal density, whereas the capacity varied with the number of lanes on the roads. In the rest of the book we concentrated on another pure case, namely a vast country with only scattered nuclei of congestion and high land acquisition costs, so that we could disregard these factors, because they can be avoided when a route is chosen or when a road is built. Instead, we concentrated on the detour-saving property of increased road capital. It should be stressed that the difference in time and space devoted to the two cases does not imply any judgement on their relative importance. The simple fact is that, when we have developed all the concepts and methods in connection with the exploration of one case, the treatment of the second can be made very brief because all the tools needed are already at hand.

The reader may ask why I did not combine the two cases in one more general case. The answer is that whereas this generalization is straightforward and the conclusions easily conjectured to be somewhere in between those for the two cases treated, the combined model would turn out to be much more clumsy than either of the two pure cases.

The detour-reducing effect, with the characteristic of decreasing returns from successive increments of road capital, was formalized in a hyperbola relation between transfer cost (=actual network distance per unit of Euclidean distance) and road capital, with one constant term and one term reciprocal to road capital.

We derived this relation formally from a network model in the limit when the network was made so dense that the size of the mesh vanished. We were able to demonstrate that the hyperbola could actually be derived for a regular network where the mesh unit was an equilateral triangle. The choice of this network type was motivated by the fact that it was the most efficient of the regular networks (triangular, quadratic and hexagonal), the efficiency being evaluated in terms of the accessibility to the network and the inherent necessity of taking detours as measured by Mosler's concepts (1976b). We also demonstrated that the derivation held true if the network was mapped conformally. This, in fact, made the derivation applicable to a wide variety of network density distributions.

However, we also saw that an approximation must be introduced that made the limiting continuous transportation model isotropic. Even if the approximation did not seem serious it would be valuable to explore the possibilities of keeping the exact anisotropy in the model, possibly by a Minkowski-like measure of distance.

With this relation between transfer cost and road capital, developed in Chapter 10, we were able to deal with the remaining partial optimization problem. Which allocation of road capital minimized total transportation costs with a given traffic distribution? This optimization was easy to carry out and resulted in a rule that road capital should be proportionate to the square root of traffic.

Hence, we could be sure that total transportation costs, being equal to a surface integral of the product of transfer cost and traffic, in fact possessed a minimum if we kept the distribution of road capital constant and let traffic vary and, conversely, if we kept the distribution of traffic constant and let road capital vary. Owing to the independence of the constraints for the two partial minimizations, we concluded that there should in fact be an equilibrium-optimum in the model. This was the case with a region that was a unit disk with a constant population.

To discover the degree of road capital concentration for such a simple region we carried out a sequence of simulations with a special class of transfer cost functions. We concluded that equilibrium-optimum road capital and traffic were concentrated to the central parts and that the optimal paths were all convex. We also carried out another simulation procedure to find out whether there were strongly opposed interests among people inhabiting locations of varying centrality. Surprisingly, there was a high degree of consensus. The degree of capital concentration that minimized total transportation costs minimized transportation costs for almost anybody.

To complement these simulations, which were made for a totally cost-insensitive transportation demand, we also simulated cases with a transportation demand that displayed a short-run sensitivity to cost. We concluded that with moderate elasticity of demand (less than unity), the criterion of minimum total cost still worked in a reasonable way and actually yielded the same conclusions as the alternative criterion of the maximum number of communications.

All these simulations were, however, made for a very special class of transfer cost functions that were even to some extent in contradiction to our general assumptions. Therefore, a very important task for further development would be to get a better idea of the equilibrium distribution.

This could be done either by the construction of extensive simulation programs or by treating the whole problem analytically. I have, for example, not sufficiently explored the possibilities of discussing the whole model in terms of something that happens on a curved surface. This could, in fact, prove to be helpful for the computation of traffic distributions.

Because the total cost when road capital is distributed in proportion to the square root of traffic is a simple expression in the surface integrals of traffic and of the square root of traffic, an analytic derivation of the tradeoff between these two integrals, when different ways of satisfying the need for transportation are considered, would be most desirable.

Generalizations of the model that might give rise to interesting conclusions include changing the shape of the region from the solid circle to a solid ellipse.

In Chapter 12 we gave some empirical evidence for the model. The square root rule was tested for a subdivision of Sweden into 275 local districts for which data on transportation work and on road networks were available (with reference to 1973). The result was that the data actually fitted the square root rule surprisingly well, but the evidence from one country for one year is certainly much too limited to provide any general conclusions.

There are also a number of other possible empirical tests that I have not yet attempted. One is to use a deformed map of a region, such as that shown in Chapter 12, for the computation of distances for a sample of pairs of locations. Such a set of distances could then be compared with actual network distances.

Another possibility would be to compute average traffic on circular segments by simulation, again using the deformed map and actual population densities. Such a simulated traffic distribution could be compared to the actual one.

If the model could be regarded as having sufficient empirical support, which it does not have as yet, then it could be used for very simple benefit–cost calculations, as indicated in Chapter 12.

Chapter 16

MATHEMATICAL APPENDICES

16.1. Introduction

The following mathematical appendices are written as brief summaries of the fields of mathematics that are of most importance in this book. They are written for an imagined economist with a general knowledge of calculus in several variables and ordinary differential equations. No such material is presented in the appendices. Instead, the purpose is to survey the fields of vector analysis, complex variables, differential geometry and the calculus of variations, which are usually unknown to general economists and are regarded as the specific tools of physicists and engineers. Regional problems, however, display such similarity to physical phenomena that those instruments greatly facilitate the analysis.

Since the reader is supposed to have a knowledge of general mathematics, the appendices are not very detailed. The reader should therefore, if necessary, consult some of the books listed at the end of each appendix. I have only mentioned titles that recommended themselves by their lucidity.

If the reader wishes to know more of the fundamentals of mathematics, there are two excellent works on advanced calculus, namely *Advanced Calculus*, by M. R. Spiegel (1974) and especially volume 2 of *Introduction to Calculus and Analysis* by R. Courant and F. John (1974). They also contain much of the material surveyed in the mathematical appendices, in addition to the fundamentals of calculus in several variables.

There are, of course, a great number of excellent "modern" works that are more axiomatic and topological in character. The choice of suggested reading is a reflection of personal tastes. As a user of mathematics I find it more yielding to read old-fashioned books that concentrate on geometric and physical applications, rather than on the logical rigor of definitions. Spivak has expressed most strikingly that in modern mathematics the difficulties lie in understanding the fundamental concepts while proofs of theorems become almost trivial. In the older mathematics the situation is reversed. Personally, I feel that the older method of exposition is more useful for a person looking for possible applications. And since in this case the material dates back to the eighteenth and nineteenth centuries, there can be no harm in reading old-fashioned expositions.

16.2. A short guide to literature on tools and methods not surveyed in the appendices

As readings about graph theory we suggest Berge and Ghouila-Houri (1962) and Berge (1970). A more application-directed presentation may be found in Deo (1974). The more special topic of flows in networks or graphs and the computational methods connected with it are treated in Ford and Fulkerson (1962) and in Iri (1969).

Literature on the geometry of tesellations or periodic tilings includes the works by Coxeter (1961) and by Fejes Tóth (1969). These books are more centered on the extremum properties of regular tesellations than is usual in the relevant literature that has a strong connection to the very abstract group theory.

The only reference on econometrics that we used is Johnston (1972).

Finally, we list some relevant books on physics. Goldstein (1950) and Spiegel (1967) give authoritative surveys of classical mechanics. The chapters on particle kinematics in particular are relevant for us as analogies to the optimum path problem. In connection with the entropy model of interaction some reference is made to the statistical mechanics of multiparticle systems. The work by Huang (1963) contains all the material needed.

APPENDIX A: ELEMENTARY CONCEPTS AND THEOREMS FROM VECTOR ANALYSIS

The aim of this Appendix is to give a brief introduction to vector analysis. Actually, the problems treated by vector analysis are not different from those treated by ordinary analysis where several functions of several variables are involved. Its great benefit is in the economy of notation, where expressions that are extremely complicated when expressed in terms of partial derivatives become simple as the operators of vector analysis are introduced. Vector analysis was developed as a tool for mechanics and since physical processes take place in three-dimensional space (at least in classical, nonrelativistic mechanics) it concerns three-component vectors. As our problems are two-dimensional the material needed is much simpler than the general material in vector analysis. We also perpetrate some abuses, by regarding some vectors as scalar quantities when they only contain one nonzero component, pointing out perpendicularly from the two-dimensional plane where everything interesting happens, and when only the magnitude of this component is of interest. In Appendix D, however, we return to the correct interpretations.

We will be very brief with vector algebra, since in contrast to vector analysis it is familiar to most economists.

A.1. Dot and cross products

We only record the definitions of *dot and cross products* of two vectors. Let $\boldsymbol{a}=(a_1,a_2)$ and $\boldsymbol{b}=(b_1,b_2)$ be any two vectors. Then we define the dot product as

$$\boldsymbol{a}\cdot\boldsymbol{b}=a_1b_1+a_2b_2=ab\cos\theta,$$

where $a=|\boldsymbol{a}|=\sqrt{(a_1^2+a_2^2)}$ and $b=|\boldsymbol{b}|=\sqrt{(b_1^2+b_2^2)}$ denote the *lengths, norms, or moduli* of the vectors, and where θ is the angle between the directions of the vectors. Likewise, we define the cross product as

$$\boldsymbol{a}\times\boldsymbol{b}=a_1b_2-a_2b_1=ab\sin\theta.$$

Strictly speaking this is incorrect because the cross product of two vectors is itself a vector directed perpendicularly to the plane spanned by the two vectors multiplied. But as the cross products at present are always normal to the plane, we can neglect the direction and regard the cross product as a scalar without risk of misunderstanding. Before leaving these definitions, we must also say something about the geometric meaning of the concepts. Hence, the dot product is the product of the length of one of the vectors and the length of the projection of the other one in the direction of the former. Because the expression is symmetric, this holds true regardless of which vector we project onto which. The cross product, on the other hand, is the area of a parallelogram spanned by the two vectors. All this is obvious from the trigonometric versions of the formulae.

From this it is also obvious that a dot product is zero if the vectors are perpendicular, and that the cross product is zero if they are parallel.

We can now pass to the definition of the differential operators in vector analysis.

A.2. Gradient

The first is the *gradient*. It operates on a scalar function $f(x,y)$ and is denoted grad$f$ or ∇f. The result is

$$\nabla f = (f_x, f_y),$$

which is simply a vector of the partial derivatives. The unit vector in the direction of ∇f, i.e. $\nabla f / |\nabla f|$, where we have $|\nabla f| = \sqrt{(f_x^2 + f_y^2)}$, points in the direction of the steepest increase of f in the x,y-plane.

A.3. Divergence

The next operator on the list is the *divergence*. It operates on a vector function of a vector variable, denoted $\boldsymbol{v} = (v_1(x,y), v_2(x,y))$. The result obtained by taking a divergence is written div$\boldsymbol{v}$ or $\nabla \cdot \boldsymbol{v}$, and is defined

$$\nabla \cdot \boldsymbol{v} = \partial v_1 / \partial x + \partial v_2 / \partial y.$$

This is a scalar quantity. As a gradient turns a scalar function into a vector function, or *field*, so the divergence does the reverse, i.e. turns a vector function into a scalar function.

The two operators may be combined, so that we first take a gradient of a scalar function, and then take the divergence. The result is denoted Δf or $\nabla^2 f = \nabla \cdot (\nabla f)$ and in terms of partial derivatives yields

$$\nabla^2 f = f_{xx} + f_{yy}.$$

This combined operator is called the *Laplacian*.

A.4. Curl

We need only one more operator, namely the *curl* or *rotation*, written curl $\boldsymbol{v}$, or rot $\boldsymbol{v}$, or $\nabla \times \boldsymbol{v}$. As can be seen, it operates on a vector function and, in a strict sense, it results in a vector function. But again the direction is always normal to the plane where everything interesting happens, and thus we deal with it as if it resulted in a scalar function. In terms of partial derivatives

$$\nabla \times \boldsymbol{v} = \partial v_2/\partial x - \partial v_1/\partial y,$$

where a direction right out from the plane is implicitly understood.

As we applied the divergence to the gradient we can also apply the curl to a gradient. The result of this, however, has no name like the Laplacian, since it is identically zero. This follows from the definitions, namely

$$\nabla \times (\nabla f) = f_{yx} - f_{xy} \equiv 0.$$

A vector field obtained as the gradient field of some function, often called the *potential function* because of its association with Newtonian mechanics, has zero curl or rotation and is called "irrotational". If the divergence of the field is zero, then it is called "solenoidal". When both divergence and curl are zero then, because the zero curl implies that the field is a gradient field, the Laplacian is zero. Putting it equal to zero leads to the Laplacian differential equation, which has many important applications in physics. The closest analogy to our use of vector analysis is its application to hydrodynamics, where the vector field $\boldsymbol{v}$ represents the flow of particles of a liquid, the components being velocity components. The unit vector $\boldsymbol{v}/|\boldsymbol{v}|$ then gives the direction of the flow and $|\boldsymbol{v}| = \surd(v_1^2 + v_2^2)$ is the speed. The divergence $\nabla \cdot \boldsymbol{v}$ has the important interpretation that it shows how many particles are added to the flow (if the divergence is positive and there is a "source") or withdrawn (if the divergence is negative and there is a "sink") in each point. The curl has a similar interpretation. It shows to what extent a small needle, floating on the liquid, turns around its axis as it is floating away with the stream.

A.5. Two identities

Before passing on to the most important part of this appendix, namely Gauss's theorem, some identities are briefly recorded that the reader may check, now that the definitions have been given, namely

$$\nabla \cdot (f\boldsymbol{v}) = \nabla f \cdot \boldsymbol{v} + f \nabla \cdot \boldsymbol{v}$$

and

$$\nabla \times (f\boldsymbol{v}) = \nabla f \times \boldsymbol{v} + f \nabla \times \boldsymbol{v}.$$

The verification is straightforward in terms of ordinary calculus. We make good use of these relations in the text.

A.6. Green's, Stokes's and Gauss's theorems

We can now pass on to Gauss's theorem which is probably the mathematical theorem that has had the most application in the text. Actually Gauss's theorem is one of several related theorems, like Stokes's and Green's theorems. Both the number of related theorems and the multiplicity of proofs offered demonstrate their importance. The theorem is usually not proved by methods from vector analysis, and hence its place here may seem odd, but this appendix is the natural place for it because it has important applications just in vector analysis. The theorems mentioned usually concern three-dimensional space. In two dimensions the matter is much simplified so that we are able to give a simple outline of a proof.

A.7. Line integrals

Consider a *line integral*

$$\int_C P(x,y)\,\mathrm{d}x + Q(x,y)\,\mathrm{d}y$$

interpreted as an ordinary integral along a path C, given by the parametric functions $x(t), y(t)$. If these are substituted into the integrand together with $\mathrm{d}x = x'(t)\,\mathrm{d}t$ and $\mathrm{d}y = y'(t)\,\mathrm{d}t$, then we obviously end up with an ordinary integral in the parameter t on some interval. This is the interpretation of a line integral written in the above, somewhat unfamiliar manner, when one does not want to emphasize the particular parameterization of the curve C.

Now, assume that the curve C is a simple, closed curve without self-intersections enclosing a definite region of the plane. To begin with, the region is supposed to be convex. Denote the region enclosed by C as R. When the region is convex we can define its boundaries by two curves, $y_1(x)$ and $y_2(x)$, defined on the interval (a,b), and such that $y_2(x) > y_1(x)$, except at a and b where they are equal. Observe that if we give C a certain *orientation*, so that we define a positive direction for getting around it, conventionally so that the interior R is on the left, then this results in a positive direction when x increases along $y_1(x)$, but a negative direction when x increases along $y_2(x)$ (see fig. A.1).

We now want to evaluate the double integral $\int\int \partial P/\partial y\,\mathrm{d}x\,\mathrm{d}y$ on R. First, we obviously get $\int\int \partial P/\partial y\,\mathrm{d}x\,\mathrm{d}y$ equal to the expression $\int(P(x, y_2(x)) - P(x, y_1(x)))\,\mathrm{d}x$, where the integration is on the interval (a,b). This, however, equals the line integral $-\int P\,\mathrm{d}x$ along C, when it is taken into consideration that integrating with respect to x along $y_2(x)$ is in the negative direction.

In the same manner, we can regard the boundary C as being made by two curves, $x_1(y)$ and $x_2(y)$, defined on the interval (c,d), and such that $x_2(y) > x_1(y)$, except at the endpoints where equality holds. In an analogous manner we can then show that $\int\int \partial Q/\partial x\,\mathrm{d}x\,\mathrm{d}y$ on R equals $\int Q\,\mathrm{d}y$ along C. Collecting the results we have

$$\int\int_R (\partial Q/\partial x - \partial P/\partial y)\,\mathrm{d}x\,\mathrm{d}y = \int_C P\,\mathrm{d}x + Q\,\mathrm{d}y.$$

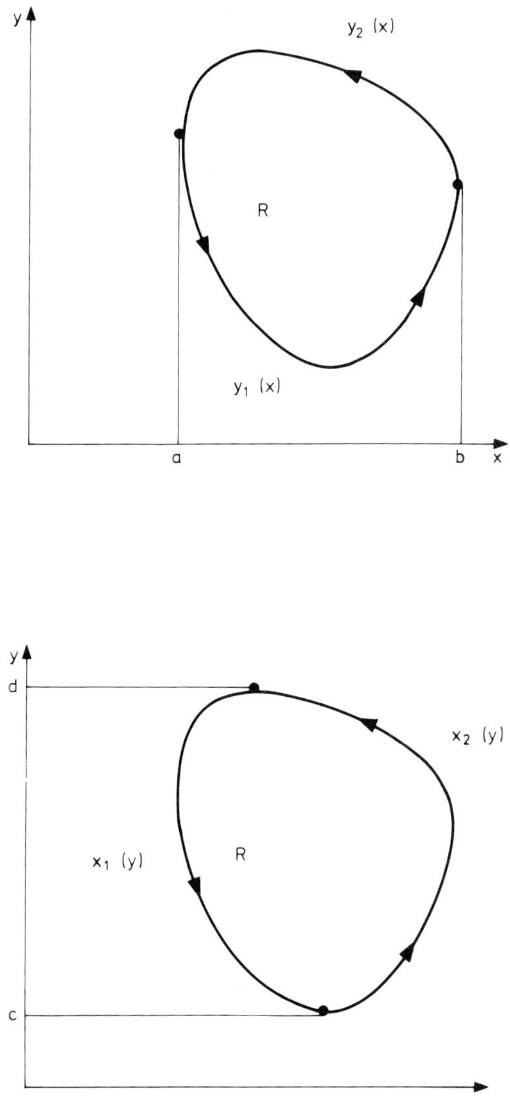

Figure A.1

This is usually called *Green's theorem in the plane*. It is not difficult to generalize it to nonconvex regions, or regions that have "holes", by dividing the region into convex subregions, applying the theorem, and observing that the line integrals along the inner boundaries that separate the subregions vanish as they are taken twice and in opposite directions.

In terms of vector analysis this important theorem has two interpretations. First, put $P = v_1$ and $Q = v_2$, and define a tangent vector to the boundary curve,

$\boldsymbol{t}=(\mathrm{d}x/\mathrm{d}s, \mathrm{d}y/\mathrm{d}s)$. From this we observe that $\partial Q/\partial x - \partial P/\partial y = \nabla \times \boldsymbol{v}$, whereas we have $P\,\mathrm{d}x + Q\,\mathrm{d}y = \boldsymbol{v}\cdot\boldsymbol{t}\,\mathrm{d}s$. Hence,

$$\iint_R \nabla \times \boldsymbol{v}\,\mathrm{d}x\,\mathrm{d}y = \int_C \boldsymbol{v}\cdot\boldsymbol{t}\,\mathrm{d}s.$$

This variant usually goes under the name of *Stokes's theorem*. It shows that the double integral of a curl of any vector field over a region equals the line integral of the tangential component of the vector field along the boundary. This latter integral gives the circulation along the boundary. If we shrink the region together to a point we understand that the curl is a measure of circulation or rotation in the point.

Another way of using Green's theorem is to put $P = -v_2$ and $Q = v_1$, and to define the outward normal to the boundary curve, $\boldsymbol{n}=(\mathrm{d}y/\mathrm{d}s, -\mathrm{d}x/\mathrm{d}s)$. By this, $\partial Q/\partial x - \partial P/\partial y = \nabla \cdot \boldsymbol{v}$, and in addition $P\,\mathrm{d}x + Q\,\mathrm{d}y = \boldsymbol{v}\cdot\boldsymbol{n}\,\mathrm{d}s$. Green's theorem transforms to

$$\iint_R \nabla \cdot \boldsymbol{v}\,\mathrm{d}x\,\mathrm{d}y = \int_C \boldsymbol{v}\cdot\boldsymbol{n}\,\mathrm{d}s$$

which, finally, is Gauss's divergence theorem. *Gauss's theorem* shows that the double integral of the divergence of any vector field equals the line integral of the outward normal component of the field taken along the boundary. This yields an interpretation of the divergence when we shrink the region together to a point, since it then reduces to the net outflow from that point. These interpretations of Stokes's and Gauss's theorems render the interpretations of the curl and the divergence, already referred to above.

A.8. Independence of path

We add a final comment on these theorems. In the right-hand member of Stokes's formula there is a line integral along a closed boundary curve. We can now divide the boundary into two pieces by two arbitrarily chosen points on it so that the line integral along the closed curve actually equals the difference between two line integrals both taken from one of the points to the other, but along different paths. The vanishing of the line integral along the closed curve is then equivalent to the independence of path for the line integral, which only depends on the endpoints. When does the line integral along C vanish identically? The answer is obvious: when the curl of the vector field in the left-hand member is zero everywhere inside C. Hence, a line integral is independent of the integration path when the curl of the vector field is identically zero. But as we have seen, this means that the vector field is a gradient field of some potential function, i.e. $\boldsymbol{v} = \nabla f$. Then $\boldsymbol{v}\cdot\boldsymbol{t}\,\mathrm{d}s = f_x\,\mathrm{d}x + f_y\,\mathrm{d}y = \mathrm{d}f$ is said to be an exact differential, and any line integral is independent of path.

A.9. Literature to Appendix A

There are two very readable text-books on vector analysis, Marsden and Tromba (1976) and Spiegel (1959). These books are purely mathematical. More about the applications to physical problems can be found in the two volumes by Weatherburn (1943a, b) and in the very compact book by Rutherford (1948). A modern, more strict, approach using differential forms is Spivak (1965), another is Rudin (1976).

APPENDIX B: FUNDAMENTALS OF VARIATIONAL CALCULUS

In this appendix fundamental concepts and theorems from variational calculus will be given. Proofs are not presented, except for the Euler equation which is the fundamental instrument in this branch of mathematics. Economists are usually familiar with dynamic programming (developed mainly by Bellman) and optimal control theory (developed mainly by Pontryagin), which are modern instruments. It should therefore be emphasized that the calculus of variations was designed to handle problems of the same type as those handled by the more modern methods and that, even though it was developed in the eighteenth and nineteenth centuries, it contains most of the material revived in the more recent approaches. Admittedly certain problems where it is natural to specify some policy control variables are best formulated as problems of optimal control. On the other hand, the problems with which we are dealing could not be so easily treated by the modern instruments, since they are designed for optimization in time, i.e. with one independent variable, whereas we presently deal with two independent variables, namely the space coordinates. Hence, the classical methods turn out to be more adequate.

The following outline relies on the books by Elsgolc (1961) and by Fox (1950).

B.1. Functionals

The fundamental problem in variational calculus is to find an extremum of a *functional*, i.e. a rule that associates real numbers not with values of variables but with shapes of functions on certain intervals. The methods are designed in particular to handle functionals obtained as definite integrals of functions involving the unknown functions as well as their derivatives. These unknown functions whose forms are sought may be one or several, and the derivatives involved may be up to any order. They may depend on one or several arguments, which means that the functionals may be multiple integrals. There may be constraints, either involving the unknown functions and their derivatives for any combination of argument values or expressed in terms of integrals of the same form as the functional whose minimum or maximum is sought. Problems involving constraints of the latter type are usually called "isoperimetric" after the classical problem of finding the largest area enclosed by a boundary of given length.

We now specify formally the types of problems that are encountered in this book. The simplest problem is to find an extremum for the functional $\int F(x,y,y')\mathrm{d}x$ on an interval (x_0,x_1) by choosing an appropriate form of the function $y(x)$ when the endpoints are fixed as $y_0=y(x_0)$ and $y_1=y(x_1)$. As in the case of ordinary optimizations, the admitted domain of variation for the unknown must be specified. Since the unknowns in this case are functions we cannot make the specification as simple as an admitted interval. Rather, a class of admissible functions must be specified. We will return to this when the distinction between weak and strong variations is made.

Specifically, the problems of this simplest type take the form $F(x,y,y')\mathrm{d}x = f(x,y)\sqrt{(1+y'^2)}\mathrm{d}x$, where the expression $\sqrt{(1+y'^2)}\mathrm{d}x=\mathrm{d}s=\sqrt{(1+x'^2)}\mathrm{d}y$ denotes arc length along the curve $y(x)$ or $x(y)$, whichever representation is chosen. We see that in this form both representations are equivalent. Using a word borrowed from the field of optics, such variational problems, where F is a function of x,y multiplied by arc length, are called "isotropic".

In some cases we even specify $f(x,y)$ as $f(r)$, where $r=\sqrt{(x^2+y^2)}$. In such cases it is appropriate to introduce polar coordinates by $x=r\cos\omega$ and $y=r\sin\omega$, so that arc length is $\mathrm{d}s=\sqrt{(r^2+r'^2)}\mathrm{d}\omega=\sqrt{(1+r^2\omega'^2)}\mathrm{d}r$. Then the unknown function is imagined as given in polar coordinates as $r(\omega)$ or $\omega(r)$. All these representations of arc length are equivalent, because $(\mathrm{d}x)^2+(\mathrm{d}y)^2\equiv(\mathrm{d}r)^2+(r\,\mathrm{d}\omega)^2$ by definition of the polar coordinates.

A more complicated case encountered is to minimize the integral

$$\int\int F(v_1,v_2,\partial v_1/\partial x,\partial v_2/\partial y,x,y)\,\mathrm{d}x\,\mathrm{d}y$$

subject to

$$\Phi(v_1,v_2,\partial v_1/\partial x,\partial v_2/\partial y,x,y)=0.$$

In particular, we have $F=f(x,y)\sqrt{(v_1^2+v_2^2)}$ and $\Phi=\partial v_1/\partial x+\partial v_2/\partial y+g(x,y)$. All this can be written much more compactly by using vector notations. Putting $\boldsymbol{v}=(v_1,v_2)$, we have $F=f(x,y)|\boldsymbol{v}|$ and $\Phi=\nabla\cdot\boldsymbol{v}+g(x,y)$. Two functions are sought, $v_1(x,y)$ and $v_2(x,y)$, or a vector field $\boldsymbol{v}$ such that the integral is minimized.

B.2. The Euler equation

As mentioned above, the *Euler equation* is the most fundamental analytical tool in this field. We derive it for the simplest problem, i.e. to find an extremum of the integral $\int F(x,y,y')\mathrm{d}x$ on some interval (x_0,x_1). To this end, imagine that a function $y(x)$, solving the problem, has already been found. Then let $\eta(x)$ be any function, such that $\eta(x_0)=\eta(x_1)=0$. Then $y(x)+\alpha\eta(x)$ satisfies the conditions on the endpoints as $y(x)$ does. This is true for any α.

Now, assume $\eta(x)$ to be a given, but arbitrary, function. Consequently, the functional, after substitution of $y(x)+\alpha\eta(x)$ for y and of $y'(x)+\alpha\eta'(x)$ for y', becomes an ordinary function of α. If then $y(x)$ is the solution, this function of α must have an extremum with respect to variations of α when $\alpha=0$, because only then does the function substituted agree with the assumed solution. This must hold true whatever the shape of the arbitrary function $\eta(x)$. The problem now has the form of maximizing or minimizing a function, and hence we simply have to put the derivative with respect to α equal to zero, and require this to hold true when α is zero itself. Hence,

$$\int_{x_0}^{x_1} (F_y \eta + F_{y'} \eta')\, \mathrm{d}x = 0.$$

We now partially integrate the second term of the parenthesis so that it equals

$$\int_{x_0}^{x_1} F_{y'} \eta' \, \mathrm{d}x = F_{y'} \eta \,\Big|_{x_0}^{x_1} - \int \mathrm{d}F_{y'}/\mathrm{d}x \, \eta \, \mathrm{d}x.$$

However, $\eta(x_0)=\eta(x_1)=0$, and therefore only the second term remains. Substituting this we get

$$\int_{x_0}^{x_1} (F_y - \mathrm{d}F_{y'}/\mathrm{d}x)\eta \, \mathrm{d}x = 0$$

where, it must be remembered, $\mathrm{d}F_{y'}/\mathrm{d}x$ is a total derivative in which the dependence of all the arguments of F on x via $y(x)$ must be taken into consideration.

The last integral must be zero *whatever form* $\eta(x)$ *has*, provided it satisfies the boundary conditions. Now, if the parenthesis were nonzero anywhere, then it would have to be nonzero in some interval, since we suppose F to have continuous partial derivatives up to the third order. It would then be easy to design a function $\eta(x)$ that is nonzero and has a constant sign on this interval, but is otherwise zero. Then the integral could not be zero. Thus, the parenthesis must be zero everywhere. This result is often called "the fundamental lemma of variational calculus". As a consequence

$$F_y - \mathrm{d}F_{y'}/\mathrm{d}x = 0$$

must hold true everywhere, and this second-order differential equation is the *Euler equation*. For special cases it takes simpler forms. When y does not appear as an argument in F, we have $F_{y'}=\text{constant}$, and if F does not explicitly depend on x we have $F - F_{y'} y' = \text{constant}$.

B.3. Weak and strong extrema

Before passing to sufficient conditions we have to say something about *weak and strong variations and extremals*. If the extremal is the best solution within a class of similar functions, such that these similar functions come close in slope to the extremal whenever they come close in distance, then we speak of a weak variation of the extremal and of itself as a weak extremal. The variations

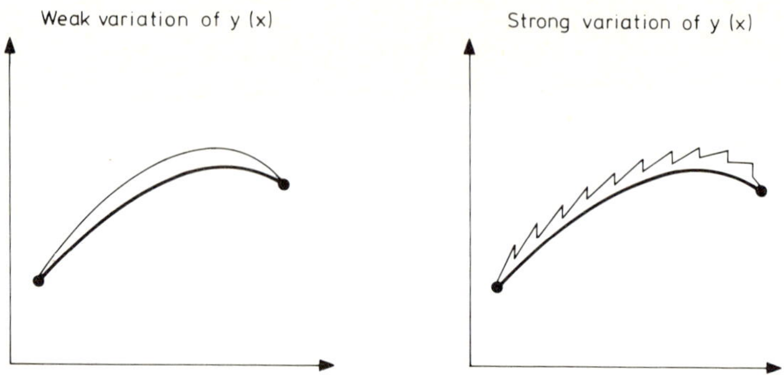

Figure B.1

introduced by adding $\alpha\eta(x)$ to the supposed extremal necessarily represent a weak variety, because $\alpha\eta'(x)\to 0$ together with $\alpha\eta(x)\to 0$ when $\alpha\to 0$.

But, if we put the formula $y(x)+\alpha\eta(x)$ in the more general form $\eta(x,\alpha)$, where $\eta(x,0)=y(x)$ and $\eta(x_0,\alpha)=y_0$, $\eta(x_1,\alpha)=y_1$ for *all* α, then $\partial\eta/\partial x$ need not approach y', even if η approaches y with α going to zero. If this is so we are dealing with strong variations.

The Euler equation, proved for weak variations, can be proved to be necessary also with strong variations, but the proof is more complicated. Weak and strong variations are illustrated in fig. B.1.

It should be emphasized that a strong extremum is, of course, better to find than a weak one, because it is the best solution within a broader class of candidates.

B.4. The Jacobi condition

The sufficiency conditions will be stated without proof. We must, however, stress that in the calculus of variations there is nothing corresponding to the theorem in ordinary calculus that states that any continuous function defined on a compact interval takes on a maximum and minimum. A variational problem may well lack a solution, although it may seem well posed.

One of the sufficient conditions is the *Jacobi test for conjugate points*. It checks that the solution curves to a Euler equation, radiating out from one fixed point of origin, constitute a so-called *central field* of curves which do not have any intersections except at the point of origin. If there were such intersections, then obviously there would be several (even neighboring) solution curves between two given points. This is illustrated in fig. B.2. The Jacobi condition eliminates this possibility.

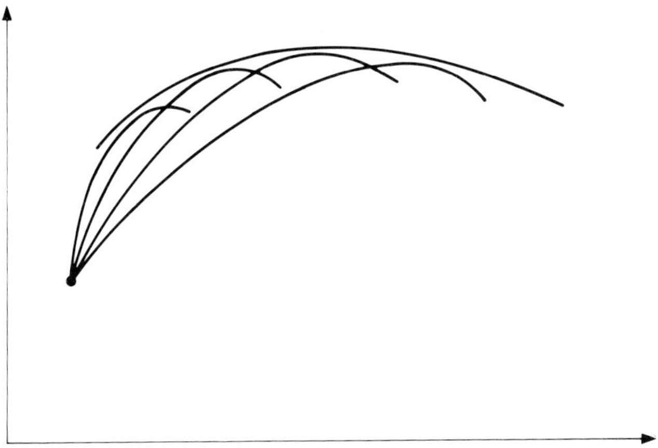

Figure B.2

There are several ways of checking the Jacobi condition. Since the Euler equation is of second order, its solution generally involves two arbitrary constants which make it possible under certain circumstances to join any two points in the x,y-plane. If we fix one point then, as already said, we obtain a central field of radiating curves. This eliminates one of the two constants. If now the curves of this field have intersections then they must be bent into each other so that they have a common envelope. The envelope is obtained, as always, by putting the derivative with respect to the remaining constant equal to zero, and using the resulting equation together with the one defining the field to eliminate the remaining constant. If we only consider the solution curves between the common starting point and the envelope, then obviously a unique central field results.

Points on the envelope are called *conjugate points* or *kinetic foci*, a term from mechanics. Then the Jacobi condition amounts to a check that there are no conjugate points to the starting point on the path. If there is no envelope then of course the central field can extend as far as one desires and no conjugate points occur.

Sometimes the best way to proceed is to construct the field and to derive the envelope, if it exists. But often this is not possible. A suitable method is then to check *Jacobi's differential equation* which is expressed in terms of the partial derivatives of F, with the solution substituted.

In the equation there also appears a variable u which in fact is the derivative of y with respect to the remaining constant. Hence, u is zero on the envelope, and it is also zero at the common starting point. Jacobi's equation reads

$$(F_{yy} - \mathrm{d}F_{yy'}/\mathrm{d}x)u - \mathrm{d}(F_{y'y'}u')/\mathrm{d}x = 0.$$

This is a new second-order differential equation that can with luck be solved. To check the Jacobi condition we then have to check that there are no zeros for u on the paths, except at the origin.

It is unlikely in practice that one would be able to solve first the Euler equation and then the Jacobi equation, both of which are of the second order. The Jacobi equation can, however, also be used for qualitative analysis. If, for example, F does not depend on y explicitly when, as we saw, $F_{y'}$ = constant is the particularly simple Euler equation, then the first part of the Jacobi equation is identically zero and only $\mathrm{d}(F_{y'y'}u')\mathrm{d}x=0$ remains. This integrates to $F_{y'y'}u'=$ constant which, if $F_{y'y'}$ has a constant sign and u is not identically zero along the curve, implies that u' has a constant sign and hence that u only has one zero. This case is particularly nice because $F_{y'y'}$ also plays an important role in the *Legendre condition* that will be dealt with presently. Fortunately, the case is relevant in the applications made here.

B.5. The Legendre condition

When we have a solution curve to a Euler equation that can be embedded in a central field so that the Jacobi conditions are satisfied, then we only need to make one more check for sufficiency. The most general way is to construct the *Weierstrass' E-function* but, as in our applications the integrand is assumed to be smooth, the *Legendre conditions* can be applied and we prefer to state them alone because of their simplicity. They state that a solution to a Euler equation is an extremum if $F_{y'y'}$ has a constant sign along the curve (with zeros admitted). The extremal yields a minimum if the derivative is positive and a maximum if it is negative. This condition, as well as the Euler equation, dates back to the eighteenth century and it was believed that it was a sufficient condition for a solution to a Euler equation to provide an extremum. Later work, however, demonstrated that this is only true if the Jacobi condition is satisfied as well.

To be more precise, the Legendre condition makes it possible to distinguish between weak and strong extrema. Written with all the arguments we have $F_{y'y'}(x,y,y')$ as the test expression. If the constancy of sign holds only for values of y' close to their actual values along the path, then we have a weak extremum; if it holds for whatever value that is substituted for y', then the extremum is strong. (For completeness we state that the constancy of sign for weak variations is required in a strong sense, without admitting zeros, whereas zeros are admitted for strong extrema. In the text we actually only deal with strong minima.)

B.6. Illustration: the isotropic case

As an illustration of the different conditions, we could use the isotropic case where the integrand is a function of the coordinates, x,y, multiplied by an arc length element. Moreover, assume that the function has circular symmetry so that we minimize $\int f(r)\sqrt{(1+r^2\omega'^2)}\,dr$, using polar coordinates. The Euler equation is then of the form $F_{\omega'}=c$, which gives $fr^2\omega'=c\sqrt{(1+r^2\omega'^2)}$. From this we can solve explicitly $r\omega'=1/\sqrt{((fr/c)^2-1)}$, so that by integration ω can be computed as a function of r.

As the integrand in the functional to be minimized does not explicitly contain ω as an argument, the Jacobi equation reduces to $F_{\omega'\omega'}u'=\text{constant}$, where we have $F_{\omega'\omega'}=fr^2/(1+r^2\omega'^2)^{3/2}$. If f is positive and u is not identically zero, then u' has a constant sign, and u can only have one zero. Hence, there are no conjugate points and the Jacobi conditions are fulfilled. At the same time, the non-negativity of $F_{\omega'\omega'}$, regardless of the value substituted for ω', fulfills the Legendre condition for strong minima. We conclude that a solution obtained from the Euler equation is indeed the extremal sought.

B.7. Transversality

As mentioned above, we assume that the F-function that is integrated to obtain the functional possesses continuous partial derivatives up to the third order. This is understandable since the third-order derivatives occur in the Jacobi equation. On the other hand, the solution $y(x)$ sought need not have such regularity. It must, of course, be continuous, because we want a solution curve made in one piece, but already its tangent may have sudden changes, so that the solution curve possesses a number of kinks. In order that such kinked curves may be extremals there are additional conditions to be satisfied at the kinks, called *transversality conditions*. They simply require that at the discontinuity for y' the expressions $F_{y'}$ and $F-F_{y'}y'$ be invariant with respect to which of the two different values of y' are substituted.

We will give one example of this. Take again the minimization of $\int f(r)\sqrt{(1+r^2\omega'^2)}\,dr$, where the Euler equation was $fr^2\omega'=c\sqrt{(1+r^2\omega'^2)}$. For $c=0$, $\omega'=0$ is an obvious solution. We can then ask whether a solution curve made up of two radial straight lines, $\omega=\omega_0$ and $\omega=\omega_1$, joined at the origin, could be an extremal. If $\omega_1\neq\omega_0$, the tangent has a discontinuity at the origin. We have to check the transversality conditions there. For both radials, $\omega'=0$, and in the origin $r=0$. Hence, $F_{\omega'}=fr^2\omega'/\sqrt{(1+r^2\omega'^2)}=0$ for both radials and $F-F_{\omega'}\omega'=f/\sqrt{(1+r^2\omega'^2)}=f(0)$ for both as well. We conclude that a pair of radials is a possible solution.

B.8. Extrema for double integrals

We close this appendix by stating the Euler equation for the more complicated double integral case. We do not give a proof because it is much too complicated for reproduction. Nor do we discuss any sufficient conditions. Our objective was to minimize

$$\iint F(v_1, v_2, \partial v_1/\partial x, \partial v_2/\partial y, x, y)\, \mathrm{d}x\, \mathrm{d}y,$$

subject to

$$\Phi(v_1, v_2, \partial v_1/\partial x, \partial v_2/\partial y, x, y) = 0.$$

To solve this problem we first state that it may be transformed into a problem of unconstrained minimization of the integral $\iint (F+\lambda\Phi)\,\mathrm{d}x\,\mathrm{d}y$, where a Lagrange function $\lambda(x,y)$ is introduced. This is done exactly as in ordinary constrained optimizations. When the constraint itself is given in integral form, i.e. when we deal with an isoperimetric problem, then λ is a constant. When the constraint is not in integral form, as at present, then λ is a function of the coordinates x,y.

For convenience of expression we now put $G=F+\lambda\Phi$ and $p_1=\partial v_1/\partial x$, $p_2=\partial v_2/\partial y$. Hence, we can write the integrand in the unconstrained problem as $G(v_1, v_2, p_1, p_2, x, y)$. As a general rule there is one Euler equation for each function sought. In our case there are two equations. Their form is greatly simplified by the fact that the derivatives of v_1 with respect to y and of v_2 with respect to x are missing:

$$\partial G/\partial v_1 - \partial G_{p_1}/\partial x = 0,$$

$$\partial G/\partial v_2 - \partial G_{p_2}/\partial y = 0.$$

When $F=f(x,y)\sqrt{(v_1^2+v_2^2)}$ and $\Phi = p_1 + p_2 + g(x,y)$ then

$$f v_1/\sqrt{(v_1^2+v_2^2)} - \partial\lambda/\partial x = 0,$$

$$f v_2/\sqrt{(v_1^2+v_2^2)} - \partial\lambda/\partial y = 0.$$

Put in the simple language of vector analysis, the solution to the problem of minimizing $\iint f|\boldsymbol{v}|\,\mathrm{d}x\,\mathrm{d}y$ subject to the constraint $\nabla\cdot\boldsymbol{v}+g(x,y)=0$ is

$$f\boldsymbol{v}/|\boldsymbol{v}| = \nabla\lambda.$$

This, if anything, illustrates the neatness of the language of vector analysis.

B.9. Literature to Appendix B

The literature on the calculus of variations is relatively old. Two works that we have followed closely in the exposition are Elsgolc (1961) and Fox (1950). More extensive works are Bolza (1904), volume 1 of Courant and Hilbert (1953), Forsyth (1927) and Kneser (1900). All this literature is mainly concerned with single integrals. Double integrals are touched on, but the specific case with a constraint is only to be found in Coral (1931–32). More recently the calculus of variations has taken on the shape of optimal control theory which is a familiar tool for economists. Remnants of variational calculus can also be found in modern works on functional analysis as applications of the otherwise very abstract theory. A reference is Wloka (1971).

APPENDIX C: ELEMENTARY COMPLEX CALCULUS

The need for this appendix is that although economists often use calculus with functions of one or several real variables, they usually are unfamiliar with complex calculus.

A complex function of a complex variable, $w = f(z)$, is a rule that associates complex numbers to complex numbers. Complex numbers can be represented as two-dimensional vectors, or points in the complex plane. This is emphasized by the expressions $z = x + iy$ and $w = u + iv$ where, by definition, $i = \sqrt{(-1)}$. We can thus regard z as a vector with real components (x,y) and w as a vector with components (u,v). Then all the usual arithmetical rules for vectors can be employed. But it is often simpler to take the representations $z = x + iy$, $w = u + iv$, and use the rules of scalar arithmetics along with the rule $i^2 = -1$, treating terms involving i as something that must be kept apart from terms that do not involve i.

Then all the rules of algebra are straightforward. For example, $z^2 = (x + iy)(x + iy) = (x^2 - y^2) + i2xy$, where we have simply multiplied term by term and used the fact that $i^2 = -1$. This is also an example of a complex function $w = z^2$, where the components of w are $u = x^2 - y^2$ and $v = 2xy$. Therefore, since a complex function relates two-dimensional vectors to two-dimensional vectors, it could seem to be equivalent to a pair of functions of two arguments, i.e. $w = f(z)$ could be replaced by $u(x,y)$ and $v(x,y)$, and one might then ask what is special about complex analysis as compared to real analysis.

C.1. Cauchy–Riemann equations

The answer is given when we come to differentiability. If we want to talk of analysis or calculus it must be possible to differentiate the functions at least once. Now, differentiability for a complex function is by no means equivalent to the existence of partial derivatives for the functions $u(x,y)$ and $v(x,y)$. To show this let us take the derivative of $f(z)$ in the usual manner by keeping y constant and letting two values of x get close together. Then

$$f'(z) = \lim_{\Delta x \to 0} \left\{ \frac{u(x + \Delta x, y) - u(x,y)}{\Delta x} + i \frac{v(x + \Delta x, y) - v(x,y)}{\Delta x} \right\},$$

which is

$$f'(z) = \partial u / \partial x + i \, \partial v / \partial x.$$

On the other hand, we could just as well keep x constant and let two values of y get close together. Then we would have

$$f'(z) = \lim_{\Delta y \to 0} \left\{ \frac{u(x,y+\Delta y) - u(x,y)}{\mathrm{i}\Delta y} + \mathrm{i}\frac{v(x,y+\Delta y) - v(x,y)}{\mathrm{i}\Delta y} \right\}.$$

But, $1/\mathrm{i} = \mathrm{i}/\mathrm{i}^2 = -\mathrm{i}$, by virtue of $\mathrm{i}^2 = -1$, and thus

$$f'(z) = \partial v/\partial y - \mathrm{i}\,\partial u/\partial y.$$

If the limit exists it must be the same no matter how $\Delta z = \Delta x + \mathrm{i}\Delta y$ goes to zero, through Δx or $\mathrm{i}\Delta y$. The two expressions for $f'(z)$ must be equal. This equality must be interpreted so that the real and the imaginary parts are equal, or

$$\partial u/\partial x = \partial v/\partial y \quad \text{and} \quad \partial v/\partial x = -\partial u/\partial y.$$

These are the *Cauchy–Riemann differential equations*. Differentiability of the component functions is not sufficient for differentiability of the complex function. In addition these differential equations must be satisfied by the component functions.

Obviously, differentiability is a much stronger requirement in complex analysis than in real analysis. The benefit of this, however, is an enormous wealth of results: any such function can be differentiated as many times as desired; it can be expanded in Taylor series; and its value can be determined by Cauchy's integral formula inside any closed area if it is known on the boundary, as can all of its derivatives. Such differentiable functions are called *analytic*.

If we differentiate the Cauchy–Riemann equations with respect to x and y respectively and add we get

$$\partial^2 u/\partial x^2 + \partial^2 u/\partial y^2 = 0.$$

Doing the same reversely we likewise get

$$\partial^2 v/\partial x^2 + \partial^2 v/\partial y^2 = 0.$$

This demonstrates that the component functions are *harmonic*, which means that they satisfy just these equations, called *Laplace's differential equations*. In appendix A we encountered the Laplacian operator, which was the divergence of a gradient of some function. The Laplace equation is obtained simply by putting the Laplacian equal to zero.

We will not go into the important field of complex analysis any further. We simply state that all the elementary functions, e.g. power, root, exponential, logarithmic, sine and cosine, to mention a few, may be extended from the real functions to analytic complex function, and that *all the familiar rules for differentiating and integrating them hold true.*

C.2. Conformal mapping

As a conclusion of this appendix we look at the mapping property of a complex function. Because it maps points in the plane on other points in the plane, we can see how geometrical objects like curves or angles or areas are affected. For analytic functions that have a nonvanishing derivative, i.e. $|f'(z)| \neq 0$, which implies that the real and imaginary parts of the derivative are not zero at the same time, the term *conformal mapping* is used.

For conformal maps important theorems hold true. So, *the angles between intersecting curves are not altered, and the linear magnification factor is the same in all directions*. This linear magnification factor is just $|f'(z)|$. Areas, on the other hand, are changed by the square of the magnification factor. The modulus of the derivative is calculated as for any vector. So,

$$\begin{aligned}|f'(z)| &= \sqrt{((\partial u/\partial x)^2 + (\partial v/\partial x)^2)} \\ &= \sqrt{((\partial u/\partial y)^2 + (\partial v/\partial y)^2)},\end{aligned}$$

depending on which expression for the derivative we take. In any case, by virtue of the Cauchy–Riemann equations, they are equal. The square, i.e. the areal magnification factor, is

$$|f'(z)|^2 = \begin{vmatrix} \partial u/\partial x & \partial v/\partial x \\ \partial u/\partial y & \partial v/\partial y \end{vmatrix} = \partial(u,v)/\partial(x,y),$$

which is the Jacobian of the mapping. From what has been said a conformal mapping maps geometrical figures on congruent figures, whatever the shape, and the areal distortion is given by the Jacobian. Of course, we are speaking only of geometrical figures of infinitesimal size since all the properties discussed are local.

C.3. Example: the quadratic

Let us give an example of a complex analytic function. We already encountered one at the beginning of this appendix, namely $w = z^2$. The discussion is facilitated if we use the polar and exponential notations for complex numbers. If we introduce polar coordinates, $x = r\cos\omega$ and $y = r\sin\omega$, we can write $z = r(\cos\omega + \mathrm{i}\sin\omega)$. But in elementary calculus it is demonstrated, by expanding the trigonometric and exponential functions in Taylor series and using $\mathrm{i}^2 = -1$ whenever it appears, that the identity

$$\mathrm{e}^{\mathrm{i}\omega} \equiv (\cos\omega + \mathrm{i}\sin\omega)$$

holds true. Hence, we also have the exponential representation of a complex number, $z = r\mathrm{e}^{\mathrm{i}\omega}$.

From this $z^2 = r^2\mathrm{e}^{\mathrm{i}2\omega}$ which, by using the identity above once more, equals $r^2\cos 2\omega + \mathrm{i}r^2\sin 2\omega$. Hence, the coordinates for w are $u = r^2\cos 2\omega$ and $v = r^2\sin 2\omega$. The verbal interpretation is that angles are doubled by the function at the same time as radii vectors are squared. By this rule the image point of any point can easily be found. This also works for any power function z^n which equals $r^n\cos n\omega + \mathrm{i}r^n\sin n\omega$.

Returning to the special case z^2, we note that it equals $(x^2-y^2)+i2xy$. Checking the Cauchy–Riemann equations for $u=(x^2-y^2)$ and $v=2xy$ we get $u_x=v_y=2x$ and $v_x=-u_y=2y$. Thus, the conditions for conformality are fulfilled. We can also calculate the derivative as $u_x+iv_x=v_y-iu_y=2x+i2y$. As expected, from the fact that the familiar rules for differentiation and integration hold true, the derivative of z^2 is $2z$. As to the mapping properties we note that the mapping represented by the quadratic complex function is conformal, except for one point, namely the origin where the derivative is zero. There is thus a singularity at the origin, so that any region on which the function is used as a mapping must exclude the origin.

Otherwise we can see that the coordinate curves for $u=x^2-y^2$ constant and for $v=2xy$ constant represent families of hyperbolas that intersect at right angles, as do the corresponding families of vertical and horizontal straight lines in the w-plane.

It can also be seen that if the coordinate curves for constant u,v are drawn with regular intervals that are not too large, then small approximately quadratic figures are mapped onto quadrats, with an areal magnification factor of $|2z|^2=4r^2$. Thus, the areas of the image quadrats are all equal, whereas the areas of the original "quadrats" decrease with the distance from the origin. This can be seen in fig. C.1.

The reader may note several interesting features in the figure. The fact that approximately quadratic figures are mapped on quadrats is true only for areas that do not enclose the origin. For the innermost figure in the z-plane, as well as for the whole diagram, it holds that an approximately "octagonal" figure is mapped on a quadratic one. The similarity of mapped figures therefore only holds true for such that do not enclose the singular point at the origin.

Another thing to observe is that the eight edges in the z-plane are mapped on four edges in the w-plane, and that the total of 49 subregions in the former are mapped on $(49-1)/2+1=25$ subregions in the latter. This halving of edges and regions is understandable if we consider that the upper half of the "octagon" *alone* is mapped on the whole quadrat, and that the same is true for the lower half. Hence, the quadrat is actually covered twice by the mapping. The eastern edge of the "octagon" is mapped on the eastern edge of the quadrat, but so is the western edge of the "octagon". Equally, both the shaded areas in the "octagon" are mapped onto the same shaded area in the quadrat.

If we look at the inverse mapping to the one illustrated, namely the square root mapping $z=\sqrt{w}$, then obviously the mapping is not single-valued, since there are several image points in the "octagon" corresponding to each point in the quadrat. To visualize such double coverings a so-called *Riemann surface* can be introduced, so that the image under the mapping is pictured on different sheets that lie one on top of another but are joined into one continuous surface. A material model in the present case could be made so that we would take two identical quadrats and slit them up along the same line and glue the cut edges together so that the quadrat makes two sheets. This is shown in fig. C.2.

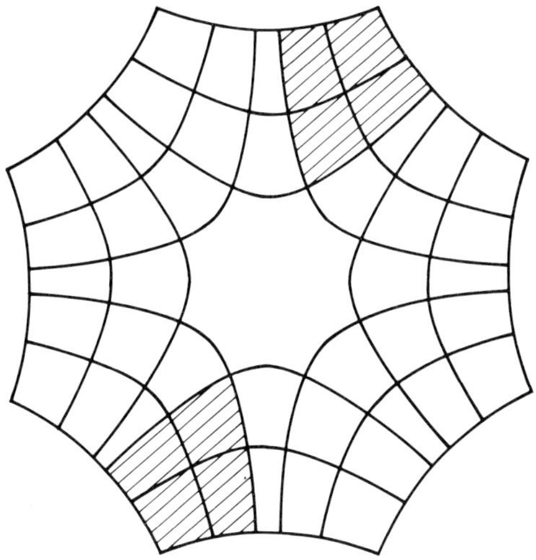

(a) z-plane.

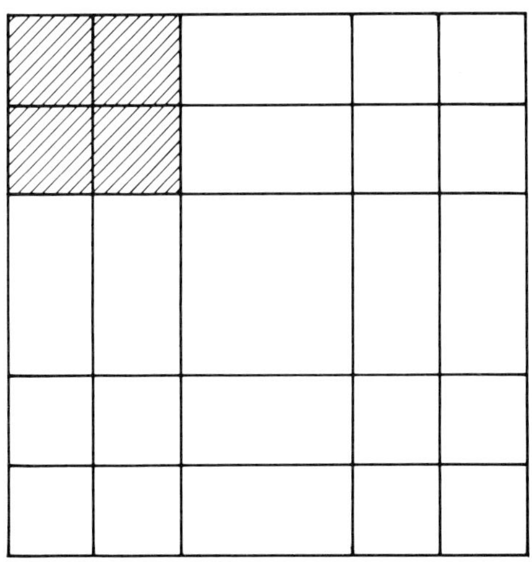

(b) w-plane.

Figure C.1.

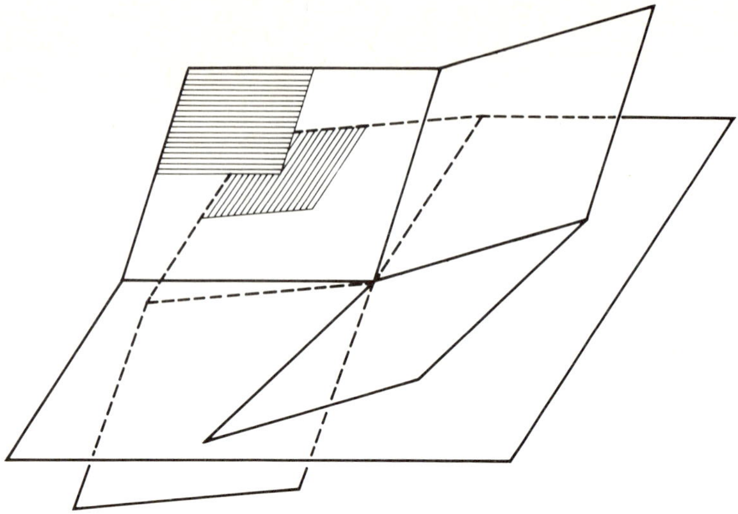

Figure C.2.

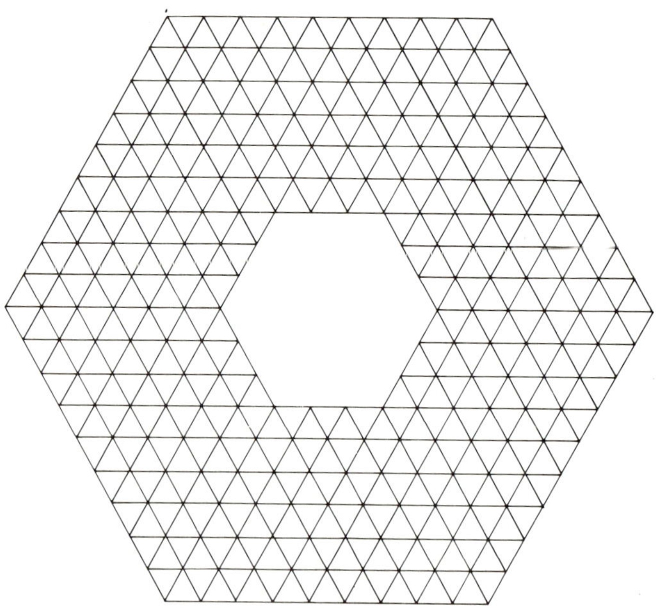

Figure C.3.

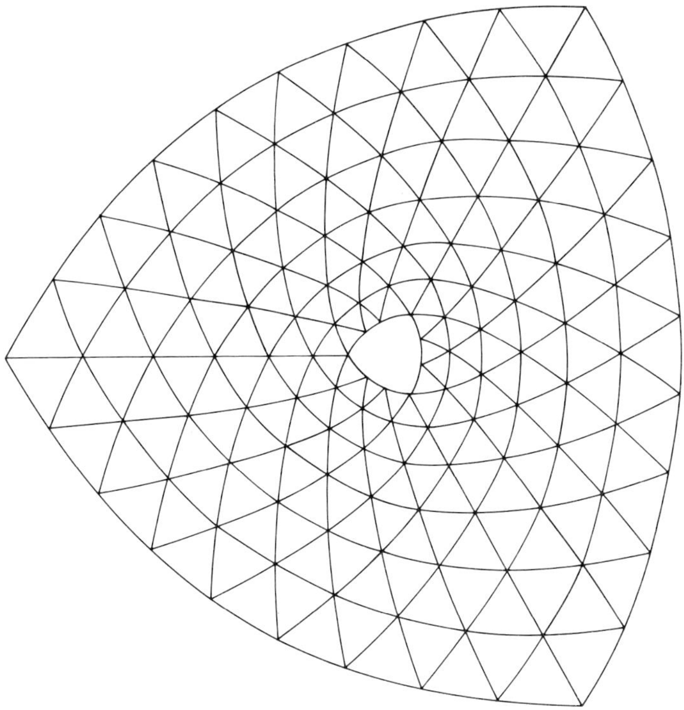

Figure C.4.

As we make a round in the z-plane, the corresponding point in the w-plane first makes a complete round on the bottom sheet of the quadrat and then makes another on the top sheet. As demonstrated in the diagram, the shaded area in the w-plane is not one but two different areas, one on top of the other. Seen in this way the mapping is one-to-one, because points in each branch have unique images.

Strictly speaking, the figure does not represent a quite correct Riemann surface. This is so because the two loose edges, remaining after the slit, should be joined together (across the already continuous sheet), since only then does one return to the starting point after a round on both sheets. In Chapter 4 the reader can find an example of a correct Riemann surface, drawn from a three-dimensional model.

Before continuing we must say something more about the fact that conformal mappings map congruent figures. The assertion that "approximate" quadrats are mapped on quadrats may not seem convincing, as the similarity is indeed "approximate". The answer to a possible objection is that the congruence is a local property that holds true better the smaller the size of the figures compared. Exact congruence only holds in the limit.

Figs. C.3 and C.4 display a somewhat better congruence, due to a finer mesh. In particular this is true for the parts that lie at some distance from the origin.

C.4. Literature to Appendix C

On complex analysis or the "theory of functions", as it is also called, our main references are Marsden (1973) and Spiegel (1964). Other references are Ahlfors (1966) and Knopp (1945). For the particular subject of conformal mapping we suggest Bieberbach (1953) and Courant (1950).

APPENDIX D: ELEMENTS OF DIFFERENTIAL GEOMETRY

D.1. Introduction

Before entering the subject of differential geometry, we have to give the generalized (correct) definitions of vector products. Let $\boldsymbol{x}=(x_1,x_2,x_3)$ and $\boldsymbol{y}=(y_1,y_2,y_3)$ be two vectors in three-dimensional space.

D.1.1. Dot and cross products

The dot product is a straightforward generalization

$$\boldsymbol{x}\cdot\boldsymbol{y}=x_1y_1+x_2y_2+x_3y_3.$$

The cross product, on the other hand, can most easily be defined as a determinant. Let us therefore define unit vectors in the three orthogonal right-handed coordinate directions $\boldsymbol{e}_1=(1,0,0)$, $\boldsymbol{e}_2=(0,1,0)$, and $\boldsymbol{e}_3=(0,0,1)$. Using this notation we have

$$\boldsymbol{x}\times\boldsymbol{y}=\begin{vmatrix} \boldsymbol{e}_1 & x_1 & y_1 \\ \boldsymbol{e}_2 & x_2 & y_2 \\ \boldsymbol{e}_3 & x_3 & y_3 \end{vmatrix}$$

or, expanding,

$$\boldsymbol{x}\times\boldsymbol{y}=(x_2y_3-x_3y_2)\boldsymbol{e}_1+(x_3y_1-x_1y_3)\boldsymbol{e}_2+(x_1y_2-x_2y_1)\boldsymbol{e}_3.$$

When we deal with two-dimensional vectors, as in Appendix A, then in the dot product the last term simply disappears, as $x_3=y_3=0$, but the cross product is $(x_1y_2-x_2y_1)\boldsymbol{e}_3$. The nonzero component agrees with the scalar formula used above, but the fact that the cross product is a vector, makes the difference.

D.1.2. Triple product

As we have now introduced the correct definitions, we can also define the *triple product* $\boldsymbol{x}\cdot(\boldsymbol{y}\times\boldsymbol{z})$. Its value can most easily be evaluated if we write

$$\boldsymbol{x}=x_1\boldsymbol{e}_1+x_2\boldsymbol{e}_2+x_3\boldsymbol{e}_3$$

and

$$\boldsymbol{y}\times\boldsymbol{z}=(y_2z_3-y_3x_2)\boldsymbol{e}_1+(y_3z_1-y_1z_3)\boldsymbol{e}_2+(y_1z_2-y_2z_1)\boldsymbol{e}_3.'$$

Recording that $\boldsymbol{e}_1\cdot\boldsymbol{e}_1=\boldsymbol{e}_2\cdot\boldsymbol{e}_2=\boldsymbol{e}_3\cdot\boldsymbol{e}_3=1$ and $\boldsymbol{e}_1\cdot\boldsymbol{e}_2=\boldsymbol{e}_1\cdot\boldsymbol{e}_3=\boldsymbol{e}_2\cdot\boldsymbol{e}_3=0$, we see that we can put the triple product too in determinant form, which has great mnemonic advantages. Hence

$$\boldsymbol{x}\cdot(\boldsymbol{y}\times\boldsymbol{z})=\begin{vmatrix} x_1 & y_1 & z_1 \\ x_2 & y_2 & z_2 \\ x_3 & y_3 & z_3 \end{vmatrix}.$$

From the algebra of determinants we know that if there is any linear dependence among the columns, for example when two columns are proportionate, then the determinant is zero. In the sequel the triple product occurs at the definition of geodesic curvature.

The absolute value of the triple product has a geometric interpretation as the volume of a parallelepiped that has the three component vectors as sides. The determinant can differ from the volume measure by a negative sign. We also note that, if we disregard changes of sign, the triple product is independent of the order in which the three vectors are arranged. The absolute value is given at the same time as the vectors, irrespective of order.

D.1.3. Spanned planes and their normals

Assume now that we define a vector

$$\boldsymbol{z}=\alpha\boldsymbol{x}+\beta\boldsymbol{y},$$

where α,β are some scalar variables. Then, by letting these scalar variables take on all real values, we generate a plane in space by the $\boldsymbol{z}$-values. This plane contains the origin and the two points in space represented by the coordinates of the two vectors, $\boldsymbol{x},\boldsymbol{y}$. If we regard vectors as directed lines or arrows from the origin to the coordinate points in question, then the plane is the plane containing the two vectors $\boldsymbol{x}$ and $\boldsymbol{y}$, or "spanned" by them.

Let us now compute the triple product

$$(\boldsymbol{x}\times\boldsymbol{y})\cdot\boldsymbol{z}=\begin{vmatrix} x_1 & y_1 & \alpha x_1+\beta y_1 \\ x_2 & y_2 & \alpha x_2+\beta y_2 \\ x_3 & y_3 & \alpha x_3+\beta y_3 \end{vmatrix}=0.$$

It is zero because the last column is a linear combination of the other two. However, this implies that the dot product of the two vectors $\boldsymbol{x}\times\boldsymbol{y}$ and $\boldsymbol{z}$ is zero. Since the dot product was the product of the norms and the cosine of the angle between the vectors, it follows that if none of the vectors is zero then they must be perpendicular.

The conclusion is that $\boldsymbol{x}\times\boldsymbol{y}$ is a vector perpendicular to the plane spanned by the vectors $\boldsymbol{x}$ and $\boldsymbol{y}$, or a normal to it. Hence, $\boldsymbol{x}\times\boldsymbol{y}/|\boldsymbol{x}\times\boldsymbol{y}|$ is a unit normal to the plane spanned.

D.2. Curves

This appendix gives a very brief introduction to the most fundamental concepts in differential geometry. We start with curves. A *regular parameterized curve* is a vector function $\boldsymbol{x}=\boldsymbol{x}(t)$, with component functions $x_1(t)$, $x_2(t)$, and $x_3(t)$, such that $|\boldsymbol{x}'(t)|\neq 0$ everywhere. Here, t is the parameter. The curve is often regarded as a geometrical object, independent of the parameterization, and hence a whole class of possible parameterizations must be considered. However, since we are concerned only with the most elementary parts of differential geometry we need not enter into the subject of allowable parameter changes. There is one exception. We must mention representation in terms of a *natural parameter, the arc length*, usually denoted s. We will keep to this symbolism, so that s always denotes the arc length.

Given a parameterization by t, we can easily define the function

$$s(t)=\int_{t_0}^{t}|\mathrm{d}\boldsymbol{x}/\mathrm{d}t|\,\mathrm{d}t$$

which, inverted, gives $t(s)$. This substituted for the original parameter yields a natural parameterization. The parameterization by arc length is unique, except for orientation and choice of zero.

To a regular parameterized curve we can define a *tangent vector*. In terms of the parameter t, we get the tangent vector $\mathrm{d}\boldsymbol{x}/\mathrm{d}t$ with components $\mathrm{d}x_1/\mathrm{d}t$, $\mathrm{d}x_2/\mathrm{d}t$ and $\mathrm{d}x_3/\mathrm{d}t$. The length of the tangent vector depends on the choice of parameterization, but the direction does not. We might wish to reduce the arbitrariness involved by defining a *unit tangent vector*, i.e. a vector of unit length pointing in the direction obtained. For this purpose we only need to divide the tangent vector, obtained by differentiating with respect to t, by the length of the tangent vector, i.e. $|\mathrm{d}\boldsymbol{x}/\mathrm{d}t|$. Hence, the unit tangent is

$$\boldsymbol{t}=\mathrm{d}\boldsymbol{x}/\mathrm{d}t/|\mathrm{d}\boldsymbol{x}/\mathrm{d}t|,$$

where

$$|\mathrm{d}\boldsymbol{x}/\mathrm{d}t|=\surd\left((\mathrm{d}x_1/\mathrm{d}t)^2+(\mathrm{d}x_2/\mathrm{d}t)^2+(\mathrm{d}x_3/\mathrm{d}t)^2\right).$$

We note that if the curve has been parameterized by arc length, then the length of the tangent vector is unity and we need not carry out the division. Hence, $\boldsymbol{t}=\mathrm{d}\boldsymbol{x}/\mathrm{d}s$. Unfortunately, we seldom have curves parameterized by arc length from the outset.

D.3. Curvature and torsion

The next concept to be introduced is *curvature*. The curvature vector is simply defined as $\mathrm{d}\boldsymbol{t}/\mathrm{d}s$, and tells how much the tangent is pulling away from its original direction as we move along the curve. When the parameterization is not in terms of arc length, then we must again divide by $|\mathrm{d}\boldsymbol{x}/\mathrm{d}t|$. We have

$$\boldsymbol{k}=\mathrm{d}\boldsymbol{t}/\mathrm{d}t/|\mathrm{d}\boldsymbol{x}/\mathrm{d}t|,$$

where $\boldsymbol{k}$ is the traditional notation for the curvature vector.

Its length $|\boldsymbol{k}|=\kappa$, is called the curvature. It is zero for a straight line and in a point of inflection. The reciprocal is called the "radius of curvature" and, in fact, is the radius of the circle that can be best fitted to the curve at a given point. Fitting a circle, a so-called "osculating circle" is no more odd than fitting a straight line as tangent. Instead of two points from the curve we can take three. Now, through any three points a unique circle can be determined. As in the limit the three points get closer and finally coincide, the circle approaches the osculating circle, and its radius is the reciprocal of the curvature.

As $\boldsymbol{t}$ is of unit length, we have $\boldsymbol{t}^2=1$. Differentiating, we get $\boldsymbol{t}\cdot\mathrm{d}\boldsymbol{t}/\mathrm{d}t=0$, or $\boldsymbol{t}\cdot\boldsymbol{k}=0$. Hence, the tangent and curvature vectors are orthogonal and we could, by putting a unit vector in the direction of $\boldsymbol{k}$, determine a *unit normal* to the curve. The problem with this conjecture is that when we have a point of inflection separating the convex and concave parts of a curve, then the unit normal would make a sudden jump from one direction to the opposite in the point of inflection, whereas it cannot even be defined at the point itself. If one wants a continuously changing unit normal one should change the sign of the normal $\pm\boldsymbol{k}/|\boldsymbol{k}|$ at each point of inflection. In this way a unit principal normal can be defined that is continuous. We denote it by $\boldsymbol{n}$. Obviously, we can then obtain a signed curvature measure by the product $\boldsymbol{k}\cdot\boldsymbol{n}=\pm\kappa$.

For the sake of completeness, we should also mention the *binormal vector*, defined by the cross product $\boldsymbol{b}=\boldsymbol{t}\times\boldsymbol{n}$. By definition, it forms a right-handed coordinate system together with the tangent and normal vectors. With plane curves it is without interest since it always points perpendicularly out from the plane, but in the context of space curves it is of importance for defining the concept of *torsion*, which measures how fast a curve is pulling away from the tangent plane. A plane curve is confined to the tangent plane and hence has zero torsion. Torsion is formally obtained in the following manner. It is first seen that the derivative $\mathrm{d}\boldsymbol{b}/\mathrm{d}s$ points in the same (or opposite) direction as $\boldsymbol{n}$. The latter is of unit length. We can define $\mathrm{d}\boldsymbol{b}/\mathrm{d}s=\tau\boldsymbol{n}$, where τ is the conventional symbol for torsion. Sometimes torsion is defined with an extra minus sign. For illustration, we mention that a circular helix confined to a cylinder has constant torsion. The sign depends on whether it is like a right-handed or a left-handed screw.

D.4. Surfaces

As with curves we start by defining what a *regular parameterization* means. It is a mapping $x(u,v)$ from two-dimensional u,v-space to three-dimensional x_1,x_2,x_3-space. It can be given by three coordinate functions, $x_1(u,v)$, $x_2(u,v)$, and $x_3(u,v)$, where we now have two parameters instead of one. The regularity condition, corresponding to that of a nonvanishing derivative in the case of curves, is now that the matrix obtained by the derivatives of the coordinate functions $[x_u, x_v]$, of order 3×2, has rank 2. There are many intricacies connected with the fact that one cannot always use a single parameterization to cover a whole regular surface, and with the general character of surfaces as geometric objects independent of parameterization, but we will not enter into these matters. Instead, we pass directly to the Gaussian theory of surfaces. If we keep the parameters u and v constant at values changing with regular intervals, then we can cover the surface with a net of coordinate lines. The derivatives $x_u = \partial x/\partial u$ and $x_v = \partial x/\partial v$ are then three-dimensional tangent vectors pointing along the coordinate lines for v and u constant.

D.5. The metrics

We now define the dot products,

$$E = x_u \cdot x_u; \qquad F = x_u \cdot x_v; \qquad G = x_v \cdot x_v,$$

which are called the *first fundamental coefficients*. Then it is possible to define the *first fundamental form*, denoted $I = E\,du^2 + 2F\,du\,dv + G\,dv^2$, which is a characteristic of the surface as a geometrical object and independent of parameterization. The fundamental coefficients change with a change of parameterization, but the form is invariant.

For our purpose it is most important that the fundamental coefficients occur in definitions of lengths of curves, and measures of areas on a curved surface. As to arc length, we may imagine a curve C confined to the surface as given by two parametric functions $u(t)$ and $v(t)$. From the u,v-plane the curve is mapped onto the surface. Arc length is, as above,

$$\int |dx/dt|\,dt, \quad \text{but} \quad |dx/dt| = \surd((dx/dt)\cdot(dx/dt)),$$

and

$$dx/dt = x_u\,du/dt + x_v\,dv/dt.$$

Substituting these into the integral and employing the fundamental coefficients, we arrive at

$$s(C) = \int_C \surd\big(E(du/dt)^2 + 2F(du/dt)(dv/dt) + G(du/dt)^2\big)\,dt$$

as a general expression for arc length. Given the parameterizations of the surface and the curve, the fundamental coefficients as well as the derivatives in this expression are given functions of t and the evaluation is straightforward.

In a similar manner, areas A can be evaluated. From the vectors $\boldsymbol{x}_u\,\mathrm{d}u$ and $\boldsymbol{x}_v\,\mathrm{d}v$, small parallelograms of area $|\boldsymbol{x}_u \times \boldsymbol{x}_v|\,\mathrm{d}u\,\mathrm{d}v$ can be defined. Since, however $|\boldsymbol{x}_u \times \boldsymbol{x}_v| = \sqrt{(EG-F^2)}$, and as the complete surface can be subdivided into patches with such parallelograms as approximating tangent spaces, we arrive at the measure

$$A(R) = \int\int_R \sqrt{(EG-F^2)}\,\mathrm{d}u\,\mathrm{d}v,$$

where R is the domain of integration in the u,v-plane. It should be noticed that the measures of area and of arc length are independent of parameterization.

D.6. Conformal and isometric maps

Suppose that u,v are rectangular coordinates in the plane, where they therefore have coordinate lines that intersect at right angles. If now the parameterization of the surface is a *conformal mapping*, then the coordinate lines on the surface also intersect at right angles, and hence the vectors $\boldsymbol{x}_u$ and $\boldsymbol{x}_v$ are perpendicular. Then, according to definition, $F=0$. Moreover, E and G are the squared linear magnification factors in the directions of the coordinate lines. As with conformal maps the magnification factor is equal in all directions, including those of the coordinate lines, we have $E=G$.

Hence, the expressions for arc length and area are much simplified as

$$s = \int \sqrt{E}\sqrt{((\mathrm{d}u/\mathrm{d}t)^2 + (\mathrm{d}v/\mathrm{d}t)^2)}\,\mathrm{d}t,$$

where $\sqrt{G}$ can be substituted for $\sqrt{E}$, and $A = \int\int E\,\mathrm{d}x\,\mathrm{d}y$, where again G can be substituted for E. As $\sqrt{((\mathrm{d}u/\mathrm{d}t)^2 + (\mathrm{d}v/\mathrm{d}t)^2)}\,\mathrm{d}t$ is the arc length in the u,v-plane, and $\sqrt{E} = \sqrt{G}$ and $E = G$ are the linear and areal magnification factors, respectively, the formulae are intuitively easy to understand.

If, in addition, $E = G = 1$ then the mapping is an isometry, and neither arc lengths nor areas are affected.

D.7. Unit normal and normal curvatures

We now turn to curvature. First, from the vector product

$$N = \boldsymbol{x}_u \times \boldsymbol{x}_v / |\boldsymbol{x}_u \times \boldsymbol{x}_v|$$

we can define a unit normal to the surface. Then, we regard all the curves obtained as intersections between the surface and different planes containing the normal. To all these curves we may associate a measure of curvature, called *normal* curvature. The Gaussian theory of curved surfaces now states that there are two orthogonal positions for this plane where the curvature takes a maximum and a minimum value. Depending on whether the signed principal curvatures have the same or opposite sign, one may differentiate between elliptic points (where the surface is "convex") and hyperbolic points (where the surface is a "saddle"). Degenerate points called planar or parabolic depending on the degree of degeneracy occur in intermediate cases.

In fig. D.1 a surface with its normal vector and two normal sections is shown. The intersection curves in the two planes are drawn. Their normal curvatures may be computed by the methods outlined above. Observe that these two normal curvatures correspond to curvature vectors that point in the direction of the normal. This is the reason for the term normal curvature.

Formally, the normal curvatures can be obtained in the following manner. In the same way as we defined the first fundamental coefficients, we define the *second fundamental coefficients*, i.e.

$$L = \boldsymbol{x}_{uu} \cdot \boldsymbol{N}; \qquad M = \boldsymbol{x}_{uv} \cdot \boldsymbol{N}; \qquad N = \boldsymbol{x}_{vv} \cdot \boldsymbol{N}.$$

Now, the normal curvatures are obtained as ratios of the second and first

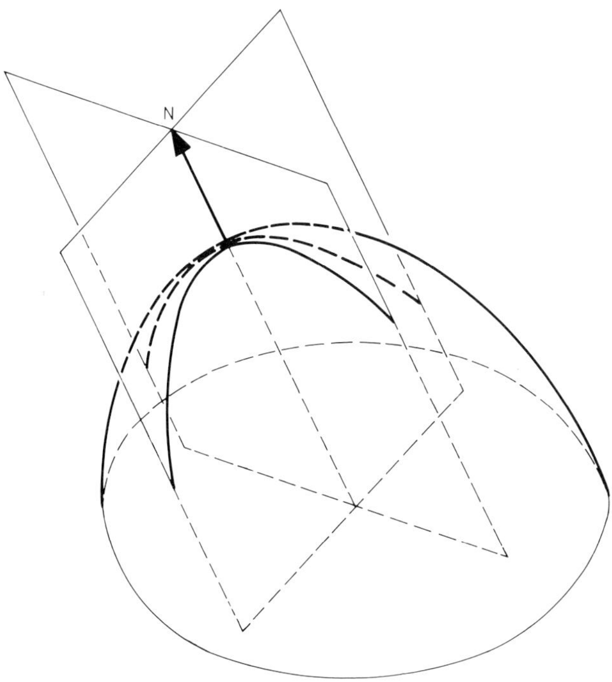

Figure D.1

fundamental forms, i.e.

$$\kappa_n = \frac{L(\mathrm{d}u/\mathrm{d}t)^2 + 2M(\mathrm{d}u/\mathrm{d}t)(\mathrm{d}v/\mathrm{d}t) + N(\mathrm{d}v/\mathrm{d}t)^2}{E(\mathrm{d}u/\mathrm{d}t)^2 + 2F(\mathrm{d}u/\mathrm{d}t)(\mathrm{d}v/\mathrm{d}t) + G(\mathrm{d}v/\mathrm{d}t)^2}.$$

Given the point where the fundamental coefficients are determined, the normal curvature depends only on the direction $\mathrm{d}v/\mathrm{d}u$ in which the derivatives are taken (with reference to the parameter plane).

D.8. Principal curvatures and directions

The *principal curvatures* and *principal directions* are now obtained by solving the equations

$$(L-\kappa E)\mathrm{d}u + (M-\kappa F)\mathrm{d}v = 0$$

and

$$(M-\kappa F)\mathrm{d}u + (N-\kappa G)\mathrm{d}v = 0.$$

Obviously such a homogeneous system of equations has a nontrivial solution only if the determinant of its coefficients is zero. Computing this determinant and equating it to zero then yields a quadratic equation in κ, with two *real* roots, κ_1 and κ_2, representing the principal curvatures. The principal directions $\mathrm{d}v/\mathrm{d}u$ can then be solved from the linear equations for the two roots of κ obtained. Two frequently used concepts are the *mean curvature*, defined as the mean of the two roots obtained, and the *Gaussian curvature*, defined as the product of the roots.

D.9. Geodesics and geodesic curvature

Even more important in our applications than the normal curvatures is the *geodesic curvature*. It is not a property of the surface only, but of the curve on the surface. Take a point on such a curve and fit a tangent plane to the surface at that point. Then take an orthogonal projection of the curve onto the plane. In general this produces the image of a curve with nonzero curvature. This curvature is the geodesic curvature when it is taken at the point of tangency. For a *geodesic*, i.e. a shortest path on the surface, the geodesic curvature must vanish everywhere along the curve.

Formally, we can compute the geodesic curvature as

$$\kappa_g = \boldsymbol{k} \cdot (\boldsymbol{N} \times \boldsymbol{t}),$$

where $\boldsymbol{t}$ and $\boldsymbol{k}$ are the tangent and the curvature vectors, respectively, as computed by the formulae in sections D.2–3, and where $\boldsymbol{N}$ is the unit normal to the surface.

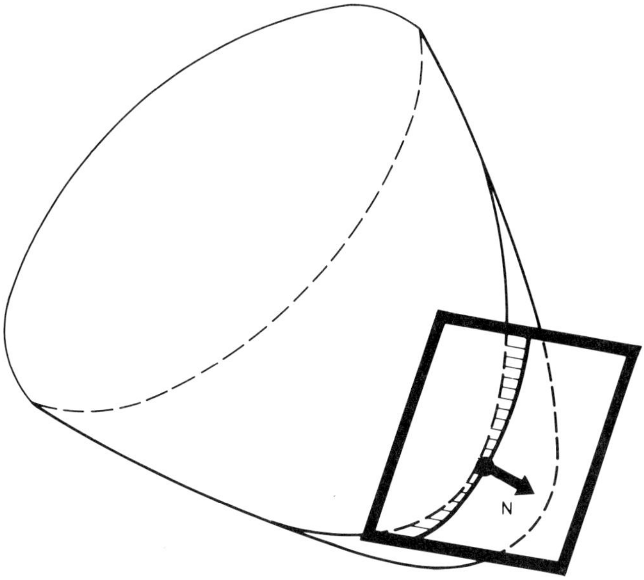

Figure D.2

The idea is illustrated in fig. D.2. The paraboloid-like surface contains a curve which is projected perpendicularly onto the tangent plane. The geodesic curvature is the curvature of the projected curve. As the curvature is not zero, the curve is obviously not a geodesic.

D.10. Example: helices on a cylinder

As an exemplification, let us discuss the surface of a cylinder of unit radius. It can be parameterized by the coordinate functions $x_1=\cos u, x_2=\sin u, x_3=v$. We have $\boldsymbol{x}_u=(-\sin u, \cos u, 0)$ and $\boldsymbol{x}_v=(0,0,1)$. Moreover, $\boldsymbol{x}_{uu}=(-\cos u, -\sin u, 0)$, $\boldsymbol{x}_{uv}=(0,0,0)$ and $\boldsymbol{x}_{vv}=(0,0,0)$. Also, $\boldsymbol{x}_u \times \boldsymbol{x}_v=(\cos u, \sin u, 0)$, and $|\boldsymbol{x}_u \times \boldsymbol{x}_v|=1$. This implies that $\boldsymbol{N}=(\cos u, \sin u, 0)$, and we can compute the fundamental coefficients $E=1$, $F=0$, $G=1$, and $L=-1$, $M=N=0$. The first fundamental coefficients show that the parameterization represents an isometric mapping. The curvatures are then simply $\kappa_n=-(\mathrm{d}u/\mathrm{d}t)^2/((\mathrm{d}u/\mathrm{d}t)^2+(\mathrm{d}v/\mathrm{d}t)^2)$. As to the principal curvatures the case is degenerate or, more specifically, parabolic, and the equations for the principal curvatures and directions reduce to $-(1+\kappa)\mathrm{d}u=0$ and $-\kappa\,\mathrm{d}v=0$. From these we can see directly that u=constant and v= constant are the principal directions. Using this information in the formula for κ_n with v constant we get $\kappa_1=-1$, and with u constant we get $\kappa_2=0$. The result is intuitively obvious. With the mapping employed the coordinate lines for constant v are unit circles. Since their osculating circles are the unit circles themselves the radius of curvature and the reciprocal curvature measure are unitary. The minus sign shows that the curvature is directed inwards, to the origin. The coordinate lines with u constant, on the other hand, are straight lines that go vertically up along the cylinder. The curvature of a straight line, however, is identically zero.

Let us now look at a class of curves confined to the cylinder, namely helices. We can define them by $u=at$, $v=bt$, where a,b are some constants. The three-dimensional image of the curve is hence given by $\boldsymbol{x}(t)=(\cos at, \sin at, bt)$. We have $\mathrm{d}\boldsymbol{x}/\mathrm{d}t=(-a\sin at, a\cos at, b)$, and $|\mathrm{d}\boldsymbol{x}/\mathrm{d}t|=\sqrt{(a^2+b^2)}$. Hence, $\boldsymbol{t}=(-a\sin at, a\cos at, b)/\sqrt{(a^2+b^2)}$. Next, we get $\boldsymbol{k}=(-a^2\cos at, -a^2\sin at, 0)/(a^2+b^2)$. We notice that $|\boldsymbol{k}|=a^2/(a^2+b^2)$, which exceeds unity, unless b is zero and the helix degenerates into a circle. Anyhow the curvature is a constant. As $\boldsymbol{N}=(\cos u, \sin u, 0)$ we find $\boldsymbol{N}\times\boldsymbol{t}=(b\sin at, -b\cos at, a)/(a^2+b^2)$ and hence $\kappa_g=\boldsymbol{k}\cdot(\boldsymbol{N}\times\boldsymbol{t})=0$. Hence, for all helices, including circles and straight lines, the geodesic curvature is zero, and the paths are geodesics (see fig. D.3).

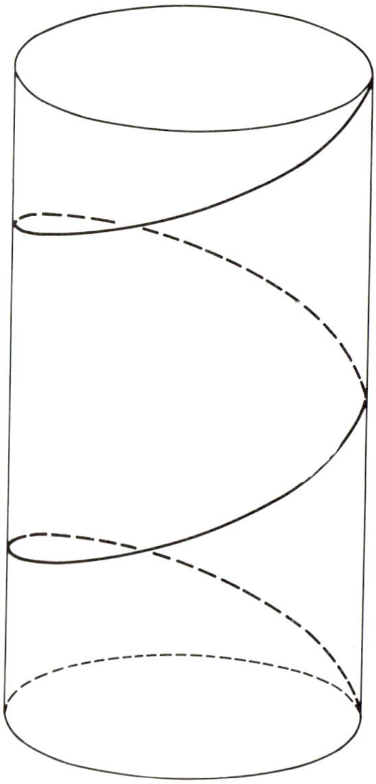

Figure D.3. Geodesic (circular helix) on a cylinder.

D.11. Example: great circles on a sphere

Let us next parameterize the surface of a sphere of unit radius. There are several ways of doing this, but most of them can only work on single patches of the whole surface. Hence, if we take $x_3 = \pm\sqrt{(1-x_1^2-x_2^2)}$, $x_2 = \pm\sqrt{(1-x_1^2-x_3^2)}$, and $x_1 = \pm\sqrt{(1-x_2^2-x_3^2)}$, which is the most obvious way of parameterization, we actually need all six of them, because each one only works for the arguments within strong inequalities. If we only took the first pair, then a great circle would be left uncovered. Adding the next pair still leaves two poles uncovered, so that we must add even the third one.

An interesting way of mapping the surface of a unit sphere onto the plane is to put the sphere tangentially on the plane, and to project its points by rays radiating from the north pole. If we add the point "at infinity" of the plane we get a one-to-one mapping, including even the north pole. Such a sphere, called the *Riemann sphere* is employed in mathematics to illustrate complex numbers. The mapping is called *stereographic projection*.

The parameterization of the sphere in a stereographic projection in terms of the coordinates of the projection plane is $x_1 = 4u/(4+u^2+v^2)$, $x_2 = 4v/(4+u^2+v^2)$, $x_3 = 2(u^2+v^2)/(4+u^2+v^2)$. We get

$$\mathbf{x}_u = (16-4u^2+4v^2, -8uv, 16u)/(4+u^2+v^2)^2$$

and

$$\mathbf{x}_v = (-8uv, 16+4u^2-4v^2, 16v)/(4+u^2+v^2)^2.$$

Hence, the first fundamental coefficients are $F=0$ and $E=G=16/(4+u^2+v^2)^2$, which means that the mapping is again conformal, but this time not isometric.

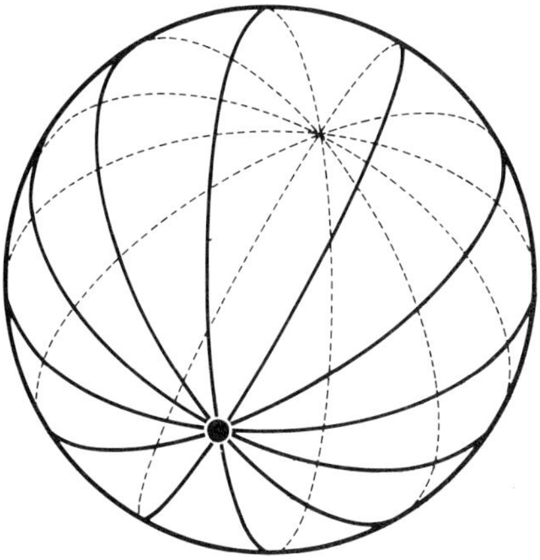

Figure D.4

The nonunitary linear magnification factor is $4/(4+u^2+v^2)$. We also get $\boldsymbol{N}=-(4u,4v,u^2+v^2-4)/(4+u^2+v^2)$. The reader can see that this equals $-(x_1,x_2,x_3-1)$. The normal vector thus points at the center of the sphere, as might be expected.

Now, take a great circle on the sphere, i.e. a circle of unit radius, obtained as an intersection between the surface of the sphere and any plane through its center. The osculating circle of such a curve is the circle itself, and hence the curve has unitary curvature. The curvature vector too points at the center. Thus, the curvature vector of the great circle equals the (inward) normal to the surface. As the geodesic curvature is $\kappa_g=\boldsymbol{k}\cdot(\boldsymbol{N}\times\boldsymbol{t})$, it is zero because $\boldsymbol{k}=\boldsymbol{N}$, no matter what $\boldsymbol{t}$ is. For this reason we need not bother with any parameterization of the great circles. We can see directly that for them the geodesic curvature is zero, which means that they are geodesics (see fig. D.4).

D.12. The Gauss equations and the Christoffel symbols

We continue the discussion by setting down a few important relations, the *Gauss–Weingarten equations*. Above, we have discussed the tangent vectors to the coordinate lines for u, v constant. These were denoted $\boldsymbol{x}_u$ and $\boldsymbol{x}_v$. We are now going to discuss the second-order derivatives $\boldsymbol{x}_{uu}$, $\boldsymbol{x}_{uv}=\boldsymbol{x}_{vu}$ and $\boldsymbol{x}_{vv}$. We note first that all vectors in three-dimensional space, subsumed the second-order derivatives, can be expressed as linear combinations of three independent basis vectors. Now, $\boldsymbol{x}_u$, $\boldsymbol{x}_v$ are independent vectors in the tangent plane, whereas $\boldsymbol{N}$ is a vector normal to the tangent plane and hence independent of the two aforementioned. The three vectors are thus linearly independent and can be taken as a basis.

This means that we can express the second-order derivatives as linear combinations of the two tangent vectors and the unit normal vector as in the following three equations.

We can see directly what three of the nine coefficients are. We have defined the second fundamental coefficients as $L=\boldsymbol{x}_{uu}\cdot\boldsymbol{N}$, $M=\boldsymbol{x}_{uv}\cdot\boldsymbol{N}$ and $N=\boldsymbol{x}_{vv}\cdot\boldsymbol{N}$. Thus, they can be obtained by taking the dot product of each of the three equations with the normal vector $\boldsymbol{N}$. But as $\boldsymbol{N}\cdot\boldsymbol{x}_u=\boldsymbol{N}\cdot\boldsymbol{x}_v=0$ and as $\boldsymbol{N}^2=1$ we conclude that the coefficients in the third column must indeed be L, M and N. These coefficients have therefore been inserted into the equations from the outset:

$$\boldsymbol{x}_{uu}=\Gamma^1_{11}\boldsymbol{x}_u+\Gamma^2_{11}\boldsymbol{x}_v+L\boldsymbol{N},$$

$$\boldsymbol{x}_{uv}=\Gamma^1_{12}\boldsymbol{x}_u+\Gamma^2_{12}\boldsymbol{x}_v+M\boldsymbol{N},$$

$$\boldsymbol{x}_{vv}=\Gamma^1_{22}\boldsymbol{x}_u+\Gamma^2_{22}\boldsymbol{x}_v+N\boldsymbol{N}.$$

Only six of the coefficients, the Γ^k_{ij}, remain to be determined. These are important concepts, called the *Christoffel symbols of the second kind*, and will be needed in Appendix E when we want to write the equations of a geodesic in compact form.

Through differentiating $E=\boldsymbol{x}_u\cdot\boldsymbol{x}_u$, $F=\boldsymbol{x}_u\cdot\boldsymbol{x}_v$, and $G=\boldsymbol{x}_v\cdot\boldsymbol{x}_v$ with respect to u,v and some algebraic exercise we can solve for the Christoffel symbols. The result is merely stated since the derivation does not present anything of particular interest.

$$\Gamma^1_{11}=\frac{GE_u-2FF_u+FE_v}{2(EG-F^2)};\quad \Gamma^1_{12}=\frac{GE_v-FG_u}{2(EG-F^2)};\quad \Gamma^1_{22}=\frac{2GF_v-GG_u-FG_v}{2(EG-F^2)},$$

$$\Gamma^2_{11}=\frac{2EF_u-EE_v+FE_u}{2(EG-F^2)};\quad \Gamma^2_{12}=\frac{EG_u-FE_v}{2(EG-F^2)};\quad \Gamma^2_{22}=\frac{EG_v-2FF_v+FG_u}{2(EG-F^2)}.$$

D.13. The Weingarten equations

Related to the three Gauss equations are the two *Weingarten equations*. They express the partial derivatives of the normal vector in the coordinate directions as linear combinations of the same three basis vectors as those used in the Gauss equations. Since these partial derivatives, like the normal itself, are three-dimensional vectors, this can be done:

$$\boldsymbol{N}_u=\beta_1^1\boldsymbol{x}_u+\beta_1^2\boldsymbol{x}_v,$$

$$\boldsymbol{N}_v=\beta_2^1\boldsymbol{x}_u+\beta_2^2\boldsymbol{x}_v.$$

The coefficients of the third column vanish as $\boldsymbol{N}\cdot\boldsymbol{N}_u=\boldsymbol{N}\cdot\boldsymbol{N}_v=0$, $\boldsymbol{N}^2=1$ and $\boldsymbol{N}\cdot\boldsymbol{x}_u=\boldsymbol{N}\cdot\boldsymbol{x}_v=0$:

$$\beta_1^1=\frac{MF-LG}{EG-F^2};\quad \beta_1^2=\frac{LF-ME}{EG-F^2};\quad \beta_2^1=\frac{NF-MG}{EG-F^2}\ \text{and}\ \beta_2^2=\frac{MF-NE}{EG-F^2}$$

are the formulae for the four remaining coefficients. The five equations together furnish a set of differential equations for $\boldsymbol{x}_u$, $\boldsymbol{x}_v$ and $\boldsymbol{N}$ as soon as the six fundamental coefficients are known functions of u,v. They can be integrated to give the surface, provided the surface exists.

D.14. The Teorema egregium

Assume that we are given any six functions $E(u,v)$, $F(u,v)$, $G(u,v)$, $L(u,v)$, $M(u,v)$, and $N(u,v)$. To simplify the formulae we only deal with the special case where the surface is conformal to the plane, i.e. $E=G=f(u,v)^2$, because this is the case we will encounter. For this case $\Gamma^1_{11}=f_u/f$, $\Gamma^1_{12}=\Gamma^1_{21}=f_v/f$, $\Gamma^1_{22}=-f_u/f$, $\Gamma^2_{11}=-f_v/f$, $\Gamma^2_{12}=\Gamma^2_{21}=f_u/f$ and $\Gamma^2_{22}=f_v/f$, as the reader may easily check.

Owing to a famous theorem by Gauss, the *Teorema egregium*, a relation among the second fundamental coefficients, namely $LN-M^2$, is completely determined by the first fundamental coefficients and their derivatives. Because of this the ratio $K=(LN-M^2)/(EG-F^2)$, which is called the *Gaussian curvature* and equals the product of the two principal curvatures, also is determined by the E, F, G functions. For the conformal case the relation can be written

$$LN-M^2=-f^2\nabla^2 f.$$

It must be emphasized that in general the relation is much more complicated. The simple form depends on the fact that the Christoffel symbols can be expressed as simply as above.

D.15. The Mainardi–Codazzi equations

The preceding equation is the first one of the *compatibility* equations. As said, it is due to Gauss. There are two more compatibility equations, the *Mainardi–Codazzi equations*, which in the conformal case read

$$N_u-M_v=(L+N)f_u/f$$

and

$$L_v-M_u=(L+N)f_v/f.$$

All three compatibility equations arise from the fact that the mixed partial derivatives of the third order of $\boldsymbol{x}$ with respect to u,v are independent of the order of differentiation.

D.16. Bonnet's fundamental theorem

We can now state the *fundamental theorem of surfaces* due to Bonnet. If E, F, G and L, M, N are *any* functions of u,v, differentiable twice and once, respectively, such that the three compatibility equations are fulfilled, then they determine a real surface, unique except for orientation in space, provided that the first fundamental form is positive definite. This last prerequisite is fulfilled in the conformal case since E, G and $EG-F^2$ are then positive. If so, there is a special case of this theorem when the first fundamental coefficients are given functions, whereas the choice of the second fundamental coefficients is free. Then it is *always* possible to choose these second fundamental coefficients so that the compatibility equations are fulfilled and so that the surface exists *locally*.

APPENDIX E: TENSOR CALCULUS AND GEODESICS ON CURVED SURFACES

In Appendix D we defined the concept of geodesic curvature, and stipulated it to be zero for a geodesic, i.e. a shortest path. This concept can be used to check that a curve suspected of being a geodesic, such as a helix on a cylinder or a great circle on a sphere, really has this property. But then we must from the outset have an idea of what the geodesic looks like.

Therefore, we need a method by which a geodesic can be found from differential equations of the Euler type. We have the mathematics needed for this already at hand but, if we do not introduce any new concepts, the resulting formulae will turn out to be extremely clumsy. For this reason we will introduce the concept of a *tensor*.

E.1. Tensors

Let us consider a scalar, i.e. a single number, a vector of N elements, and a square matrix of N^2 elements. All these are familiar concepts. There is, however, no reason to stop with the matrix. We can take N square matrices of N^2 elements and place them one behind the other to form a three-dimensional block. We could continue the process beyond geometric space. All these objects, the scalar, the vector, the matrix, can be examples of tensors of zero, first and second orders, respectively.

But it is not correct to say that tensors are simply generalizations of vectors and matrices. They are geometric objects related with spaces and surfaces at given points, that remain invariant under coordinate transformations, or that transform according to certain specified rules. The meaning of this will be clarified later.

First we have to introduce certain conventions of notation that will save a lot of writing. We put all coordinate numbers as superscripts instead of as subscripts, so that a vector $[x^1, x^2, \ldots, x^N]$ specifies a point in some coordinate system. Secondly, we agree that x^r itself denotes the whole vector so that the *free index* r takes on all values from 1 up to N. Thirdly, we take it as implicit that whenever the same index appears twice in a product, once as a superscript and once as a subscript, then summation with respect to that *dummy index* is implied. Hence, for example, $a_{mn}x^m x^n$ is automatically a double sum of N^2 terms, i.e. a quadratic form. The two summation signs, the summation indices m and n, and the range of summation, 1 to N for each, are simply deleted.

Let us now look at a coordinate change, given by the functions $x'^r = f^r(x^1, x^2, \ldots, x^N)$ for $r = 1,2,\ldots, N$. We suppose the Jacobian to be nonzero and finite, so that we can solve explicitly for $x^r = g^r(x'^1, x'^2, \ldots, x'^N)$, $r = 1,2,\ldots,N$, and so that we can pass without problems from one coordinate system to the other and back again.

The components of a tensor are changed by this change of coordinates. Let us say that a_{mn} is a tensor expressed in x^r coordinates. If the components of the tensor when expressed in the x'^r coordinates are obtained by the transformation formula

$$a'_{rs} = a_{mn} \frac{\partial x^m}{\partial x'^r} \frac{\partial x^n}{\partial x'^s},$$

then the tensor in question is *covariant*. If instead we have a tensor a^{mn} in x^r coordinates and obtain its components in x'^r coordinates by the transformation

$$a'^{rs} = a^{mn} \frac{\partial x'^r}{\partial x^m} \frac{\partial x'^s}{\partial x^n},$$

then the tensor is called *contravariant*. Both tensors exemplified are of the second order, i.e. are matrices.

The transformations can equally well be applied to vectors. Let b_m denote a vector in x^r coordinates. If its components in x'^r coordinates are transformed by the formula

$$b'_r = b_m \frac{\partial x^m}{\partial x'^r},$$

then we speak of a *covariant* vector. If instead we transform a vector b^m by

$$b'^r = b^m \frac{\partial x'^r}{\partial x^m},$$

then the vector is *contravariant*.

We notice that tensors, whether of matrix or vector character, are indexed by subscripts when they are covariant and by superscripts when they are contravariant. From the second order onwards we can speak of *mixed* tensors as well, such as

$$a'^{\cdot s}_{r} = a^{\cdot n}_{m} \frac{\partial x^m}{\partial x'^r} \frac{\partial x'^s}{\partial x^n},$$

$$a'^{r}_{\cdot s} = a^{m}_{\cdot n} \frac{\partial x'^r}{\partial x^m} \frac{\partial x^n}{\partial x'^s},$$

with one covariant and one contravariant index. Mixed tensors are mentioned merely for the sake of completeness. We also mention that any scalar, i.e. any zero-order tensor, transforms according to

$$c' = c$$

from x^r to x'^r. A scalar is therefore an *invariant*.

E.2. Tangent and gradient vectors as tensors

We are now ready to supply examples of tensors of different kinds. Suppose we have a path in N-dimensional space parameterized by the x^r coordinates. The path is supposed to be given by N regular equations of a parameter t, not necessarily arc length. Consider the tangent vector $[\mathrm{d}x^1/\mathrm{d}t, \mathrm{d}x^2/\mathrm{d}t, \ldots, \mathrm{d}x^N/\mathrm{d}t]$. Let us tentatively write the tangent vector, abbreviated in tensor notation as $\mathrm{d}x^r/\mathrm{d}t$ and ask what its components are in x'^r coordinates. Obviously, by the chain rule

$$\frac{\mathrm{d}x'^r}{\mathrm{d}t} = \frac{\mathrm{d}x^m}{\mathrm{d}t}\frac{\partial x'^r}{\partial x^m}.$$

Hence, we were justified in writing the components of a tangent as a contravariant vector because it transforms like one when the coordinate system is changed.

Next, consider a function $f(x^1, x^2, \ldots, x^N)$, and take the vector of its partial derivatives, i.e. the gradient. It is readily obtained as $[\partial f/\partial x^1, \partial f/\partial x^2, \ldots, \partial f/\partial x^N]$. We write it provisionally as a tensor $\partial f/\partial x^r$. In passing to x'^r coordinates, it is easy to see that, again by the chain rule,

$$\frac{\partial f}{\partial x'^r} = \frac{\partial f}{\partial x^m}\frac{\partial x^m}{\partial x'^r}.$$

The tensor notation was thus justified because the components of the gradient transform like a covariant vector.

We have now seen examples of both contravariant and covariant vectors, namely the tangent vector and the gradient vector.

E.3. Metric tensors

Let us now consider a curved surface in three-dimensional Euclidean space. The surface itself is a two-dimensional manifold that has no Euclidean character, and it is only this manifold and its intrinsic properties that matter. Embedding in three-dimensional Euclidean space aids visualization but is without importance. Let the surface be regularly parameterized by the three functions $x^1(u^1,u^2), x^2(u^1,u^2)$ and $x^3(u^1,u^2)$. The tangent vectors are $[\partial x^1/\partial u^1, \partial x^2/\partial u^1, \partial x^3/\partial u^1]$ and $[\partial x^1/\partial u^2, \partial x^2/\partial u^2, \partial x^3/\partial u^2]$, respectively. Denote them by $\boldsymbol{x}_{u^1}$ and $\boldsymbol{x}_{u^2}$. Above, the first fundamental coefficients of a surface were defined as $E = \boldsymbol{x}_{u^1}\cdot\boldsymbol{x}_{u^1}$, $F = \boldsymbol{x}_{u^1}\cdot\boldsymbol{x}_{u^2} = \boldsymbol{x}_{u^2}\cdot\boldsymbol{x}_{u^1}$ and $G = \boldsymbol{x}_{u^2}\cdot\boldsymbol{x}_{u^2}$. For notational simplicity we introduce the new symbols $a_{11} = E$, $a_{12} = a_{21} = F$, $a_{22} = G$. We consider the 2×2 matrix of these fundamental coefficients and denote it a_{mn} as a tensor.

To prove the tensor character we introduce a coordinate change from u^1, u^2 to u'^1, u'^2. Now, by the chain rule for derivatives, we get $\boldsymbol{x}_{u'^1} = \boldsymbol{x}_{u^1}\partial u^1/\partial u'^1 + \boldsymbol{x}_{u^2}\partial u^2/\partial u'^1$ and $\boldsymbol{x}_{u'^2} = \boldsymbol{x}_{u^1}\partial u^1/\partial u'^2 + \boldsymbol{x}_{u^2}\partial u^2/\partial u'^2$. Hence, we easily find

$$a'_{rs} = a_{mn}\frac{\partial u^m}{\partial u'^r}\frac{\partial u^n}{\partial u'^s}$$

so that we are indeed dealing with a covariant tensor of the second order, comprised by the first fundamental coefficients. This important tensor is usually called the *covariant metric tensor*.

We can also exemplify a contravariant tensor of the second order by inverting the matrix $[a_{mn}]$. We write the components of the inverse matrix a^{mn}, anticipating that it represents a contravariant tensor of the second order. We obviously have $a^{11}=G/(EG-F^2)$, $a^{12}=a^{21}=-F/(EG\text{-}F^2)$ and $a^{22}=E/(EG-F^2)$. The components of a^{mn} transform according to

$$a'^{rs}=a^{mn}\frac{\partial x'^r}{\partial x^m}\frac{\partial x'^s}{\partial x^n}$$

so that we are indeed dealing with a contravariant tensor of the second order. It is called the *contravariant metric tensor*.

E.4. Arc length as an invariant

Invariants, i.e. tensors of zero order, should need no exemplification, but we can easily write down one that will be used in the equations for a geodesic. Again consider a surface in three-dimensional Euclidean space, given by $x^1(u^1,u^2)$, $x^2(u^1,u^2)$, and $x^3(u^1,u^2)$. We also take a parameterized curve $u^1(t)$, $u^2(t)$ and define

$$w=\sqrt{\left(a_{mn}\frac{\mathrm{d}u^m}{\mathrm{d}t}\frac{\mathrm{d}u^n}{\mathrm{d}t}\right)},$$

where a_{mn} is the metric tensor. We can interpret $w\,\mathrm{d}t$ as an arc length element so that the length of a curve on the surface is

$$\int_{t_0}^{t_1} w\,\mathrm{d}t.$$

Now, w is an invariant. Shifting coordinates from x^r to x'^r we obtain by the chain rule

$$w'^2=a'_{rs}\frac{\mathrm{d}u'^r}{\mathrm{d}t}\frac{\mathrm{d}u'^s}{\mathrm{d}t}=a_{rs}\frac{\mathrm{d}u^r}{\mathrm{d}t}\frac{\mathrm{d}u^s}{\mathrm{d}t}=w^2.$$

Observe that in all the formulae the indices range from 1 to 2 since we are dealing with a two-dimensional space defined in various curvilinear coordinates. The fact that the surface is embedded in three-dimensional Euclidean space is completely irrelevant, as we have already stressed.

E.5. Geodesics

By the methods used in Appendix B we could now easily obtain the minimum of $\int w\mathrm{d}t$ by a Euler equation that reads

$$\frac{\mathrm{d}}{\mathrm{d}t}\frac{\partial w}{\partial p^r}-\frac{\partial w}{\partial u^r}=\frac{1}{2w}\frac{\mathrm{d}w}{\mathrm{d}t}\frac{\partial w}{\partial p^r},$$

where we have defined $p^r = \mathrm{d}u^r/\mathrm{d}t$. The derivation is not reproduced. Since w is an invariant, the geodesic is obviously, as it should be, independent of how the surface is parameterized. It is also easy to see that the geodesic does not depend on the choice of parameterization of the curve. For the parameter we could thus choose arc length s, which simplifies the problem. The previous equation transforms to

$$\frac{\mathrm{d}}{\mathrm{d}s}\frac{\partial w}{\partial p^r} - \frac{\partial w}{\partial u^r} = 0.$$

These two differential equations (for $r = 1,2$) can be transformed to

$$\frac{\mathrm{d}^2 u^r}{\mathrm{d}s^2} + \Gamma^r_{mn}\frac{\mathrm{d}u^m}{\mathrm{d}s}\frac{\mathrm{d}u^n}{\mathrm{d}s} = 0,$$

where the symbols Γ^r_{mn} are the *Christoffel symbols of the second kind*.

For the present case the Christoffel symbols are

$$\Gamma^1_{11} = \frac{GE_1 - 2FF_1 + FE_2}{2(EG - F^2)};\quad \Gamma^1_{12} = \frac{GE_2 - FG_1}{2(EG - F^2)};\quad \Gamma^1_{22} = \frac{2GF_2 - GG_1 - FG_2}{2(EG - F^2)},$$

$$\Gamma^2_{11} = \frac{2EF_1 - EE_2 + FE_1}{2(EG - F^2)};\quad \Gamma^2_{12} = \frac{EG_1 - FE_2}{2(EG - F^2)};\quad \Gamma^2_{22} = \frac{EG_2 - 2FF_2 + FG_1}{2(EG - F^2)},$$

as the reader will recall from Appendix D. For convenience we define $\Gamma^r_{mn} = \Gamma^r_{nm}$. These definitions of the Christoffel symbols work when we deal with two-dimensional surfaces in three-dimensional Euclidean space. In general, we can define the symbols by the tensor equation

$$2\Gamma^r_{mn} = a^{rs}\left(\frac{\partial a_{sm}}{\partial u^n} + \frac{\partial a_{sn}}{\partial u^m} - \frac{\partial a_{mn}}{\partial u^s}\right),$$

where a_{mn} and a^{mn} denote the covariant and the contravariant metric tensors to the surface, respectively. This definition works with manifolds of more than two dimensions and is hence used in Riemannian geometry and in Einstein's general relativity theory. Here, we can use it as a mnemonic device, since the Christoffel symbols are otherwise difficult to memorize.

E.6. Geodesics on a sphere again

We finish this appendix by exemplifying how the method of finding geodesics by tensor calculus works with a sphere. Suppose we have a unit sphere that is parameterized by the usual spherical coordinates ϕ, θ, so that

$$x^1 = \sin\phi\cos\theta,$$

$$x^2 = \sin\phi\sin\theta,$$

$$x^3 = \cos\phi.$$

We take $u^1=\phi$ and $u^2=\theta$. Then

$$\boldsymbol{x}_{u^1}=(\cos\phi\cos\theta, \cos\phi\sin\theta, -\sin\phi)$$

$$\boldsymbol{x}_{u^2}=(-\sin\phi\sin\theta, \sin\phi\cos\theta, 0),$$

which gives the fundamental coefficients

$$E=1; \qquad F=0; \qquad G=\sin^2\phi.$$

When we compute the Christoffel symbols we note that all the terms involving F or any of the derivatives of E, F and G, except $G_1=2\sin\phi\cos\phi$, are zero. Hence, there are only two nonzero Christoffel symbols, namely

$$\Gamma^1_{22}=-\sin\phi\cos\phi \quad \text{and} \quad \Gamma^2_{12}=\Gamma^2_{21}=\cos\phi/\sin\phi.$$

Hence, we obtain two Euler equations for the geodesics:

$$\frac{\mathrm{d}^2\phi}{\mathrm{d}s^2}-\sin\phi\cos\phi\left(\frac{\mathrm{d}\theta}{\mathrm{d}s}\right)^2=0$$

and

$$\frac{\mathrm{d}^2\theta}{\mathrm{d}s^2}+2\frac{\cos\phi}{\sin\phi}\left(\frac{\mathrm{d}\phi}{\mathrm{d}s}\right)\left(\frac{\mathrm{d}\theta}{\mathrm{d}s}\right)=0.$$

If we multiply the first equation by $\mathrm{d}\phi/\mathrm{d}s$ and the second by $\sin^2\phi\,\mathrm{d}\theta/\mathrm{d}s$ and add, we get

$$\mathrm{d}/\mathrm{d}s\left((\mathrm{d}\phi/\mathrm{d}s)^2+\sin^2\phi(\mathrm{d}\theta/\mathrm{d}s)^2\right)=0.$$

Hence, the expression within the parentheses must be constant. It is, in fact, because it is identically equal to $(\mathrm{d}s/\mathrm{d}s)^2=1$ on the unit sphere when we parameterize the curve by arc length. This "particular first integral" holds true in general, i.e. in the tensor symbolism $a_{mn}p^m p^n=1$.

If we take the second differential equation and again multiply by $\sin^2\phi\,\mathrm{d}\theta/\mathrm{d}s$, we see that it can be written

$$\mathrm{d}/\mathrm{d}s(\sin^2\phi\,\mathrm{d}\theta/\mathrm{d}s)=0$$

or

$$\sin^2\phi\,\mathrm{d}\theta/\mathrm{d}s=\text{constant}.$$

Two cases are obvious solutions. If we put $\phi=\pi/2$ and $\theta=s$, we obviously have the constant equal to unity. The solution curve is then the "equator" of the sphere. If we put θ constant, we deal with a great circle through the "north–south axis". In general we can obtain all the great circles as solutions.

E.7. Literature to Appendices D and E

There are three different "languages" in which differential geometry can be explained: that of classical analysis; that of differential forms; and that of tensor analysis. In Appendix D we used the classical exposition, especially adapted to the case of two-dimensional (by themselves non-Euclidean) surfaces embedded in three-dimensional Euclidean space. Relevant literature for this classical Gaussian theory is DoCarmo (1976), Coxeter (1961), Lipschutz (1969) and Struik (1950). A very simple intuitive exposition of the main ideas can be found in Hilbert and Cohn-Vossen (1932).

The tensorial language, touched upon in Appendix E, is suitable for the study of the intrinsic properties of surfaces regardless of embedding. Its main purpose is the generalization of problems beyond geometric space, which is irrelevant for us. The language is, however, useful also in our case, due to the facility of formulating equations for geodesics. Literature on tensor analysis includes Dodson and Poston (1977), Lipschutz (1969) and Synge and Schild (1949). Differential geometry explained in tensorial calculus can be found in Laugwitz (1977) and in the comprehensive five-volume work by Spivak (1970–75).

We have not employed the very neat language of alternating differential forms, even though for example the relations among multiple integrals related to Gauss's theorem could most elegantly be exposed in it, and we have made no use of it in differential geometry. There is, however, a necessary reference to a work on differential geometry using this language, namely Guggenheimer (1963), because Bonnet's fundamental theorem for the case when there is free choice of the second fundamental coefficients can (to my knowledge) only be found there.

Differential topology is the necessary foundation of modern differential geometry. Two references are Bröcker and Jänich (1973) and Wallace (1968).

Finally, it should be emphasized that the related field of integral geometry (or geometric probability) could prove most valuable for the problems treated. An authoritative reference, including a large bibliography, is Santalò (1976).

SYMBOLS

As far as possible I have tried to keep a consistent symbolism throughout the book. However, because of the multitude of symbols needed and the fact that special mathematical concepts have a traditional notation that aids understanding, it has been necessary to make a number of exceptions from this ideal. Some symbols have more than one meaning, which seems to be unavoidable. For the convenience of the reader I have listed the most important symbols below:

A, B = balancing factors in gravity and entropy models
A, B = occasionally transformed space coordinates to facilitate integration
A = area of S or part of it
$B(,)$ = the beta function
a, b = various constants, as in transfer cost function or in solutions of differential equations
a, b = occasionally transformed space coordinates to facilitate integration
$\boldsymbol{b}$ = binormal vector to a curve
$C(\xi, \eta)$ = total transportation cost from a given location of origin
c = constant with various meanings
$D(x,y)$ = density of destinations in gravity and entropy models
E, F, G = first fundamental coefficients of a surface
$E(r)$ = complete elliptic integral of the second kind
e = number of edges or arcs in a network
F, G = occasional notation for integrands in functionals to be minimized
$f(l)$ = detour dependent local transfer distance function
G = boundary of the region S
$g(i/l)$ = congestion-dependent local transfer time function
I = transportation cost between two points obtained as an integral of transfer distance (= cost) along some path
i = local traffic obtained as an integral of $|\boldsymbol{v}|$ with respect to ξ, η
i = occasionally $\sqrt{-1}$
J = total traffic obtained as an integral of i with respect to x,y
K = occasional constant
$\boldsymbol{k}$ = curvature vector for a parameterized curve
L, M, N = second fundamental coefficients for a surface
L = total road capital obtained as an integral of l with respect to x,y
l = local road capital
m = (in p = constant r^m) exponent in specification of population density

N = total communication or number of trips (synonymous with T in one of its meanings)
$\boldsymbol{N}$ = normal vector to a surface in three-dimensional space
n = (in $f = r^n$) exponent in a power curve specification for transfer cost
$\boldsymbol{n}$ = unit normal vector to a curve
$O(\xi,\eta)$ = density of origins in gravity and entropy models
P, Q = as $P(x,y), Q(x,y)$ parts of a line integral
P = total population obtained as an integral of p with respect to x,y
$p, \bar{p}$ = local population density at x,y and ξ,η
p = number of polygons in a network
$R = r^{n+1}$ transformed polar space coordinate
r = polar radius coordinate for x,y
S = the region considered
S', S'' = various parts of the region
s = arc length parameter
s = side length of a regular polygon in a regular network
T = total transportation work for the whole region or a part of it
T = total number of trips in the entropy model
$[T_{ij}]$ = matrix of trips between a finite number of locations in the entropy model
T', T'' = parts of a chord of a unit circle
t = arc length parameter
$\boldsymbol{t}$ = tangent vector to a curve
u, v = occasionally transformed space coordinates
u = occasionally the dependent variable in Jacobi's differential equation
v = number of vertices or nodes in a network
$\boldsymbol{v}$ = vector field representing the flow of traffic from a given origin ξ,η
$|\boldsymbol{v}|$ = partial (local) intensity of traffic passing in one direction across the point for which it is specified
$\boldsymbol{v}/|\boldsymbol{v}| = (\cos\theta, \sin\theta)$ unit tangent vector to a path
$w = u + iv$ point in the complex plane
X, Y = transformed space coordinates
x,y = space coordinates
$Z = z^{n+1}$ point in the complex plane where the optimal paths for $f = r^{n+1}$ are mapped onto straight lines
$z = x + iy$ point in the complex plane

α, β = occasional constants
β = coefficient in distance dependence in the entropy model
Γ = occasional inner boundary to delimit a part of the region
$\Gamma(\ )$ = the gamma function
γ = coefficient in the partially optimal road capital distribution
γ = occasional integration variable (an angle)

ε = distance elasticity in the gravity model
ξ, η, ζ = coordinates for a point in three-dimensional space
θ = direction angle for a transportation path
κ_n = normal curvatures
κ_g = geodesic curvature
λ, μ = Lagrange multipliers
μ, σ = occasionally mean and standard deviation of a spatial density distribution
ξ, η = coordinates for the origin of a transport
ρ = occasional integration variable
σ = arc length parameter
τ = arc length parameter
Φ, Ψ = sets of admissible functions
ϕ = occasional integration variable
$\Omega = (n+1)\omega$ transformed polar angle coordinate
ω = polar coordinate for the point x,y

∇ = gradient
$\nabla \cdot$ = divergence
$\nabla \times$ = curl or rotation
∇^2 = Laplacian
$|\ |$ = Euclidean norm or modulus of a vector
bar($\bar{\ }$) = above a complex number denotes the complex conjugate
$\partial(,)/\partial(,)$ = Jacobian of a mapping

Indices
0, 1 on $X, Y, x, y, R, \Omega, r, \omega, z, w$ denotes endpoints for a path. 1, 2, 3 on x denotes occasionally three space coordinates (synonymous with ξ, η, ζ).

REFERENCES

Ahlfors, L. V. (1966) *Complex Analysis* (McGraw-Hill, New York).

Alonso, W. (1965) *Location and Land Use* (Harvard University Press, Cambridge, Mass.).

Angel, S. and G. M. Hyman (1970) "Urban Velocity Fields", *Environment and Planning* 2, 211–224.

Angel, S. and G. M. Hyman (1971) "Urban Travel Time", *Papers and Proceedings of the Regional Science Association* 26, 85–99.

Angel, S. and G. M. Hyman (1972a) "Urban Spatial Interaction", *Environment and Planning* 4, 99–118.

Angel, S. and G. M. Hyman (1972b) "Urban Transportation Expenditures", *Papers and Proceedings of the Regional Science Association* 27, 105–123.

Angel, S. and G. M. Hyman (1976) *Urban Fields – A Geometry of Movement for Regional Science* (Pion, London).

Batty, M. (1974) "Spatial Entropy", *Geographical Analysis* 6, 1–31.

Beckmann, M. (1952) "A Continuous Model of Transportation", *Econometrica* 20, 643–660.

Beckmann, M. (1953) "The Partial Equilibrium of a Continuous Space Market", *Weltwirtschaftliches Archiv* 71, 73–89.

Beckmann, M. (1965) "Uber den optimalen Standort eines Verkehrsnetzes", *Zeitschrift für Betriebswirtschaft* 35, 65–80.

Beckmann, M. (1968) *Location Theory* (Random House, New York).

Beckmann, M. (1974) "Entropy, Gravity and Utility in Transportation Modelling", in: G. Menges, ed., *Information, Inference and Decision* (Reidel, Dordrecht).

Beckmann, M. (1976) "Equilibrium and Stability in a Continuous Space Market", *Operations Research Verfahren* 14, 48–63.

Berge, C. (1970) *Graphes et Hypergraphes* (Dunod, Paris).

Berge, C. and A. Ghouila-Houri (1962) *Programmes, Jeux et Réseaux de Transport* (Dunod, Paris).

Bieberbach, L. (1953) *Conformal Mapping* (Chelsea, New York).

Bolza, O. (1904) *Lectures on the Calculus of Variations* (The University of Chicago Press, Chicago).

Bröcker, T. and K. Jänich (1973) *Einführung in die Differentialtopologie* (Springer, Berlin).

Bunge, W. (1966) *Theoretical Geography* (Gleerups, Lund).

Christaller, W. (1935) *Die zentralen Orte in Süddeutschland* (Fischer, Jena).

Coral, M. (1931-32) "The Euler–Lagrange Multiplier Rule for Double Integrals", in: *Contributions to the Calculus of Variations*, Vol. 1.

Courant, R. (1950) *Dirichlet's Principle, Conformal Mapping and Minimal Surfaces* (Springer, Berlin).

Courant, R. and D. Hilbert (1953) *Methods of Mathematical Physics* (Interscience, New York).

Courant, R. and F. John (1974) *Introduction to Calculus and Analysis*, Vol. 2 (Interscience, New York).

Coxeter, H. S. M. (1961) *Introduction to Geometry* (Wiley, New York).

Deo, M. (1974) *Graph Theory with Applications to Engineering and Computer Science* (Prentice Hall, Englewood Cliffs).

DoCarmo, M. P. (1976) *Differential Geometry of Curves and Surfaces* (Prentice Hall, Englewood Cliffs).

Dodson, C. T. J. and T. Poston (1977) *Tensor Geometry* (Pitman, London).

Elsgolc, L. E. (1961) *Calculus of Variations* (Pergamon, Oxford).

Fejes Tóth, L. (1969) *Regular Figures* (Pergamon, Oxford).

Ford, L. R. and D. R. Fulkerson (1962) *Flows in Networks* (Princeton University Press, Princeton).

Forsyth, A. R. (1927) *Calculus of Variations* (Cambridge University Press, Cambridge).

Fox, C. (1950) *Introduction to the Calculus of Variations* (Oxford University Press, London).

Goldstein, H. (1950) *Classical Mechanics* (Addison-Wesley, Reading, Mass.).

Guggenheimer, H. W. (1963) *Differential Geometry* (McGraw-Hill, New York).

Hilbert, D. and S. Cohn-Vossen (1932) *Anschauliche Geometrie* (Springer, Berlin).

Holtgrefe, A. A. I. (1975) *An Optimizing Medium-Term Planning Model for the Netherlands Railways* (Universitaire Pers, Rotterdam).

Huang, K. (1963) *Statistical Mechanics* (Wiley, New York).

Iri, M. (1969) *Network Flow, Transportation and Scheduling* (Academic Press, New York).

Johnston, J. (1972) *Econometric Methods* (McGraw-Hill, New York).

Kansky, K. J. (1963) "Structure of Transportation Networks", University of Chicago, Department of Geography, Research Report no. 84.

Kirby, H. R. (1970) "Normalizing Factors for the Gravity Model – An Interpretation", *Transportation Research* 4, 37–50.

Kneser, A. (1900) *Lehrbuch der Variationsrechnung* (Vieweg, Braunschweig).

Knopp, K. (1945) *Theory of Functions* (Dover, New York).

Lam, T. N. and G. F. Newell (1967) "Flow Dependent Traffic Assignment on a Circular City", *Transportation Science* 1, 318–361.

Laugwitz, D. (1977) *Differentialgeometrie* (Teubner, Stuttgart).

Launhardt, W. (1869) *Rentabilität und Richtungsfestellung der Strassen* (Hannover).

Lighthill, M. J. and G. R. Whitham (1955) "Theory of Traffic Flow on Long Crowded Roads", *Proceedings of the Royal Society* 229:1178, 281–345.

Lipschutz, M. M. (1969) *Differential Geometry* (McGraw-Hill, New York).

Lloyd, P. E. and P. Dicken (1972) *Location in Space – A Theoretical Approach to Economic Geography* (Harper & Row, New York).

Lösch, A. (1962) *Die räumliche Ordnung der Wirtschaft* (Teubner, Stuttgart).

Marsden, J. E. (1973) *Basic Complex Analysis* (Freeman, San Francisco).

Marsden, J. E. and A. J. Tromba (1976) *Vector Calculus* (Freeman, San Francisco).

Melut, P. and P. O'Sullivan (1974) "A Comparison of Simple Lattice Transport Networks for a Uniform Plain", *Geographical Analysis* 6, 163–173.

Mosler, K. C. (1976a) "Minimum Cost Location of Branched Networks for Transportation to a Center", in: M. Roubens, ed. *Second European Congress on Operations Research* (North-Holland, Amsterdam).

Mosler, K. C. (1976b) *Optimale Transportnetze – Zur Bestimmung ihres kostengünstigsten Standorts bei gegebener Nachfrage* (Springer, Berlin).

Niedercorn, J. H. and B. V. Bechdolt (1969) "An Economic Derivation of the 'Gravity Law' of Spatial Interaction", *Journal of Regional Science* 9, 273–283.

Nijkamp, P. (1975) "Reflections on Gravity and Entropy Models", *Regional Science and Urban Economics* 5, 203–225.

Nijkamp, P. (1978) "Gravity and Entropy Models: The State of the Art", Wrije Universiteit, Economische Fakulteit, Amsterdam, Serie Researchmemoranda 1977-2.

Nijkamp, P. and J. H. P. Paelinck (1974) "A Dual Interpretation of Entropy Maximization Models in Regional Science", *Papers and Proceedings of the Regional Science Association* 33, 14–31.

Palander, T. F. (1935) *Beiträge zur Standortstheorie* (Almqvist & Wiksell, Uppsala).

Puu, T. (1977) "A Proposed Definition of Traffic Flow in Continuous Transportation Models", *Environment and Planning* 9, 559–567.

Puu, T. (1978a) "On Traffic Equilibrium, Congestion Tolls and the Allocation of Transportation Capacity in a Congested Urban Area", *Environment and Planning* 10, 29–36.

Puu, T. (1978b) "Towards a Theory of Optimal Roads", *Regional Science and Urban Economics* 8, 225–248.

Puu, T. (1978c) "On the Existence of Optimal Paths and Cost Surfaces in Isotropic Continuous Transportation Models", *Environment and Planning* 10, 1121–1130.

Rudin, W. (1976) *Principles of Mathematical Analysis* (McGraw-Hill, New York).

Rutherford, D. E. (1948) *Vector Methods* (Oliver and Boyd, Edinburgh).

Santalò, L. A. (1976) "Integral Geometry and Geometric Probability", *Encyclopedia of Mathematics and its Applications* (Addison-Wesley, Reading, Mass.).

Schweizer, U. and P. Varaiya (1976) "The Spatial Structure of Production with a Leontief Technology", *Regional Science and Urban Economics* 6, 231–251.

Smith, T. E. (1975) "A Choice Theory of Spatial Interaction", *Regional Science and Urban Economics* 5, 137–176.

Solow, R. (1972) "Congestion, Density and the Use of Land in Transportation", *The Swedish Journal of Economics* 74, 161–173.
Solow, R. and W. Vickrey (1971) "Land Use in a Long Narrow City", *Journal of Economic Theory* 4, 430–447.
Spiegel, M. R. (1959) *Vector Analysis* (McGraw-Hill, New York).
Spiegel, M. R. (1964) *Complex Variables* (McGraw-Hill, New York).
Spiegel, M. R. (1967) *Theoretical Mechanics* (McGraw-Hill, New York).
Spiegel, M. R. (1974) *Advanced Calculus* (McGraw-Hill, New York).
Spivak, M. (1965) *Calculus on Manifolds* (Benjamin, New York).
Spivak, M. (1970-75) *A Comprehensive Introduction to Differential Geometry* (Brandeis University).
Steenbrink, P. A. (1974) *Optimization of Transport Networks* (Wiley, New York).
Stewart, J. Q. (1947) "Empirical Mathematical Rules Governing the Distribution and Equilibrium of Population", *Geographical Review* 37, 461–485.
Struik, D. J. (1950) *Differential Geometry* (Addison-Wesley, Reading, Mass.).
Synge, J. L. and A. Schild (1949) *Tensor Calculus* (University of Toronto Press, Toronto)
Wallace, A. (1968) *Differential Topology – First Steps* (Benjamin, New York).
Wardrop, J. G. (1966) "Journey Speed and Flow in Central Urban Areas", *Traffic Engineering and Control* 9, 528–532.
Wardrop, J. G. (1969) "Minimum Cost Paths in Urban Areas", *Strassenbau- und Strassenverkehrstechnik* 86, 184–190.
Warntz, W. (1967) "Global Science and the Tyranny of Space", *Papers and Proceedings of the Regional Science Association* 19, 7–19.
Weatherburn, C. E. (1943a) *Advanced Vector Analysis* (Bell & Sons, London).
Weatherburn, C. E. (1943b) *Elementary Vector Analysis* (Bell & Sons, London).
Werner, C. (1968) "Research Seminar in Theoretical Transportation Geography", in: F. Horton, ed. in *Geographic Studies of Urban Transportation and Network Analysis* (Northwestern University).
Werner, C. (1966) *Zur Geometrie von Verkehrsnetzen* (Abhandlungen des 1. Geografischen Instituts der FU, Berlin).
Williams, H. C. W. L. and J. D. Orthuzar Salas (1976) "Some Generalizations and Applications of the Velocity Field Concept", *Transportation Research* 10, 65–73.
Wilson, A. G. (1967) "A Statistical Theory of Spatial Distribution Models", *Transportation Research* 1, 253–269.
Wilson, A. G. (1970) *Entropy in Urban and Regional Modelling* (Pion, London).
Wingo, L. (1961) *Transportation and Land Use* (Resources for the Future, Washington).
Wloka, J. (1971) *Funktionalanalysis und Anwendungen* (Walter de Gruyter, Berlin).
von Thünen, H. (1921) *Der isolierte Staat* (Waentig, Jena).
Zitron, N. R. (1974) "A Continuous Model of Optimal-Cost Routes in a Circular City", *Journal of Optimization Theory and Applications* 14, 291–303.

AUTHOR INDEX

SUBJECT INDEX